The
Biddle Street Bridge

by Jack Lundon as told to Fred L. Miller

SlingShot t/m

This edition printed in 1999 by
Slingshot Publishing Company
P.O. Box 208 Arnold, Maryland 21012
Library of Congress Catalog Card Number 98-96841
Soft Cover: ISBN NUMBER 0-9668962-0-3
Case Bound Hard Cover: ISBN NUMBER 0-9668962-1-1

Dedicated to my family and the city of my childhood, Baltimore

The Biddle Street Bridge

Table of Contents

Tenth Ward East Baltimore

Most folks have the opportunity to visit the neighborhood where they grew up and even introduce their children to the place they used to call home. To be able to stand, reflect and perhaps talk to some of the old residents. Not so with my old neighborhood. My neighborhood was put in the hands of the once-notorious blockbusters. They were out to scare the homeowner into a quick sale before the whole area went down.

"This may be your last chance to get a fair price for your house," was their pitch and all too often the homeowner would sell fast, knowing full well that home value plummeted after the initial sale. Yes, prejudice fueled the panic, but it was also an economic truth that many homeowners lost home equity to these cynical operators. We were renters. We were also one of the last families to move.

My old neighborhood was not physically demolished, but it was, nevertheless, "torn down" to make way for a slum. It may have been on its way out when we moved in, in 1944. If so, I guess World War II put the movement on hold. When the exodus did start, it raced like a juggernaut and, by 1957, the neighborhood as I knew it was gone.

Share my memories of growing up in an environment that produced both devils and angels. It was a time when the automobile was a luxury and not a necessity. The neighborhood was close to everything. You could walk to the big five-and six-story department stores, see both stage and motion picture show in combination at one of the many theaters. In a time when it was fashionable to dress up, you too, could be part of the exciting but long forgotten Easter Parade on Charles Street. In the evenings of the springtime you may be entertained by St. James Drum & Bugle Corps marching past your house. During the summer, the Saturday morning air was filled with the sound of Singing Sam, the Watermelon Man, selling red-to-the-rind watermelons. Mounted on the cab of a huge red truck was an obese black man. With a megaphone pressed to his lips, Singing Sam would sing "Pennies from heaven" and insert refrains about his watermelons, "Every time it rains I get melons from heaven." He'd plug them to prove they were red. Singing Sam was an institution and we would wait for him to appear before making a watermelon purchase.

Bordering on the south of our neighborhood was the Maryland State Penitentiary and the Baltimore City Jail. Across the street and, half a block away was a large garage with a second floor used for gambling. There were times when the police, who gathered on the corner, were asked to take a walk as their presence was bad for business. East of the jail was a large railroad yard where freight cars were parked for short periods while awaiting routing. The presence of the jail shadowed many of the freight car break-ins. The west side of the neighborhood was separated by a railroad and two very wide streets that converged and perhaps served as a moat protecting those folks who lived to the west of us.

Neighbors to the north were protected from us by factories and a 24-square- block graveyard that served as a personal petting zoo for the locals. There you could dig up snakes and catch rats if you were into that sport.

I have named my book after the Biddle Street Bridge because it was central to the lives of those kids growing up in the Tenth Ward area of East Baltimore. It was torn down recently and replaced by something more modern, but I'm sure none of our gang will ever forget it. To our gang, the Biddle Street Bridge was a haven and a source of strength and protection from the environment and the cops. That old concrete and stone bridge had a hollow street. Two manholes provided an access to a "fort" under the sidewalk that only we boys and a few selected girls were aware of. The underside of the bridge was large enough to house several catwalks, side tunnels and a quick getaway through the ash tunnels to an open field on Preston Street. When it came to hiding stolen loot, there was no better place. If you longed for winter sports, no problem. Snow that had slightly thawed and then refrozen would remain for days and you could go ice skating on the bridge. The hillside that was visible from the bridge was a favorite place for sleighing. In inclement weather, we remained inside the fort and engaged in indoor sports such as climbing the interior walls, playing stick ball, catching and roasting pigeons, building a fire or seeing who could piss the highest up a wall.

Sit back, relax, and take a tour with me through my old neighborhood. True, it's gone, but the memories will linger forever. At times they come back to haunt me. I long to be able to sit on the steps and share the experiences and antics of those old places. The neighborhood, a one square mile area of East Baltimore, was known as the Tenth Ward.

The Beginning

East Baltimore 1944

My sister and I had just completed construction of our cardboard fort and went in for lunch when a cry of "FIRE" came from the back yard. The Abbot kids had struck. This, on my first day in a new neighborhood, was a harbinger of years to follow; a never-ending parade of characters and screwups and the beginning of a total shock treatment for a sheltered kid such as me.

This was the Tenth Ward, a lower to middle income area of Baltimore that encompassed about one square mile of East Baltimore. It also housed the Baltimore City Jail (known to all as the Fallsway Apartments) and the Maryland State Penitentiary. I learned that being a member of the community was like living in a protective shell that shielded us from outside forces. This seems odd considering the harshness of our lives, but it was.

Some two hundred boys, in my own age group of five to eight years lived in the Tenth Ward. Talk about diversity! The neighborhood comprised Italian, German and Irish families, with regiments of kids. I had one sister and three brothers, a fourth brother died when I was young. The neighborhood was home to the roughest, toughest gangs in the city. We seldom fought among ourselves, but never gave a second thought to fighting any other part of town.

How old was I when the Abbott kids set my fort ablaze? A petrified six years old. The Abbotts; were the epitome of ill breeding. A meaner bunch was not known to me. They were from Illinois and rumor had it they were escorted to the Illinois border by the sheriff and each state followed suit until they got to Baltimore. The father, Mr. Abbott was a paper hanger and sported a mustache like that of Adolph Hitler. This alone made him suspect. There were two girls in this family and they were as tough as any male members. Dorothy and Peggy, nick named the Rhea sisters, Dia and Gonneah. I saw them beat the living hell out of one of the sister's beaus.

The fires continued to burn and tended over to other escapades until I fought, one by one, each of the two Abbott boys. In a fair fight I could have beaten either, they knew this so they made sure they were both present. Eventually they decided to pick on someone who didn't fight back. The main role model for the two Abbott boys was an older brother Billy. Billy was like taking a trip to a comic farm, he had a freckled face on a fat head with red hair and a mouth with teeth only on one side. I recall him once taking away my water gun and pissing in it. That day he was a menace to the community. I told my mom and she went after him, followed by his bucktoothed fat-assed sister Dorothy, who challenged my mom to a fist fight.

I actually recall hate when thinking about members of the Abbott Bunch. The three boys, Billy, Franny and Richard were like night, day and in between. The oldest brother Billy was a combination of both only dumber. Richard, older than Franny, was the meek one. Franny, a psychotic nut, outweighed Richard by some twenty pounds. Many times I would witness Richard being beat upon by brother Franny. When separated they were manageable, when together, a living hell on the loose. Playing baseball with the Abbotts was a memorable occasion, too. Franny would make up the rules as the game went on, five and six outs for his side and four and five strikes or no strikes until he actually hit the ball.

Do you remember when another kid would ask for a taste of your candy bar? Franny never had that problem. He would lick his candy bar and no one would even think of asking for any part of it.

One summer the Millsaps, cousins to the Abbotts, came to Baltimore for a visit. I don't recall anybody having the time of their life that summer, because most didn't come out of the house. I went for a walk with the Abbotts and Millsaps through a neighborhood just west of us. Soon I found myself running out the back of a closed gasoline station like a bat out of hell, carrying an air hose. The air hose was a prize handed to me by one of the Millsaps. What a prize, I stole an air hose and for what? But that was the kind of fun in store for any kid in the company of the Abbotts.

Once the Italian kids got the idea to gang up on the Abbotts and I helped lead the charge by punching Richie (Richard) on the nose, that's when Franny made a promise to get each of us when we were alone, putting a sour note on the whole plan. Franny was always a menace. Among some of the nutty stuff he would do, was to tie a string on the neck of a broken bottle, spin the broken bottle in a large circle over his head. He terrified anyone in his way. To my knowledge, he never cut anyone with this antic, but that doesn't mean he wouldn't have. Franny became a complete nuisance to the whole neighborhood and began vandalizing neighborhood businesses, was caught and sent to a reform school. As for the rest of their bunch, they moved away. Rumor was they were last seen being escorted by the Delaware sheriff to a boat on the Atlantic seaboard.

The Misadventures of Kenny Zin

World War II was ending, but not too soon for me. It was 1945 and my brothers would be coming home to protect my family from the likes of the Abbotts. Had mom known the crap I learned from the Abbotts (stealing, breaking and entering, and a host of window breaking to name some) it would surely have sent her to an early grave. Fortunately, I never got caught. Besides, I was terrified at the thought of being put away in St. Mary's or the Maryland Reform School for Boys. Today when I see what's going on in my old neighborhood, the drugs, truancy, and all that, I wonder what it would be like if these kids had the threat of a formal education at St. Mary's hanging over their heads.

Anyway, we knew this one kid named Kenny Zin who for a long time lived in the railroad tunnel high up under the Fallsway. The Fallsway was an elevated road that transverses the railroad yards. He wore a green uniform and was said to have escaped from reform school. We used to go up there and eat fruit he heisted from railcars and listen to the most unbelievable stories. Like the time he stole a Hudson automobile and drove all the way to Florida before ditching it and hitching his way home. Of course he was picked up by this beautiful lady who ravished him from Savannah to Charleston. Kenny was about fourteen years old, I think. He told me a story about running away from the reform school and showed a cut on his leg that he claimed was made when the guards shot at him. I really believed him but, I don't think it was a possibility. Once he told me about how he managed to get locked up. It went this way:

"I was a rich kid living with my beautiful and rich mother. My mother married this mean bastard who was after her money and he hated me. The reason he hated me was, I knew he was a bum and married her just for money. The old bastard was always beating on me and my mother. One day, after eating a double bowl of a special cereal, that they don't sell any more cause it makes you too tough, I beat him up. He then paid the cops to send me away. They put me in St. Mary's but I still had enough of the strength from the cereal in me and I beat up all the guards there. When I was asleep, they injected me with a special needle of sleeping stuff. When I awoke, I was in Maryland Training School. They also shaved my head to make me weak until the cereal worked off. Plus they put an iron ball on my legs, make that two iron balls to be sure. That's it, it was two iron balls, each weighed a hundred pounds. My mother is now poor and my stepfather is rich. The old bastard is living in Spain, where he has his own army, paid for with my mother's money."

In fact, Kenny's mother was a prostitute who let him fend for himself. His fending always had a lot of glory to it. In one on his most glorious fends, he stole a watermelon boat from the docks and claimed to be headed for Cuba. I don't know how far the boat would have floated on its own. It was pushed from the docks and set adrift. Franny Abbott was his first mate and I was the cabin boy. Along with two of the Solon brothers we made up the crew. I remember there was a slop jar on the boat and before we took off, Kenny lit an M-80 fire cracker and threw it in the slop jar. We ran for cover to keep the shit and whatever else from splattering us. About a minute went by and nothing happened, the firecracker refused to explode. Franny went over to peer into the slop jar to investigate, when all of sudden the delayed fuse happened. Franny was facially covered in brown and green GOO.

After washing his face in harbor water, Franny produced a sandwich he had tucked in a bag under his shirt. A convenient place to carry something, that is, if you're a kid. Then a scuffle broke out. Franny was thrown overboard by Kenny when he refused to give up his lunch. In fact, Kenny threw the lunch overboard, too, after biting into it. I started to cry for being scared. The two Solon brothers jumped overboard for fear that Kenny had gone nuts. The boat rammed a dock a few streets east of where we started. I got off, running nonstop until I reached my house. When I got there, I went in and took a bath. Later on, I found that Kenny abandoned ship when his crew mutinied.

I recall when Kenny and Franny had an urge to find a gun. They were breaking into parked police cars in their search. Once they stole a briefcase from a police car parked at Biddle Street and the Fallsway. They snatched it from an open window. When I came upon them, they were burning the evidence. They probably cost that poor cop a mound of trouble since all that was left was a pile of papers.

They did eventually find a gun. A small silver revolver. The find was in a tool box in a shed at the railroad yard turntable. What it was doing there will have to remain a mystery. The gun fortunately was not loaded. Franny and Kenny were entering into a short-lived experience of being highwaymen. Kenny approached a colored lady at the bus stop on Preston Street and the Fallsway and demanded her pocketbook. The would-be victim, while reaching for the gun said, "Give me that cap pistol you fucking little cracker." And with that, she hit Kenny so hard with her pocketbook it knocked him down. Franny screamed as she hit him directly in the face with her deadly packed pocketbook. Blood was streaming from his nose as he ran past me, while I watched from my shielded perch on the signboards across the way. Joy filled me to see Franny bleeding running and crying in fright. That incident probably saved both those kid's lives. Imagine a loaded gun in the hands of these two genuine screwy kids.

I'm not sure what became of Kenny Zin. I don't think it was too easy to become a member of the reform school, though there were quite a number of kids from the neighborhood who did.

Once I saw a movie about a reform school starring William Bendix. I remember it didn't seem to be too bad a place, but I hoped other kids didn't become inspired by it. That is, want to go there. We did a lot of bad things but we, at least I, never lost a sense of right and wrong.

The war was over, the Abbots were gone from the area and the neighborhood got a new bunch of kids from Virginia and the West somewhere. I guess that was mostly due to the large job market opening in Baltimore. Not that anyone really missed the Abbotts, but they were a group, we could all kind of hate, so in that respect, we did miss them.

I used to spend many a summer day at the city dock on Pratt Street begging for watermelons from the skippers of the watermelon boats. These boats were the famous skipjacks, a sailing vessel some fifty feet in length. During the winter, they earned their keep dredging "arsters." Most young people today don't know it, but it was illegal to dredge oysters from engine-powered boats. The law required that watermen sail and oyster at the same time. Anyway, when the boat attendant wasn't looking, I would kick a melon and ask if I could have the cracked one.

We boys would spend the winter days playing in a large field near the railroad that ran under the Biddle Street Bridge. At least, that's what we told our parents, (usually, our moms). In reality, we would be looking for hideouts in caverns under the Fallsway. Or breaking into freight cars looking for peaches, cherries or a new thing called "Frozen Strawberries by Birds-Eye"to purloin.

Trouble

Warren Grimm moved into a house on Barclay Street in 1948. I disliked him immediately. He was my age and size, sported a butch crew cut and had a dark, blemished complexion. Years later he acquired a tattoo proclaiming "Born to lose." That was true. A new kid in the neighborhood was always cause for excitement. While the movers were still unloading the Grimms' meager furniture, Warren was kicking stones along the sidewalk. Recognizing, perhaps, a kindred spirit, I ambled over to meet him.

"Hey kid, that's my ball," he yelled, meaning the rubber ball I was bouncing. "Give it here!" He reached to take it from me, so I belted him in the face. So much for meeting my new best friend. Mrs. Grimm broke us apart and, while absolving Warren of any wrongdoing, made it clear she wanted me to appreciate her son's better nature (which did not exist). Warren was her pride and joy and she allowed him to become a spoiled brat. She worked in a gin mill at night (there was no Mr. Grimm) so Warren and his sister roamed freely.

Murphy's Dime Store was a good place to shoplift, if you had the nerve, and Warren Grimm did. He'd take "orders" for the most popular toys (like the Buntline Special cap gun) and delivered them at deeply discounted prices. I admit to being a customer myself from time to time.

Eventually he graduated to the career of a burglar and was caught burglarizing Resnick's and put away for six months at Maryland Training School. Upon release, he joined the Hollywood gang and was soon the best-dressed young man in the neighborhood. Two months later, BAM, Warren was back at MTS. We didn't know the word "sociopath" back then, but we knew one when we saw one. Warren's philosophy: If you want it, take it and it's only wrong to get caught.

The Royal Crown Cola Bottling Company was only a block away from home. On warm summer days, we would go over and play on their hill. This was part of the railroad. The soft drink trucks would be returning to the plant and we would race up and pretend to be playing cowboy. Using the returning trucks for cover from make believe Indians, we'd lift an R.C. or two and make for the Biddle Street Bridge. There we would find a way to open and drink the warm soda and yoke it up. One day I sat under the Biddle Street Bridge, hidden from view, and watched some older boys hiding soft drinks, obviously stolen, and I got a brilliant idea. Steal their loot.

I made the mistake of telling Warren Grimm about an R.C. caper. On the way to school I told Grimm I had hidden a case of Nehi Orange under a piece of roofing material near the Preston Street Bridge and was going to retrieve it after school. That afternoon I was summoned to the principal's office where Miss Crocker, the principal, had Grimm and two others (not from our crowd) standing at attention. Grimm looked at me and motioned as if drinking from a bottle. Seeing this, Miss Crocker said "Gangsters! He just gave you the signal!" Gangsters?

What happened was Grimm had retrieved my loot during the lunch hour, then carried it to school and asked the janitor to hold it for him, saying "I bought this for my mom and don't want everyone trying to get some." The janitor turned it over to the principal. When confronted, the little bastard told the principal that I'd sold him the soda and he was intending to give it to his mother as a gift. The other two were there to corroborate his story. I told Miss Crocker "I never sold him anything! I just told him about seeing older boys hide the soda." She believed Grimm. "How much did you pay Jackie for the soda," she asked Warren. Without pause he lied, "Thirty-six cents, Miss Crocker, all I had."

Turning to me she demanded, "Young man, you return his money and I will hear no more about this." I was forced to give him all the money I had, about 15 cents, and promise to repay the balance. Outside her office I demanded that Grimm return my 15 cents. "No way," he said and walked off sniggering with his friends.

A favorite Grimm larceny was breaking into railcars. Once, he and another guy broke into a private car owned by the famous showman, Joe E. Brown. They stole a wristwatch, a fur coat and other valuables. Then, the goof balls took the loot home to their mothers who, in turn, called the police. Grimm was a crook; Grimm was stupid, but he was lucky. Here's how the newspaper reported it: "They found the loot hidden under the bridge and promptly notified the authorities." Mr. Brown rewarded each family with tickets to his show and they were heroes! Everyone in the neighborhood was praising Warren for his noble act. Within in a month, he was back in reform school for another burglary.

Our gang didn't go in for breaking into railcars, but we did find a lot of fun things just lying around. One such find was a large red paperboard canister filled with yellow powder. We went to the water tower where the railroad turntable was located and cooked some up. When dropped in water it would bubble, when tossed into a fire, it burned in multicolors. It also created great clouds of acrid smoke that caused three fire trucks and the police to investigate. Lucky for us, they used sirens.

Another fun spot was the big cooler box located on the loading dock of a chemical company on Guilford Avenue. The box contained dry ice, and like everything else we found, we dropped it in water or tried to burn it. When we dropped it into water it would bubble and create a fine ground fog. One day we placed chunks of dry ice in canning jars half filled with water, tightened the lids and placed them on the sidewalk as we walked along. About a block and a half away, the jars started exploding, POW . . . POW . . . POW.

Dynamite caps were readily available, too, but until Grimm showed me, I never knew where the older guys got them. They would place a cap on the tracks and the train crossing over it would cause it to explode. I believe the caps were used as a railroad signal of some type. When Grimm asked Georgie Emerson and me to go with him to pick up some dynamite caps, we went. When I found out that, rather than being hidden in tall grass near a work train, they were to be liberated from inside the caboose of the train, I froze. The first thing I thought of was doing time with Grimm at MTS, because Grimm had a habit of getting caught. Georgie Emerson was my age and easily lead by Grimm. Georgie told me to be the lookout while he and Grimm broke into the caboose. As they headed toward the unattended train, I picked up a rusty license plate and threw it toward an abandoned car. It startled Grimm and Georgie and they called back in a hushed voice, "What was that?"

"It came from over there," I lied.

"Where?"

"There. I think he's a cop."

They took off and I was right behind. When we were safely away Grimm asked, "Did you see him?"

"Yes."

"Was it really a cop?"

"I'm not sure. I thought I saw a shiny badge. Anyway, I don't want to get caught for stealing noise makers."

"Shit, man, I hear they keep dynamite sticks on those trains. Where are you going, Jackie?" I was already walking away. "Up to the Times Inn to get a hot dog with chili." While eating my chili dog I waited for a blast announcing the destruction of Grimm, Georgie and the railroad yard.

The Railroad

There was usually something going on at the railroad yard. There were a couple of hermits who were living down there, one was sort of a caretaker living in a shelter under the Fallsway. I remember, in later years, reading about a hermit who fit this guy's description and location, who became ill and died. The news reports claimed he had some fifteen thousand dollars stashed away in his dwelling with no heirs to ever claim it.

The day after the dynamite caper, I saw some older boys hiding frozen strawberries high up in the breastwork of the Fallsway. When they left, I returned with a band of guys and we set out to extract the strawberries. I remember this as if it were yesterday. We climbed to the top of the tunnel, up a large stone wall that had railroad spikes driven into it for foot placement. Mike Campo was a human fly and his talent for climbing was the stuff of legend. When we got almost to the top, we stopped. Mike would now go the rest of the way and cross a space some five feet wide and fifty feet deep. The drop was into the actual Jones Falls, an old river on which Baltimore was first laid out.

Baltimore was once called Jones Town. This inner area was, then, open spaces and country. To us boys it was the country. To reach the country, you simply went down the steps of the Biddle Street Bridge.

Mike had now reached the cache of strawberries and began chucking boxes back to us. Before he had thrown the first box, though, one of us had shouted the question, "How many strawberries are there?" to Mike. "Fifteen," he yelled back. Wow, a magic number since fifteen boys were we.

Vernon Solon was the first boy in our relay brigade. The first box came his way, but he clumsily dropped it into the abyss and hollered, "There goes Jack's." I heard the splash as my precious loot hit bottom. Vernon had pronounced the fated box of berries mine, and in response to some unwritten code, I accepted it. Someone did share a box with me and they were awful. I guess they were spoiled. There was nothing very unusual about us stealing fruit, except this fruit was stolen from thieves. We hid ourselves and waited for the older boys to return, finding they were victimized, but they never came. It's logical, now, to presume they too had tasted their booty.

Herbert the Wart and the Ears Brothers

Living in the center of this vast manufacturing area, it was not unusual to see boys running down Biddle Street with a coat rack in tow or an arms load of freshly stolen suits. It may not have happened every day, but it wasn't an unusual sight. Some of the guys took orders for the stuff on the racks, but as it is in supply and demand, the sizes were not to be counted on. The industrial building was in the 700 block of East Preston Street and contained many small-to medium-sized manufacturers; paint, printing, clothing and toys to name a few. You would be surprised at what all was being made inside. I know I was. If I owned the place, I would have charged people to collect from the trash dumpsters. Oh boy, what treasures were there. I personally ravaged their trash piles to get enough parts to build toy watches and model boats. There were engraved printer's plates with real important stuff that just had to be saved. Of course my mom would throw out some of my treasure when she cleaned under my bed. One day I was having a particularly good day at finding good stuff, as we called it when the overhead chute opened. I was almost buried in stuff. I mean everything came down, garbage, toys and empty thread spools. There was no need to be upset. I just hit the jackpot. I was thankful to be there. The commercial thread spools were welcomed by every one of the guys in the neighborhood. The spools were utilitarian. They could be used for throwing and made good slingshot targets. The whole gang had slingshots so the demand for these swell targets was ever popular.

I found myself shooting targets under the bridge one Saturday morning in hopes some of the gang would soon appear when I discovered three of the ugliest kids ever. They were holding a fourth kid down and it appeared they were trying to cut off his nose. He was screaming bloody murder. I startled the group with my appearance and the silence came over everyone, you could have heard a pin drop. I was frightened at the sight I was seeing and wondered whether this was about to happen to me. I kept my slingshot loaded with a three quarter inch marble at the ready and I'm sure the wonder of the moment was mutual. I immediately recognized the kid being held down as "Herbert the Wart Nose" from school. Herbert was not a friend of mine but an acquaintance from P.S. #32. I felt like the Lone Ranger rescuing a victimized farmer from cattle rustlers. One was taller than the next and each had ears that stood out straight like the doors of a yellow cab waiting for passengers at the train station. The tallest was every bit of fourteen years old and he demanded to know who I was and what I was doing with the loaded slingshot pointed at him. I answered by asking what was he trying to do with Herbert. Meanwhile Herbert was up and out of sight and I now was confronted with a problem that was about to make me crap my pants.

Just in the nick of time, my pal Stevie Fazzio happened under the bridge and wouldn't you know it, Stevie knew these three. They were all pals, Stevie had invited them earlier to meet us under the bridge to shoot targets. A truce was at hand and I was introduced to the Ears Brothers. There was the oldest brother known as Big Ears and he had this thing for yelling like Tarzan that became infectious. It sounded like ALL-E-ALL-E-All. The three were very skinny, lanky and with brown hair and seemed to lack an understanding for humanities, like we all did at that age. The middle brother was known as Ears and the younger one was Little Ears. Later I learned their names in respect were Leroy, Ronnie and Joe. We weren't interested in last names and I never learned theirs.

Stevie told me a story relating to the middle brother and it was probably the seed to the family problem. The one Ears brother, Middle ears or Ears, was accused of stealing money from the father of the Ears family. The father held Ears' hands over the gas range until he confessed to doing the crooked deed. As for a sense of honor, I learned firsthand there was one. When confronted by the police and in front of my mother, Ears took the blame for me after I broke a window of the post office garage. This was above and beyond what he should have done. His marbles never got even near the window.

I almost forgot to tell you what the Ears brothers were doing to Herbert the Wart Nose. Herbert had a large wart on the center point of his nose. It was a real eyesore and made him the center of torment at school. I imagine in his own neighborhood, many blocks away from mine, the kids made fun of Herbert. The Ears brothers had a piece of dry ice and were attempting to burn the wart off ole Herbert's nose when I happened on them. They were actually doing Herbert a service even though he was declining. Big Ears had appointed himself as the surgeon in charge. Later, I happened to think I may have done an unjust act to all, including Herbert the Wart Nose.

The Royal Crown Caper

We hit The R. C.

One night when we had nothing to do, we decided to inspect the Royal Crown Cola Company's new fence. The fence was installed some days before so the delivery trucks could be stocked, ready for the next working day, and not be subject to raid. In addition, a large boxer dog was left to roam the new corral. There was a lovely hill surrounding three sides of this corral and we came up with a brilliant idea about using it to our advantage. We would get large cardboard boxes, the kind toilet paper is shipped in, and flatten them into sleds for sliding down the grass hill. They would have added utility as cardboard barges to transport the loot down the hill. We decided no one at Royal Crown would think twice about a bunch of nice boys sliding down a hill. At dusk, we began sliding, whooping and hollering—it was fun and looked very much like a Norman Rockwell Saturday Evening Post cover.

Once it grew dark, we sidled over to the chain-link fence and found we were an inch and a watchdog away from all the R.C. Cola in the world. How to get at those soft drinks, which were staring us square in the eye? The dog must have gotten used to our presence, since it had yet to bark. Okay, we'll just climb the fence and take our chance with Fido, and had started doing just that when we heard someone coming. We ran to cover in some bushes near the Preston Street side of the hill and waited until two figures emerged into the sparse light cast by a single pole lamp in the loading yard. It was two boys from the neighborhood, Junyah and Little Jimmy. We were totally hidden from view as we watched these two produce a can of Big Heart dog food and a long spoon tied to a stick. This was exactly what we needed so we joined forces with them.

Again, we started our ascent up the fence only to be startled by a squeaky, rolling sound and footsteps coming from the tunnel of the Preston Street Bridge. It was the Whitey Brothers, who I disliked with a passion. We never knew the Whitey Brother's real names; we named them because they had white hair and were pure-mean. I would pound the hell out of one of them one day and they would ambush me the next. I finally put a stop to this ambushing thing by carrying a big stick and/or traveling in pairs. Wouldn't you just know it would be them? And with them, another arch enemy, Billy Kerts. Billy would buy friendships by stealing money from his grandmother and play the sport with it. It appeared he was entertaining the Whitey Brothers tonight, because nobody would hang out with Billy for free.

Another reason I didn't like Billy Kerts was because he shit in my brother's jeep and I got blamed for it. My older brother had a Willys Jeep and us boys would hide in it to smoke cigarettes. Since my brother also smoked, he never noticed the jeep being used as a smoke house until the Whitey Brothers and Billy Kerts' unauthorized use of it. Anyway, here were the Whitey Brothers and Billy Kerts with a Radio Flyer wagon in tow. Wow, that wagon would come in handy. Maybe it would be a good time for a truce.

It turned out that Junyah and Little Jimmy would play the most important part in this raid. Junyah's given name was never known to any of the gang. His mother would call to him, "Junyah" and it stuck. Anyway, my mom approved of him because he was a Seventh Day Adventist, whatever that meant. What a pair of characters Junyah and Little Jimmy were.

We had several "Jimmys" in our neighborhood, but this Jimmy was a dwarf. He was only four feet tall then, and if he is alive today, he probably isn't over five feet tall. His main characteristic was he smelled like fresh farts. We were to learn that he shit himself when excited, and he must have become excited every day. When his family moved away, he wasn't missed.

I remember when Little Jimmy's family moved in on Biddle Street. His sister was quickly noticed by all the boys since she was very pretty. All the guys, for days to come, would talk about her and who would be the first to win her hand. Then the talk turned to who would fuck her first. Fuck her? I wasn't sure just what this fuck thing was, but I wasn't about to let anyone get ahead of me. So the next time she was out in her back yard, I approached her and offered her a comic book for a fuck. Naturally, she asked her mother what it was I wanted and I soon met her father. Her father was content after he realized I didn't know what I said. However, it wasn't long before I found out what I said was worth more than a comic book.

Our spirits buoyed by the dog food, wagon and added manpower, we got to it. Little Jimmy went down the fence about ten yards. He scooped some of the dog food with his fingers that he then deposited on the spoon. The boxer stayed uninterested until Little Jimmy threaded the spoon through the fence and started making kissing noises and rattling the fence. The guard dog took notice and was soon sniffing the spoon.

We helped Junyah to the top of the fence. Junyah was a head taller than any of us, and a lot dumber. While straddling the fence and soda truck, Junyah began passing down cases of soft drinks. There was Royal Crown Cola, but Nehi Orange and Grape as well. By now Little Jimmy had made friends with the boxer dog and was petting him through the fence and feeding him treats and saying, "Good Boy," repeatedly.

We lifted at least a case or two for each of us. The Whitey Brothers were afraid we would turn on them, so they quickly loaded their loot and left by way of the railroad, the wagon loaded with soda clunking over railroad ties behind them. We hid most of the cases in the bushes and took some with us to our retreat on the Biddle Street Hill. We were about to light up some cigarettes and reminisce on what we had just pulled off, when a light shone down on us from the crest of the hill. We took off like cockroaches and I heard a man yell, "Halt." I was running pell-mell down the railroad tracks when I heard one of the boys holler, "HE HAS A GUN!" I stopped and turned toward the light, which was squarely on me, with my hands up in the air. This reminded me of a scene from a war movie, One where the Germans were rounding up the Free French. I was scared! I looked but could see no one, just silhouettes. Most of the gang got away.

My captor was a Pennsylvania Railroad cop in uniform, and not a Baltimore cop. I thought of how fortunate we were for that. For a moment, I considered taking off again but in that instant visualized my bullet-torn body being deposited at the feet of my mother. Since we had left the evidence in the tall grass, I hoped he would not know what we had just done. But Willard Rizzo and Little Jimmy had also surrendered, so now he had three of us. He asked our names and addresses first off. Willard Rizzo gave him a phony name and address. Little Jimmy gave a phony name and the correct address. Me, I gave my real name and correct address. A good thing, too. For now the policeman was going to escort us all home. The cop told my mother to keep me off railroad property as I could get hurt, there was nothing about the heisted soft drinks.

My mom was very strict and concerned with what I was doing. She would interrogate my friends and I thought for sure she was going to really let me have it for being disruptive. However, she let the lecture be enough punishment. In fact, she thanked the policeman and merely questioned whether I understood the meaning of his short lecture. I was more concerned with getting to the bathroom and depositing myself in the warm tub. I found solitude in a warm bath. By now, I imagined Little Jimmy had a good case of diarrhea and Willard Rizzo was having a memory problem. I learned a few days later that Willard told his mother that I got him to lie to the policeman and they, wanting to believe him, did just that. As for Little Jimmy, he was punished and had to shit his pants at home. Billy Kerts spent the night at the Whitey Brothers and got the living hell beaten out of him. I heard they caught him trying to steal their father's wallet. Later, he hung around with Larry Barely who set him up in pocketbook stealing. The business was a Seventy-thirty split with Billy getting the thirty and eventually a jail sentence. We never heard from him again.

Over the coming years we continued to visit the Royal Crown yards and, come to think of it, I don't think any of us ever drank a Royal Crown Cola COLD!

How to Become a Superhero and Stay Alive

Every kid I knew had a fantasy about being a superhero, and most of them did what I did, buy it. We sent away for magic decoder rings and other devices advertised on the radio, the back of cereal boxes and in comic books. Upon receipt, the ads promised, you'd be ushered into the secret world of the (sponsoring) superhero, and share his glory.

The first such product I ever ordered was a glow-in-the-dark magic ring. All kinds of wonderful powers were to be mine once I learned to master the ring's powers. The day Jimmy, our mailman, called to me from a block away to tell me he had my package, boy, oh boy! Such excitement! I was ten years old.

The ring had finally arrived and my waiting was over. It would have been terrible to think I almost missed the mail. My Aunt Peg and Uncle Paul were visiting from Cumberland, Maryland. They spent a few days. My mother, sister and I were getting into Uncle Paul's car to go back to Cumberland for a visit when Jimmy spotted me and began yelling, "I have your package." When he handed it to me, I tore open the package to display my prize. The ring was one-size-fits-all, so you knew right away it was magical. Rocket shaped, it had a removable nose piece that concealed the secret compartment containing a glow-in-the-dark "Crystal ball." Before it would glow, though, it had to be held near a light bulb.

I was so excited I asked Sis to read the instructions for me. Later, I reread the instructions, but still there was no magic. I was sure that, had we stayed home, the ring's power would have manifested, but going into the mountains had diminished the ring's power. Upon returning, a week later, I met some of the guys who had the same rings. Of course, their rings worked and I was regaled with bull crap beyond belief.

One account, told by Gene Fox, was how he "looked into the crystal-ball and saw Superman. In flight!" I said bull crap? No, then it was gospel. Furthermore, he had details like "he steers himself by pointing his hands where he wants to go." Well, that was it, then. Gene was a classmate of mine in grammar and junior high schools. I was friendly with Gene in grammar school, but saw less of him afterward.

He was a tall, skinny kid with black hair that hung down over his eyeglasses. For a while he wore a white patch over one lens, which made us think of him as being sickly. He wasn't, the patch was to correct his vision, but that is how we thought. Gene's cheeks were always rosy like he just walked in from the cold. He brought tuna fish sandwiches to school every day for his lunch, and he smelled like urine. In retrospect, he must have had a bladder problem, but at the time I blamed the smell on the tuna fish.

One day, on the Liberace Show I saw a big sick-looking man, with a womanish manner, singing and playing the piano. His sponsor? A tuna fish company! Reason number two for not liking tuna fish—it made you a sissy. One sunny morning Gene and I and some others sat on the ledge of the Ash Tunnel under the post office garage and discussed superheroes. Who was best? Superman, Captain Marvel, Green Hornet and other comic book characters who could fly. Then we discussed paratroopers, and how they would float to the ground, suspended under a parachute. Four of the older boys claimed to be paratroopers themselves. One said he regularly jumped off his third-story roof and floated to the ground using a bed sheet. Now that seemed very reasonable and I decided to try it. I would have to wait until the third-floor apartment was empty, but I would soon be the envy of the neighborhood. Meanwhile, I got in some practice jumps.

That afternoon most of us took bath towels from home and fashioned makeshift capes with them. No self-respecting superhero would be caught dead without his cape. We jumped the low ledges and imitated flying with outstretched arms.

When I went home, I practiced my paratrooper jumps off the back porch. My first jumps were from the top steps of the porch, a distance of about five feet. My next jumps were from the top of the porch rail, eight feet, with the aid of a towel. When the towel still failed to fill with air, I got my mom's umbrella. I shimmied up to the porch roof, eighteen feet above sea level, opened the umbrella and jumped. For a split second the umbrella ride was thrilling, then it inverted. I hit the ground with a mighty thump, my bottom teeth crashing against the top. It scared the crap out of me, but worse, there was the inverted umbrella. When I told mom how I came to break her umbrella by parachuting off the porch steps (I fudged a little), she hugged me. She was glad I told her and explained the law of gravity, and the false notion that, say, a bed sheet could circumvent it. She asked my promise never to try anything so foolish. How did she know my plan?

Even with my mother's warning, my adventures didn't end. One afternoon I sneaked up to the ice truck and snatched a bite-size piece. While enjoying the ice, I got another brilliant idea. (As you have noticed by now, I was full of brilliant ideas!) I would take a ride around the neighborhood on the back of the ice truck. The ice truck had a step on the back and safety handrails for the iceman to hold on to as he made his block-to-block, house-to-house run. No one was on the back of the truck when it started down Barclay Street so I jumped aboard.

The ice truck was racing up Chase Street hill in high gear and the intersections were zipping by. Panic began setting in. I was afraid I'd wind up someplace I couldn't get home from. I jumped off the truck and my feet couldn't keep up with my body. I landed and slid down the blacktop street with my left arm and elbow taking all the punishment. Blood was streaming from the wound. I had a small, one-foot flag of the forty-eight states in the pocket of my jacket. I wrapped it around my elbow and refused to stop for the many people who were urging me to let them help. I ran for home.

My mom wanted to know what happened so I told her I was jumping off garage roofs when it happened. After stopping the bleeding and bandaging my arm, my mom wanted me to show her that roof. I took her up to a group of garages a block away from our house and looked her in the eye and said, "You don't believe me, do you?" She said, "No! Because no roof fall would look like that!" I confessed the truth and again I promise never to hop rides on ice trucks. A promise that is easy to keep.

It wasn't long before the whole neighborhood had refrigerators in every house and the ice man disappeared.

My Sex Education

No matter how you look at it, our neighborhood never ran out of bully-type know it alls. Every gang had one. Our gang had several. When you first met this type, he would try to impress you with his worldly knowledge. And if you were about ten years old, I can guarantee you were impressed. I know I was.

I'll never forget the time Johnnie Spencecola, Georgie Emerson, Joey Campo and I headed for a day of play under the Biddle Street Bridge. That was when we met up with the all-knowing Hymie Glick who was at least sixteen years old. So why was, he interested in conversation with us? Was he trying to freeload or somehow take advantage of us younger kids? No. Hymie was looking for companionship since his own age group had abandoned him. They had grown tired of his stupidity.

I had seen this big mouth, large-framed bully several times. He was about six feet tall and weighed every bit of two hundred pounds. His pug nose, red face and dirty blond hair arranged such as to spell I-g-n-o-r-a-n-c-e.

My first encounter with the Great Hymie was traumatic. Our conversation immediately turned to a subject I knew nothing of—SEX. The first thing Hymie said was that I came from my mother's ass. Those words could very well have been Hymie's last. Georgie, Joey and I were ready to attack Hymie. Georgie told Hymie, "You shouldn't say something like that to Jackie or about his mother!" "You all came from your mother's ass. Hey, what'd you think, the stork brought you?" Hymie yelled at us. In defense of Hymie, Johnnie agreed that Hymie was telling us the truth. Good thing for Hymie, because the sentiment was to gang up on him. The next few hours of that sunny afternoon were dedicated to our sex education.

I remember Hymie explaining jerking off. "Jerking off," explained Hymie, "will become habit forming. Once you get the habit, you can't stop. When that happens, it will cause the softening of the brain and you'll go nuts!" I would worry about that a great deal after I turned thirteen.

When Hymie explained oral sex, his worldly knowledge soared to new heights. Hymie said, "If you do that to a girl, it will take over. You will lose the use of your dick. Your dick will die and you will never ever be able to use your dick for screwing." He also added that could happen from too much jerking off. Boy, Hymie was really smart, and we were sure lucky to have a swell guy like Hymie in the neighborhood. From that day forth, many of us would seek out Hymie's advice about worldly matters.

Once, we pitched in and Hymie bought each of us a pack of rubbers. Actually, it was two packs of three. We opened the packs and distributed them and I could hardly wait to put mine on. We all talked about using them for the purpose intended, but finally opted to put them on, urinate, tie the end closed and drop them off the Biddle Street Bridge.

Several years later, Hymie took a new moniker. The Right Reverend Hymie Glick. All the Italian boys had to attend Mass on Sundays. Every Sunday at 8:30 they would all meet on the corner of Brentwood Avenue and Biddle Street. Mustn't be late for service? This was a sight to make any parent proud. Early Sunday morning, fresh scrubbed, nattily dressed, a donation for the poor in a pink envelope, it was off to church. Saint John's Catholic Church was located on the corner of Valley and Eager Streets. However, these particular parishioners headed in the opposite direction, straight to the Right Reverend Hymie Glick's for a mass at St. Jack of Diamonds.

Hymie had organized a regular Sunday morning card game for his followers. Today, they would play the most honored of all card games, Pitch. If you were from the Tenth Ward and played cards, you played Pitch, a four-point card game involving five cards. The object of the game was to gather points. The bid cards were known as trumps and in a clockwise manner the game would run until someone opened with a bid or guaranteed he'd have points. If he played out his hand and not enough points were obtained he would lose, and in most cases it was money he was losing. The point system was High, Low, Jack and Game. High would be the protected face card or an ace. Low would be the trump card and so on. Jack was an important card to have or capture as it was an automatic point and game was the counting of captured face cards.

This one morning there were too many for playing partners and Big Jake was on a roll. He had at least twenty dollars, his whole week's pay on the line and in the play. Big Jake almost immediately laid down two points that he bid on the hand and when laying down his cards at the top of his voice he yelled, "Duckers," a term recently taught by the Reverend Glick when he had a winning hand that was conclusive. In his hand he held automatic points, an ace and deuce of trumps.

"Hold on!" shouted the Right Reverend. I have a kangaroo straight and nothing beats a kangaroo straight except a kangaroo straight royal flush, at which point he laid down trump cards in a series of two, four, six, eight and ten. Big Jake asked, "What the hell are you talking about?" His Reverence then stated it was in the official rules under jump over rules laid down long ago. "Most people never ever have a kangaroo straight and that is why it may not be familiar to youse guys." This fact was agreed upon by Larry Barely, and since Larry said it was fact, it was fact. Nobody in our gang would dare to dispute Larry and not get the living hell beat out of him. Hymie's cousin was entering the game and to ward off any hard feelings told Big Jake that both these guys were mistaken about the rule book. The rules were to be found in Tanrs book on Pitch. He furthermore said he had a copy of Tanrs at his house. I later found out that Tanrs was an acronym for There Are No RULES.

Morons live forever but not so for little boys. Most of us managed to grow older, therefore outgrowing Hymie Glick. A pity, too. For somehow I miss the humor and antics of Hymie. God bless you, Hymie. You meant no harm to anyone, you only wanted recognition .

The Rizzo Family

The Rizzos were another interesting family. There were Mama Rizzo, Poppa Rizzo and the two boys, Richie Rizzo and his big skinny brother Willard. Willard was harmless and liked to sleep with his big mutt in the backyard doghouse. His kid brother Richie, however, had a tremendous hatred for me and I don't know why. It seemed to me he lived to lie and get me in trouble. Was it because Mike Campo and I once put a milk bottle on their window sill, tied a string from it to their front doorknob, and rang the bell? When it burst against their marble steps, Mrs. Rizzo claimed the "little bastards filled the bottle with beer." That was a damn lie! Where would we get beer at ten years old? It was piss!

Maybe it was because I rang their doorbell after placing a paper bag filled with dog shit on their porch and setting it on fire. I don't think so because, as far as I know, Mr. Rizzo, who stamped the fire out, was too embarrassed to tell anyone.

If he hated me for breaking into their cellar and stealing two jars of canned pears, it was only because his brother Willard and I had done it once before. This time Richie was not home, but Mike and I were, so we just helped ourselves. After all, had Richie been home, he could have joined us. I do not know where he got the idea I was not his friend.

One day Hugh Footley had his pigeon coop broken into and his pigeons stolen, and Richie told Hugh—one of the Tenth Ward's great bullies—that I did it. That just was not so. I had no idea where Hugh lived or that he had pigeons, but he beat me up anyway.

Then there was the time Richie told the cop on the beat that I was the one who broke the windows in the post office garage. That lie almost got me locked up. It did get Richie a black eye. For that, and the Hughy incident, I neatly smacked his brother, Willard, in the mouth. My most vivid memory of the Rizzos, though, is of their venture into entrepreneurship. They were the first to open a snowball stand in their back yard. A snowball is shaved ice splashed with a flavored syrup and served in a paper cone. Mrs. Rizzo ran the operation. Mrs. Rizzo was also the first woman I saw wearing short pants, and I do mean short. Ladies wore shorts in magazines, and the features or newsreels at the movies, but not in our neighborhood. It would not be long before all the women would wear them, but

Mrs. Rizzo was the trailblazer. I must add, she was a beautiful woman. I was about five feet tall, so most grownups looked tall to me, but Mrs. Rizzo was taller than most of the ladies in the neighborhood. Her long blond hair and shapely body also made an impression on me. Thanks to my complete sex education, courtesy of Hymie Glick, and some prematurely howling hormones, I was now more appreciative of her than ever.

This Saturday morning was very hot and muggy, so the Rizzos moved their snowball stand to the basement. The Rizzo's basement was accessible by a backyard stairway. I entered the basement to buy a snowball and heard Mrs. Rizzo saying to a lady customer:

"Oh Helen, all the women will be wearing shorts this summer. I just have not had an opportunity to get out to the stores to get any. They are about the same as a man's shorts, so I borrowed Harold's."

My eyes jumped to the south of Mrs. Rizzo's waist and I was mesmerized. She was wearing a pair of men's red and white, fly-front, boxer shorts. When my turn came, she asked what flavor I wanted. "Cherry," I answered, and she started shaving the large block of ice. As she worked, the fly on the boxer shorts opened and closed in rhythm with her to-and-fro movement. Her hairy crotch was winking at me. I tried to look anywhere but there, but that winking action was magnetic; I actually began to tremble. When she handed the snowball to me. I almost dropped it while handing her my money. I turned and stumbled up the basement stairs into the yard and got the hell out of there.

I told Mike Campo about my experience and we returned to the Rizzos basement for a snowball. Soon, every kid on our block was buying snowballs from Mrs. Rizzo. I bet she set an all-time record for snowball sales that day. Alas, she soon wised up and used a large safety pin to hold her fly shut. By the way, Mrs. Rizzo was not a true blond!

My Buddies Stevie and Mike

Stevie Edwardo Fazzio

I was nine when I met Stevie Fazzio. He and his kid brother, Deano, were sitting on the large granite steps decorating the Biddle Street Bridge while Georgie, Joey and I were embarking on a day of play in the Ash Tunnel.

The Ash Tunnel was a huge fill under the post office garage where ashes were piled as high as forty feet. I have no idea where all these ashes came from, but many people in the neighborhood would lug their furnace ashes to the fill and dump them over the fence. We had lots of fun playing there, climbing high up under the garage, jumping off the substructure, and landing on the soft ashes. We would be gray from top to toe after playing on the ash pile. The post office garage was a swell place to play in, too. The Biddle Street entrance was a city block away from the main entrance on Preston, which was great. The reason it was so great? No one would hear you or bother to come to this end and chase you away, that is unless we really got noisy, and that was every time we were in there. There were hoses to squirt and parked trucks in a line to run through and everything, just lots of swell things to do. Did you ever see those shiny brass fire extinguishers? Did you know, to get them to work they have to be turned upside down? We learned about them, too. They had several there for us to learn about. We once set a small fire and put it out with one of those shiny things. We did it before the fire trucks arrived and nobody gave us any credit for putting the fire out.

The Fazzio brothers sat on the bridge eating candy bars; that caught our attention. They told us they had just moved into the neighborhood from another part of East Baltimore. The normal procedure when you met a new kid in this neighborhood was to establish who was boss. That meant picking a fight, but this was different. They were eating candy bars and extended a large brown bag filled with candy and asked if we wanted some. Of course we wanted some.

Stevie explained they lived over top of the grocery store and had to traverse the grocer's storage room to reach the stairs. That explained the candy bars. These candy bars were better than the pigeons we were planning to catch, and eat and we gobbled them up.

I liked both Stevie and Deano Fazzio. Stevie was half a year older than I; Deano was two years my junior. Mom would later call Stevie my adopted brother, and most people thought we were brothers. We both had blond hair and hazel eyes that appeared blue at times. We were both the same height and build, until we were fifteen and I grew to six feet and Stevie stayed two inches shorter.

Stevie had a problem with his front teeth, probably all of his teeth. They were starting to rot. Some of the guys would poke fun at his two rotten front teeth. Big Bob, never missing the chance to put someone down, started to make fun of Stevie. When Big Bob found out Stevie's middle name, Edwardo, he had everybody calling Stevie Eddie Pearls or Pearls S. Fazzio, pearls making reference to pearly white teeth. Stevie put a stop to it real quick by challenging everyone except Big Bob to a fight.

Stevie and I didn't have a reason to fight but we did. We only fought each other once. When we ran into each other afterward, we laughed because he had a black eye and so did I. A bond of friendship developed between us that lasted all the days we lived in the Tenth Ward.

Although Stevie's mom and dad were divorced, he loved them both very much. To hear him talk you would get the impression they all still lived together, but both had remarried. His father married a Jewish woman with a mouth as big as the Grand Canyon. His mother married a man who had one foot stuck in the local bar.

Stevie was always making up stories about his mother and real father. I knew they were made up, but he seemed to like these dreams and I never called him on them. Stevie never got to go anywhere with the gang because he had to watch his kid brother Deano, sister Carol Anne, half-brother David, and half-sister Margie. When I think about it, Stevie was the best kid in the neighborhood. He was an altar boy at St. Anne's, where he continued to attend school, and a member of the Police Boys Club. His father's new wife had two boys by their marriage. I guess Stevie's answer was to make life enjoyable by pretending to be happy.

A thought comes to me of the time Altar Boy Stevie almost got sent directly to hell. I really mean it, no passing go, no collecting $200. Just go straight to hell!

Stevie wore his hair in a high pompadour. It was well greased, too, and stood about 2 inches high. One Sunday as he was assisting the priest in Mass, holding onto a large candle holder he became amused and couldn't stop giggling. His giggling became infectious and all the altar boys became engaged with uncontrollable giggles. Why? One altar boy was to light a candle from behind the altar and proceed out with one enormous lit candle. The priest was now at a point where he loudly exclaimed in sing-song fashion, "Let one lit candle show bright throughout the world." The priest repeatedly sang out and got no response. On the priest's third sing song and with no action taking place, the altar boy that was to bring forth the light for the world, sang back, "A cat pissed on the matches." Not only the few altar boys heard this, but the priest was within earshot of the matches refrain, too. Stevie still clutching his lit candle, his person elevated on a step above, bent his head over in an attempt to hide his giggling, and set his pompadour afire.

I remember when the gang all got bicycles for Christmas. Stevie told us he got one, too. It was supposedly kept at his father's house because his mom didn't want him riding it in the street. When we got roller skates, again, the same story-the skates were at his father's.

Stevie would try to con me out of my comic books by telling me he had hundreds at his dad's house, and would get me some the next time he visited. We were poor, but there was always someone poorer, so mom suggested I let Stevie have my comic books saying, "After all, Jack, you have read them." Stevie used to pull the wool over a lot of the gang's eyes. Me, I understood him.

Twice, I got really mad at Stevie. The first was when we were both in Boy Scouts. Yes, we were Scouts. It cost my mom fourteen dollars to get me set up in Troop 164, Shawnee Patrol. Stevie got upset at the troop over something and quit. When he heard I was made bugler, his former job, he rejoined the troop. So I quit. Since I was now out of the troop, Stevie quit again. That did not make sense to me, but eventually I wrote it off as the way he was.

The second time I got mad at Stevie was when I helped his father one Sunday. They were laying floor tile in a dairy, and Stevie asked me to help. He said we would get five dollars—each—for the day. Stevie got the pay and never gave me my share. I was mad for a few days, then forgot it. Those who liked him never let his idiosyncrasies bother them.

Stevie had an uncle for everything. If my family was going on a moon-light bay cruise, Stevie was quick to say, "If I was going too, my uncle would get us on board for free. He pilots the boat." If we were going to the amusement park, his uncle was the general manager.

Stevie once invited me to an Orioles baseball game under the guise of getting in free as his mother's brother was the groundskeeper, whatever that was. He said the game started at one-thirty, and since we would be walking to the stadium, we'd better leave early. We headed up Greenmount Avenue when a streetcar passed by. "Hurry up, Jackie, or we'll miss our ride," Stevie yelled, as we raced to catch the steel-wheeled vehicle. We hopped onto the back of the streetcar, holding on all the way to the stadium. When we got to the stadium, I had no idea how we would get in. Stevie did. I still thought we would be given V.I.P. treatment by virtue of his uncle, the great big-grounds keeper. We walked right through the gates as if we belonged there. We milled around the top section, then went down to the bottom section where we saw an empty soft drink case. Stevie told me to pick it up. When we saw another one, Stevie picked it up. He looked at me and started to laugh. "Keep that case until the game starts. People will think we work here," he said.

The Shrine Circus came to town and scheduled its first circus parade since before World War II. Georgie Emerson, Stevie, and I went to the parade route, our hearts were filled with excitement. We followed along with the elephants all the way to the finish at the Fifth Regiment Armory. Georgie asked Stevie if he was going to ask his uncle, the one who was in charge of the doors, to let us in free. Without hesitation Stevie said, "Wait here, I'll see if he's in there." Stevie was gone about ten minutes when he returned saying, "You guys want to let your moms know where we'll be for the next couple of hours?" And we got in.

Stevie's kid brother, Deano, loved to play with matches, and like most of us, liked to torch old, dry Christmas trees and abandoned automobile tires. One day I found Deano rolling around in the alleyway entrance to the Fazzios' apartment. His pants were on fire and he was trying desperately to put it out. I managed to douse the flames and summon help. Help came and he was taken away in an ambulance with sirens blaring. This gave him an awful scare, but I somehow believe he enjoyed the ride. He had been at the railroad yard, setting fire to dry Christmas trees when his pants ignited. Stevie and his mom told me they would be forever grateful for my help.

I was probably in the alley entrance way that day on my way to lift a few empty soft drink bottles from the grocer's yard. That poor grocer! Often, I would sneak into his yard where he kept bottles and grab a quick cache of empty soda bottles. Then I would walk around to the front and turn my swag in for the deposit. The deposit was two cents a bottle, and admission to the Preston Theater was ten cents before two o'clock. When a six-pack came out the side door, it was a direct pass into the theater. There, for one thin dime, you could see a full-length feature, two comics, and one chapter of a serial adventure.

There was a small, green-fronted store across from the Preston Theater. I'm not sure how you would classify this store today, but there were many like it all over East Baltimore. Inside were candy cases, a cigar and cigarette rack, two phone booths, an ice cream box, jars of pickles, pickled onions and a tray of coddies. Coddies were a delight to most kids, although a gourmand would puke if offered one. The coddies were lying out in the open where anyone could finger them and flies could land. The coddie's secret ingredient, as best I could learn, was mashed potatoes and cod fish with breading, deep fried and served with mustard and crackers. After leaving the movies, a six-cent coddie was a tasty way to tide yourself over until dinner. The stores also sold racing forms. Hmm? Phones and racing forms? They would have to sell one heck of a lot of coddies to pay the rent!

Thinking back, of all the locations in the neighborhood, the grocer Resnick was probably the only establishment that wasn't into gambling although he may have purchased a package or two that fell out of the back of a truck. I knew for a fact every one of the bars and restaurants was into gambling in some form or other. There were games of chance or bookie joints at more convenient locations. The neighborhood was too poor to support all the businesses located there. Stevie was once told he couldn't see a young girl anymore as her parents wouldn't allow her to have a boy-friend. The next week her mother's beauty shop was raided by the police for bookmaking.

Mike Campo

Mike Campo was two years older than I, and I learned from him. I admired his ability to seemingly understand everything. Mike was very popular and had a magnetic personality. We were about the same height, Five foot, and I felt good when I was with him. He had thick black wavy hair, and eyes as black as coal. He, along with Stevie, was my best friend.

When I was ten, Mike told me about a wonderful restaurant on Greenmount Avenue. The food was great and, here is the best part, they liked little kids. They liked them so much that there was no charge to eat there. The place was Mamie Schreck's restaurant. We went there twice and ordered French fries with gravy. The waitress would pile the plate full, bring us catsup and water, and to our amazement, never asked us for money.

This was just great! When I got home, I told my mom about Mamie Schreck's. It wasn't like the Montgomery Ward Cafeteria, now my second favorite place in all the world to eat. There, my mom would have to pay the cashier when we got to the end of the line. This wonderful place was free. My mother was not impressed. She did not believe this "free meals for little kids" thing. This caused me great anxiety, so I coaxed her into going there with me. When we entered Mamie Schreck's, she asked to see the owner. Then, speaking very loudly with the lady who owned the place, Mom said, "My son has eaten in here."

"Yes!"

"My son said you don't charge for kids?"

"Lady, your son walked out of here without paying!"

"That's what I thought. I would enjoy a fried oyster sandwich for me and my son, and I will pay whatever it is he owes you."

* * *

A Street Arab, or huckster, sold fruits and vegetables from a horse drawn wagon. They used to be all around Baltimore, and I think one or two might still be left. "Huckster Nick" came through our neighborhood every day. Everyone took care of his horse. I would carry a bucket of water out and hold it for Jake the horse to drink from. Other times, I fed him sugar and carrots from my hand. One day Mike Campo started throwing Jake's turds like they were snowballs. He chucked one at me, and when I ducked it splattered onto Huckster Nick's vegetables while Mrs. Spencecola was buying tomatoes. "I can't buy these things," she shrieked, "they have horse crap all over them." Huckster Nick would have whacked us good had he caught up with us. We avoided Nick and Jake for the next few days

* * *

One day my brother Leroy gave me a camera and developing set to encourage me to take up photography. I got Mike Campo, and together we began learning how it all worked. By the time I had the developer mixed, we had decided to go into business and take pictures around the neighborhood for ten cents each. Then I decided that, once we perfected things, we would ask the two local drugstores to let us do their work.

Mike's older sister was our first customer, and her pictures turned out beautifully. By the next day, we would see they were even more beautiful if you liked red. Pretty soon you could not see anything but red. We had used all our supplies by this time and just said to hell with it.

* * *

One summer day our gang was playing cowboys and Indians when Mike suggested we needed a campfire. We set about collecting scraps of paper and wood. As usual, we started building on the original plan until it got out of hand, like the time one of the Whitey Brothers told us how easy it was to swipe comic books from the drug store. Soon, we were developing a plan to tunnel into the Lord Calvert Savings Bank. We always did that.

This time we decided to cook dinner on the fire, so Deano ran home to get the potatoes we would roast. Pigeon tasted good with potatoes, so Mike volunteered to catch some. With a few rocks in hand, he set off on a pigeon hunt, and in no time had four proud specimens. Pigeon catching is easy, and we did it a lot. Find a pigeon, and they were everywhere, wing it with a rock so it couldn't fly away, and grab it. We wrung their necks and pulled the feathers off, stuck a wire through them and roasted the pigeons over our fire. By now, the potatoes were black and tender. We divided the pigeon legs and breasts and divvied up the spuds. They were delicious. Years later I learned that what we called eating pigeons, the swells referred to as "dining on squab." What a laugh we would have had over that.

After our feast, we could not let this fire go to waste. After all, our original objective was to dance around the fire. We danced around it, trying to keep it going, but recent rain made it difficult to find enough dry wood. "That tire will burn," Mike said, and pointed to an abandoned tire.

An automobile tire will burn nicely once you get it started. The thick black smoke a tire produces is incredible, like a building on fire. We placed the tire on the fire, rubbed cinders on our faces to look like war paint, and danced around the fire whooping and yelping Indian sounds. Within minutes we heard fire trucks on the Fallsway and Biddle Street Bridge. We all raced up the hill so we could see what was on fire.

* * *

One Saturday I went to see a movie at the Apollo Theater. Mike and all the guys were going together, but I had to wait for my mom to come home from the market. When I arrived, the theater was packed, even though it was early matinee. That was annoying, but so was the fact that the Apollo was a higher-priced theater than the Preston we usually patronized. That day, even though I was only eleven years old, I was tall enough that the ticket seller made me pay the full price of fourteen cents. That made me break my bank.

Once inside I saw nobody I knew and figured the gang went to the Preston Theater instead, which, in fact, is what they did. I found a seat in the middle of the theater, right in front of some punks who started harassing me. The worst thing to do when outnumbered is to acknowledge that the harassing bothers you. I scrunched down in my seat and tried to concentrate on the movie. When the feature changed, all but one of my tormentors got up and left. The punk directly behind me stayed though, and he kept his feet on the back of my seat, as he had since I first sat down.

On the way to the movies I bought a pack of Embassy cigarettes and a pack of matches (Embassy was advertised, Better by Far and Less Acid Tar). I retrieved the matches from my shirt pocket and tore off a paper match. Sliding down to the floor, I surveyed the punk's shoes. The light reflecting from the movie screen clearly showed a hole in the bottom of one shoe, over which he had placed some cardboard. Peeking through the seat backs gave me a glimpse of my tormentor. Artie the Gawk. That half-wit son-of-a bitch from Warden Street. I slipped the match, oh so carefully, into this hole. The row I was sitting in had emptied, so staying low, I struck another match. Almost trembling, I lit the match in Artie's shoe and scooted out to the aisle and to the back of the theater. Suddenly, I heard loud shouting from the center of the theater. An usher ran down and ordered Artie out of the theater despite his protestations that he had, for a change, been wronged.

* * *

A carnival had been set up near Johnson's Square, and a few of our gang decided to go. Johnson's Square was not a playground, but a small park with benches located in the middle of the Ward. We were really enjoying ourselves when a kid about my size, completely unprovoked, walked up to me and slapped me in the face. Hey, it hurt and stunned me! He turned to his group and they walked off laughing. Mike was just catching up to me and asked what was going on. I explained, and Mike advised me to punch the punk and they would back me up. I caught up with the show-off and nailed him good, smack in the face. He started to yell, "I'm going to get my big brother." His brother was not long in coming either. Mike told me not to get scared and strike quickly. Taking this advice, I punched the guy when he got close enough to reach. He was stunned at first, then cried, "I'm not fighting you, you cocksucker. I'm a Catholic!"

The World's Best Ice Cream

I miss the days of waking up to the sounds of Saturday morning on Biddle Street: A hose spraying the soot off the sidewalk. The old man ringing his bell, which summoned you to bring your knives for sharpening or have your marble steps sanded. He was the city grinder, as much a part of Baltimore as the marble steps he sanded. I can see him now, a very bent old man pushing this very bent, custom-made contraption. It looked much like a wheelbarrow with a large grinding wheel placed in its middle and a bell that constantly clanged whether the contraption moved or not. The old man worked a treadle with his foot, and that powered the grinding wheel.

Dearest to me, though, were a tiny pony and cart that would race down my street as if the driver had to meet a very important schedule. A very small, old Italian man drove it. He reminded me of "Jocko, the Organ Grinder," a story I once read in school. The pony pulling the cart was so small you could think of it as a playmate for your dog. Everything seemed to match—the old man, the pony and the cart. There was a continuous sound of clanging from a small bell hanging from his cart. He sold fresh hand-dipped ice cream.

I thought I must be dreaming the first time I saw him go by on Biddle Street. I raced after him, yelling for him to stop, and then asked how much his ice cream cost. He pointed at the large sign, much too large for the tiny cart, which read eight cents. My mom, who had been standing on the front sidewalk, came to my aid. The old man climbed down from his cart and asked me, "Whata you lika boy?" I replied, "Strawberry, sir," as my mom gave me enough money to buy that delicious strawberry ice cream. She smiled and asked me, "Does it taste good?" I answered, "Oh, yes, it is delicious." She replied, "I'm sure it is, it's handmade."

I don't think any ice cream could ever duplicate the old man's handmade variety. I also believed, somehow, that this old man was special to me. That no one else could see him. We had several ice cream trucks that would visit the neighborhood two and three times a day, and I would patronize them all when I had money, but I don't remember ever seeing anyone else buy from the old man. And the speed with which the old guy passed through our neighborhood was odd for someone wanting to sell ice cream. All summer, I waited Saturday morning for the sound of the pony racing past my house. He would always stop on the Biddle Street Bridge and start to prepare a strawberry ice cream cone for me. I handed him money and he would give me ice cream, then run his fingers through my hair and say "Golda hair." Then he'd pat me on the head. I may have overslept one morning, but he stopped coming by. I remember there were times I thought I heard the pounding sound of tiny hooves on the street racing toward the Biddle Street Bridge. I would anxiously race to see him, but he never did appear, though. Too soon, things we enjoy and that become a part of our lives are no more.

Buccheri Izzo Giordano Olivarri
a.k.a. BIGO

A few doors nearer the Biddle Street Bridge lived an old, somewhat well-to-do Italian man. He would carry on long conversations with my mother and, from what I could gather, was in the realty business. He rented out the two upper floors of his house. Then he up and died. He had a son who was away at private school, and when the old man died he came home and never returned to school.

The son was fourteen years old and big, at least five feet ten inches tall. He weighed 150 pounds plus, and nobody messed with him because he could beat the hell out of you. His name was Buccheri Izzo Giordano Olivarri. We called him "BIGO"

My mom said he was under the guardianship of one of his father's renters, after somehow proving the old man had bequested it. The renters, who paid no rent now, were the Runks. What a mean bunch of rotten bastards they were. They had three sons, two in their early twenties who did nothing but knock Bigo around and make his life a living hell. He would tell me, "When I reach the age of consent, out go the Runks."

Bigo was an inventor and was always trying to invent something that would blow up. He beckoned me out to the bridge one day to see an experiment. He had mixed a concoction that would burn through concrete and demonstrated by pouring it on the sidewalk of the Biddle Street Bridge. The sidewalk was in flames immediately after Bigo set a match to it. It burned for ten minutes or so. When the flames died, however, the bridge and sidewalk were intact. I was ten years old at the time, and asked Bigo what his secret ingredients were. Bigo named about ten items from his chemistry set. The most powerful ingredient, he claimed, was from Mrs. Runk's dressing table. A liquid that was in a blue bottle and burned with a blue flame that just happened to Mrs. Runk's perfume.

Bigo was full of adventure. He volunteered to climb the great bent tree on the Preston Street hill and tie a manila hemp rope above the bend of the tree. This would become our personal swing, only to be used by those selected by Bigo and me, which meant about twenty others.

Bigo climbed to the top of the bent tree, and since the tree didn't budge under his weight, we knew it would be safe for us to swing. Bigo secured the rope and each of us got a turn at swinging out over the railroad. The swing was over forty feet from the ground and, on a good swing, you would arc over fifty feet above the tracks. We told Bigo he should have the first swing since he did all the work. We didn't mention that there was no way we were going to risk our necks until this thing had been test driven.

Rope in hand, and with plenty of slack on the ground, Bigo raced to where the earth met air at the cliff's edge, and with determination, he leaped and was airborne. We let out a mighty cheer!

He swung to the extreme limit of the rope when the knot holding the rope to the tree came undone. Bigo continued to fly upward for a moment and then, as if hitting a wall, he stopped climbing. In typified horror we watched Bigo, still grasping the rope, drop like a stone to the railroad yard below. He lay motionless. My God! Was he dead? We raced down the hill to see if he was okay, but he was out cold. We ran to summon help but when we got back, Bigo had already gotten up and gone home.

The next morning, I went over to the Runks' to find out how Bigo was doing. Mrs. Runk said, "He's not here. He left early this morning. I thought he might be with you." I went to the far side of the Biddle Street Bridge where you could see in several directions. Bigo was again airborne on the swing. This time, the knot holding the rope looked as big as a bowling ball.

* * *

One of the guys thought he was very clever when he added an "N" to Bigo, making his name Bingo. That cost the guy a broken nose. Even then, the jerk started singing the Bingo song, you know the one, ". . . had a little dog and Bingo was his name, sir." We did enjoy calling out to Bigo from across the room at the church bingo games. But only when he was across the room.

* * *

Bigo and I built a pigeon coop in my back yard. I don't know if raising pigeons was a regular thing for Italians, but there were a lot of pigeons in our neighborhood. We found ourselves constantly trying to catch every pigeon that landed on Barclay Street. There was a granary at the foot of the Fallsway. A large red building with a huge number "2" painted on both the north and south sides of it. We would take a trip to the number 2 building and gather grain that was spilled during the loading process. Eventually, we purchased a few racing pigeons and talked about the prospect of raising them for profit. We let a few other guys join us in our venture, and that was our undoing. One of the rookies decided to find out whether or not they were homing pigeons, and opened the coop. He proved they were, indeed, homing pigeons when they all went home. Wherever that was.

One day, while walking down Barclay Street, I saw a beautiful red and gray pigeon with a band on its leg, lying on the ground. I carefully approached the bird and picked it up. Believing it to be a pigeon with an important mission, I took it home where it could rest and feed before continuing its journey. My mother constantly complained that the pigeon was sick, so after a few days I decided to release it. I wrote a note stating I had cared for the bird and included my name and address in the bird's banding, and sent the pigeon airborne. A few days later my trained canary, the one that would eat from my hand, lay dead in its cage. The next day four finches were also dead.

* * *

Bigo had a '41 Olds left to him by his father. It sat in front of his house for a long time since Bigo was not old enough to drive. We would sit in the car and daydream of taking trips as soon as Bigo came of age. Bigo had just turned fifteen and it was my eleventh summer, we were thirsting for adventure. One day we decided we would wait no longer. We had been talking with an old man who told us tales of the "Old West," and we just had to go. We would head out Biddle Street and make a left at Maryland Avenue. From there we would go down Cathedral Street until we got to the Y.M.C.A., make a right turn onto U.S. Route 40 and keep on going until we were in the "Old West."

We decided to get a load of dried beef for the trip. After all, dried beef was what the cowboys in the movies took on trips. When they got hungry, they simply pulled a hunk out of their pocket and bit off a chew. Resnick's sold dried beef, so we sent the little seven year old Runk kid there to get two packages of it. There were five of us making the trip and two packs of beef sounded just fine. He would charge them to his mother's account. "Get some eggs, too," we hollered as he ran toward the store. Hard-boiled eggs would go nicely with the beef.

Soon, Horatio Runk (as the little Runk was christened), returned with a large bag of provisions for our trip to the "Old West." Opening the bag, we saw Horatio had purchased a dozen eggs and the beef. He had also bought a pint of oysters and a dozen Hershey bars with nuts. Horatio said that since we were leaving, we might as well go in style. That explained the chocolate, but he could not explain the oysters other than saying, "I like oyster stew."

We placed the bag of provisions on the back window ledge of the car, up and out of the way. Our canteens were loaded with Kool-Aid and placed in the car as well. We would leave for the "Old West" first thing in the morning. In the meantime we sat and talked about all the great things we were going to find in the ghost towns. Silver saddles, boots, and even six-shooters all lying there just waiting for us to take them. Stevie Fazzio said, "My uncle owns a gas station out on Route 40. If we need gas, we can get it there." We assured him that would not be a problem. The gas gauge was on full and that would last a long time.

It's nine-thirty, Saturday morning, and we were ready to go when Stevie showed up with his kid brother, Deano. We would be on short rations of beef if he came along, but we wouldn't refuse him. We got in the car and waited for Tony Vespi to show. Stevie asked if the battery was hot. "Yes, I start this thing every day and run it for five minutes," responded Bigo.

Tony had a bag of sandwiches. He told his mom we were going on a picnic and she packed sandwiches and sliced cake for each of us.

Bigo started the car, lowered the clutch pedal and let it out with a jerk. The car jumped the curb and stopped running. Again Bigo started the car. Cursing, he stomped on the clutch and shifted into reverse. He backed the car off the curb and shifted into forward. With a heavy foot to the gas pedal, he engaged the gearshift, again jumping the curb. He crashed into the marble steps of my house. I guess that was when we all realized Bigo didn't know how to drive.

I noticed a very disagreeable odor in the car and thought someone crapped his pants. We climbed out of the car and pushed it off the curb. Fortunately, none of the audience that was assembling around us was family—yet. A man came from across the street and re-parked the car. He asked what was going on. We told him we were trying to get it closer to the sidewalk to wash it. He resounded, "Well, you'd better wash the inside, too."

We opened the door to get in and the odor knocked us over. In our initial excitement over the trip, none of us had noticed the smell earlier, besides some kids stink. I don't know how we missed it, because the smell was god awful. We retrieved the bag in the back window. The trip to the "Old West" was forgotten, but with the sandwiches Tony brought and our larder, we would have a fine picnic.

Opening the bag of dried beef was a sickening chore. The odor was worse than a dead rat, and there was goo in the bag. It was rotten hamburger.

"Horatio, what the heck is this stuff?"

"Two pounds of ground beef."

"Ground beef? We told you dried beef."

"Maybe he only had the wet kind? I'll take it back and have Resnick take it off my mom's bill. I'll tell him she opened it last night after he closed and went somewhere else for the right stuff."

"Okay, good idea." It wasn't long after Horatio entered Resnick's that he reappeared. Mr. Resnick, leading Horatio by the arm, was headed toward the Runk house. Resnick carried the beef in his other hand and was grimacing over the smell.

First Time at Bat or Young and Horny

We were young detectives, unswerving in our dedication to solving the mysteries of sex. It mattered little whether you were a boy or a girl, we wanted to examine that which sat, or hung, between our legs. I was eleven years old, as were most of my pals. I never gave much importance to age, only thinking alike and shared interests mattered.

One day we were measuring our dicks to see who had the longest. We did this often since, at age eleven, things could change rapidly. These comparisons would occasionally have a contested jerk-off that we called a "circle jerk." If someone had a nudist magazine and was willing to sacrifice it by laying it on the ground, the contest ended quicker than if we had only the stimuli of our imaginations. Actually, it was more a "line" jerk than a "circle" jerk. The orgasmic shooter muscle in an adolescents penis is wondrous. During one of our early "circle" exercises, Stevie let go with a wad that hit Tony Meatball in the face, a good six foot-shot. Anyway, after that we stood in a straight line.

One day during recess I was standing at the urinal when I glanced down at Lenny "Auggie" Auggusto's wang. Here was a kid my age holding a piece of meat bigger than the Polish sausage Mom made for dinner. I couldn't believe what I was seeing.

"What are you looking at?" Auggie asked when he noticed my fascination with his wang.

"Shit! Auggie" I exclaimed, "that's the biggest fuckin' dick I've ever seen."

It was too.

Zipping up his pants, Auggie, on the verge of bawling, sniveled, "Hey, it's not my fault. I was born that way and it's not nice to make fun of people." And he stormed out. Make fun of him? Shit, I was ready to ask him to hang out with me. I've since often wondered if, on his wedding night, he warned his wife, "Please don't make fun of my giant dick."

Lest you think we were interested only in male sexuality, we weren't. There was just a great lack of female genitalia to analyze. Most of what we saw was courtesy of guys who had sisters, like Tony "Meatball" Lardeo. One night I was going in the door when Tony saw me and yelled for me to come over. I was in a hurry because I wanted to watch Arthur Godfrey's Talent Scouts on television, and it was about to start. "What's up Tony?" I asked.

"Come on, but be quiet," he answered and we crossed the street and went down the alleyway next to his house. When we got to the back stairs, he turned and gave me the index-finger-to-the-lip "be quiet" sign, and we crept carefully up the stairs. Crouched against the bricks under the bathroom window he whispered, "My sister's taking a bath and I opened the window a crack and raised the shade. Be fuckin' quiet." My heart went to 190 beats in a flash.

His sister Carmella was fifteen, and better than average looking. I peeked through the one-inch opening into the bathroom and saw Carmella, bending partially over the tub and pull the plug out of the drain. She was beautifully naked! My breath caught and I had trouble breathing for a moment. This was paralyzing. Carmella took a towel and turned, facing us directly, not five feet away. She had the most beautiful breasts with pink nipples! After wiping her face, she started drying her body and removed a swatch of soapy foam that clung to her pubic hair. Holy shit! She had jet black pubic hair, thick enough to make you want to grab for it. We stayed motionless until Carmella, clad in a pink flannel night shirt, left the room.

Once home, I had just two thoughts. Carmella was the most beautiful girl I had ever seen, and how could that fucking pervert Tony let me look at his sister? Tony was sexually pathological. When he learned the art of jacking off, he stayed home from school for at least three weeks. He amassed a huge collection of nudist camp magazines and would lay in bed while jacking off on them. He'd bring them out to show us and, at first, we couldn't figure out why the pages were stuck together. None of the guys wanted to go into Tony's house, and entering his bedroom was out of the question! Tony told me I could borrow a few of his books. They were hot stuff, but there was no way I'd touch them.

I once saw him in the Times Theater, sitting in the front row. He'd peek back every so often, then move to another seat. Afterward, I asked what that was all about. He answered, "I was trying to look up that broad's dress behind me and she kept shifting her legs."

Tony told Floon and me about a girl's dance studio near Calvert Street, saying he'd stopped and looked in the window. "I swear to God, these girls undressed and you could see everything!"

Now Floon, as well as every guy I knew, had been apprized of our reconnaissance on Tony's sister, so this was treated as gospel. On the way to the dance studio we met Everett and he joined us—after paying Tony the price of an ice cream for the information.

Arriving at the dance studio, we stationed ourselves at the window, which was under a fire escape and in full view of the street. The window was open and the room well lit. Inside was a long bench and sounds of music and girl's voices were plainly heard. It was nighttime, but we were worried someone would see us. Retreating to the back alley, we found a very-large cardboard box. We cut most of one side out in order to peer in the window, then a few holes in the street side for keeping a watch on passersby. Once in position we sat for a long time with nothing happening.

Suddenly, we heard something on the street side of the box. It sounded like someone running a hose. Everett peeked out a surveillance hole to see a drunk pissing from the shadows, right down on us! He was pissing on us and we couldn't say a word. Man, did it stink! Everett was getting the worst of it and finally yelled, "Hey, stop it!" With that the drunk upchucked right into the top of the box. We started climbing out. The drunk hollered, "Shit! What the fuck you doing in there? I'm calling the cops!"

* * *

Phil Mahoney was a nice kid, but he would walk around with his index finger in his right nostril. By the time he was fifteen years old, his nostril was so distorted we all called him "Torn Horn." Phil really hated me, and were situations reversed, I might, too.

Phil's sister, Ann, was a year my senior. I didn't know her very well because she went to a different school. Stevie Fazzio, however, did know Ann. As a matter of fact, in some ways, he knew her better than her brother did. One day I was headed for the railroad when I saw Stevie and Ann. Stevie said, "Hey, Jackie, you want to see Ann's pussy?" Taken off guard, I muttered "Huh?"

"You want to fuck me?" Ann asks.

"When?"

"Right now, stupid."

"Where?" I asked.

Ann pointed under the Biddle Street Bridge. "Over there, near the Ash Tunnel."

I casually nodded assent, but my body was all a quiver. We entered the Ash Tunnel and Ann disrobed. Her tits were smallish, but what interested me most was her pubic region. She had reddish-brown hair on her crotch and under her arms. Suddenly I realized that I was in over my head. "What is it I should do here?" I asked myself.

"You want to go first?" Stevie asked.

"Sure."

Since I had been educated about "S-E-X" by Hymie Glick, I think "I can do this." Well, I certainly try. I dropped my pants and let them fall over my shoes. I guess I looked very stupid with my tiny bat sticking straight out. I didn't have any pubic hair, and I didn't know that fucking while standing up is an art. We stood around for an awkward few minutes, that's all. Ann was a good, if mixed up, girl. She didn't know what to do either. Stevie said he'd give it a try, but the best he did was stand and hug her. He asked, "Do you want to suck her tits?" I was already very disappointed and said no. We got dressed and then sat and told stories until it was time to go home for supper.

The next day, Moe Thompson came over to my house, and while we were talking, Ann walked by. She waved and said "Hi!" Moe asked "Who's that, she's cute?" I replied, "Just some girl Stevie and I fucked." Moe stayed with me all that day.

Curious about the girl he asked so many questions, I even made up answers and they almost got me killed. The very next day I was helping my older brother clean the trunk of his car when suddenly, WHAM! A club hits me in the back of the head. I turned around to see Ann's brother, Phil, swinging a stick and screaming, "You fucked my sister!" There were some guys with him, so lucky for me, my big brother walked up. At least the fight would be clean. We fought like hell. I was defending myself admirably when here came Stevie Fazzio running down the street. He told Phil that I don't know his sister from Stevie's cousin. "It was my cousin we screwed," he explained, and Phil bought it. Good old Stevie Fazzio, best bullshitter in all the Tenth Ward.

Chef Jack

I became a chef at age eleven. Summer vacation was beginning when some girls in my class told me they were signing up for a cooking class. It was sponsored by the Red Cross and was to be held through June and July. There were only a few girls in my neighborhood, if there were more, I hadn't noticed them. I had noticed these girls however, and instantly had an idea about this cooking school. Most guys went to the church dances to find girls, but I figured this cooking class would be a "girl store." If they let me sign up, WOW! I'd have them to myself. Stupidly, however, I told Everett about my idea. He told his cousins, Billy Gene and Jimmy McCarthy, which was like telling the Tenth Ward. Billy Gene was stockily built and a mean character. His kid brother Jimmy fell just short of being an idiot.

The first day of cooking class was loaded with guys—Everett, Billy Gene, Jimmy, and a bunch more. As we progressed through the first week however, I found the class was becoming very interesting. We learned food handling and preparation, and did some actual cooking and baking. Jimmy McCarthy did nothing right. He would add too much of this, not enough of that, and try to fix it by adding more water, and then more flour, until he had a total mess. As I said, Jimmy was an idiot. I really enjoyed that class, though I went for the wrong reason.

After the class, I started cooking as a hobby. My mother joked that I would now require Duncan Hines-caliber cuisine. Hey man, I now was using words like hors d'oeuvre and Garde Manger.

I got an opportunity to display my new talent to my pals. We were going on a hike to Lake Roland and each guy was to bring some food. Anxious to show off, I volunteered two dozen home-baked muffins for the trip. Muffins could be eaten en route and would need no additional preparation. I worked very hard all Thursday evening preparing for the trip. I had not, however, asked my mother's permission.

The next day I had a knapsack loaded with delicious muffins prepared by the great Chef Jack. I told my mother good-bye, explaining I was going on a hike with the gang. She told me that, under no circumstance, was I going on that trip, and I knew she meant business. I gave the knapsack filled with muffins to Mike Campo and explained that I was not going. Mike expressed his heartfelt sympathy and, walking away, took out a muffin ate it. He yelled back that it was the best he had ever eaten. Reluctantly,

I went into the house. When I looked out the window a few minutes later, I was extremely hurt to see the whole gang throwing my muffins at each other like snowballs. Mortified, I went into the kitchen where there was one more tray of muffins. I had saved these for my mom. I took a muffin and bit into it. It tasted like pure salt. I gathered the remainder and went out to the Biddle Street Bridge. As I approached the gang, Mike said, "That fuckin' Jackie couldn't go on the hike so he tried to poison us!" I threw some muffins at them and the fun really began. We had a great time muffin-fighting.

First Worst Job?

We went into the wood selling business. There was a seemingly endless supply of wooden crates along the railroad tracks and every home had a wood and coal burning furnace. We filled bushel baskets (used for hauling washed clothes and found on nearly every back porch) with the broken-up crates and sold them for a quarter.

Two boys walked door-to-door taking orders while the rest gathered the wood. Business was great, but the "endless" supply of crates was rapidly being depleted. We loathed quitting because the demand was so great and we had gotten used to the money. While filling the baskets one day, Stevie came up with a heady idea. Stack the larger pieces of wood up to near the top and lay scraps of the fresh cut white pine on top. The basket was only half full, but looked look full up. That swindle hit rocks its first time out. The customer hefted her purchase and could tell she was being bamboozled. We came up with another idea. We were running this operation from behind the billboards on the Biddle Street Bridge. They were made of wood and we needed wood. So what if the wood was painted green? Wood is wood. With saws borrowed from home, we carefully cut alternating braces from the scaffolding. We continued selling wood this way until, clearly, removing another sliver would cause the billboards to topple over. Eventually they did.

As we were nearing the end to our wood selling venture, a new opportunity presented itself. It was late in the morning when Stevie and Deano came back carrying a basket with its lid inverted. There was wood piled on the lid giving it the appearance of being full. Underneath, however, were posited three quarts of milk, lifted from an unsuspecting customer. Henceforth, a new business.

That night we replaced the note from Doc Busch's milk bottle. It originally read "No milk through Tuesday, I will be away." Now it instructed "6 quarts of chocolate." Drinking our chocolate milk the next morning, we decided to expand. For the next few days the Cloverland Dairy, Rices Bakery and the Bond Bread delivery men saw sales skyrocket. When weekly bills were submitted, however, the resultant furor convinced us to return to pigeon hunting.

The first money I earned, on my own, was by making Christmas decorations from pine and holly branches. I tied a bunch together, splashed on some gold paint, and they looked good. After arranging them in baskets, I loaded the merchandise into a wagon and pulled them up to Charles Street where I had no trouble selling them. I'd walk into a bar, look for a woman, place the decoration near her shoulder and say, "Lady, that looks good on you!" She, or a gentleman friend, would buy every time.

One day I was pulling my wares up Charles Street when a colored lady stopped, rolled down her car window, and asked "Are you selling those?" She was, she explained, a school teacher who wanted to show my work to her class. She told me many of her students had never seen pine and holly before. I thought it was really dumb, a kid that never saw a pine or holly tree? I sold her one for twenty-five cents.

Later, I began to reflect on what it must be like being a colored kid. Having to live in a concrete section of Baltimore, without trees or streams, just dirty alleys to play in, and houses with five or six families living in them. Wow. The thought was genuinely depressing. Then, I began feeling better. Was I ever lucky to live in a neighborhood as nice as the Tenth Ward!

Christmas passed, and with it my Christmas decoration business. I tried selling newspapers on Charles Street, keeping one step ahead of the badge man, an investigator from the Child Labor Board. You had to be eleven to sell papers, and to sell them you needed a newsboys badge. I was only nine. Mike Campo was caught selling papers without a badge, but he was two years older than I, so was thus able to get his newsboy's badge. When his badge was approved, we went into business together.

We set up on Charles Street, right in front of the "Bloody Bucket," a bar known for knife fights. It was a prime corner, but every Saturday night we were evicted by "Big Bob." He and some older guys sold the big Sunday papers on that corner, and Sunday papers were a very lucrative business. They told us to leave, then cursed us when we didn't, and finally began threatening our well-being. We were no match for Big Bob and his thugs (they were all of high school age), plus, they could stay out all night and we couldn't. We finally acquiesced, but not without a payback. Big Bob was Georgie Emerson's older brother. Georgie had three older brothers in the same age group as my own brothers. However, no match. Big Bob should have been named Big Boob as he was certainly stuck head over heels on himself. He was bigger than the elder brothers and quite stupid. This fact was probably brought through his own growing-more energy was given to muscle than brain cells.

Lying in bed that night, it came to me how we could get back at Big Bob. When I woke up earlier than usual Sunday morning, I knew it was God's will. It was still dark when I slipped out the back door, down the stairs, grabbed my wagon and made a beeline for Greenmount Avenue and Preston Street. Old Blind Charlie's paper stand. Each Sunday morning a mountain of papers was dropped on that corner, where an older kid sold them to people going home from church. The kid paid Charlie for the use of his stand on Sunday mornings. The papers were waiting for me when I reached the corner. I snatched two bundles of papers, loaded them into my Radio Flyer and got out of there.

Reaching home, my conscience started to bother me. Maybe I should take the papers back. Alas, the missing papers would be blamed on thieves and the kid wouldn't have to pay for them. He'd simply report them missing to the Sun and News Companies and the delivery driver would bring him more. I know this to be true from experience, because Mike and I have been in the same situation. I put my mind at rest, determined with the fact I was on a kind of mission from God to punish that big prick Big Bob. I covered my stash with pieces of tar paper and sneaked back into the house. The entire operation took 45 minutes.

My plan was to wait until next Sunday when I would dump the bundles at Big Bob's corner on Charles Street, hopefully causing him to sell last weeks newspapers to his customers, and hopefully causing him to get pounded. When I later told Mike, he thought my plan was terrific.

"But how do we get the papers dropped off he asked." "Won't he get suspicious when we bring the papers by?"

Whoops, hadn't thought that far ahead.

How we did it was we showed up on our old corner the next week with the load of papers. We would act as though, threats be damned, we were competing for this spot. When the inevitable threats came (Your mama's gonna find you floating in the harbor), we would act terrified and run off, leaving our papers behind. Big Bob, of course, in his greed, would look on our abandoned papers as a windfall, and sell them. Success would depend on his not noticing that he was peddling last week's news, but he would have to be able to read, something we doubted he was capable of. It turned out easier than that.

When we arrived, we saw that Big Bob had his papers stuffed and ready for sale, but there was no Big Bob, and no goons. Mike suggested that, after stuffing their papers (the Sunday paper was distributed in sections, and had to be "stuffed") he had gone somewhere to screw around until traffic started. Whatever, it was our good fortune. Rather than pile our stale papers on top of his, we replaced the front page of our papers with the front page from his. The result was a very deceptive "sandwich" of fresh bread and tainted meat. Now, even if Big Bob could read, there was nothing to tip him off. We loaded the carcasses of his original supply and skedaddled.

To this day I don't know what happened. I'm positive the bogus papers were sold, and equally sure that some very angry customers came back and demanded refunds. At the time we were satisfied with the vision of a car pulling up and spraying Big Bob & Co. with a machine gun.

Having now gained Mike's confidence, he taught me to "use the system." He said, "If you want to make money, you have to hustle." So, we took turns at the hustling thing. For example, I'd catch a city transit bus—drivers let newsboys ride free—and work my way to the rear of the bus "barking" papers. I'd stay on for several stops, exit, then catch a return bus and repeat the process. I could look out the bus window and see all the news stops we were taking business from.

Other times, when there was a lot of foot traffic, I'd stay and take care of our "spot." I always remained a stone's throw from the corner to avoid getting caught by the badge man. I could keep an eye on the papers and money lying there on the honor system, and make my escape if necessary. Mike and I made some decent money doing this, but eventually, one or the other of us got bored, and our business association ended. I did learn a lot about hustling though.

The summer I turned thirteen, I went over to the Royal Crown Cola Company and applied for a job. I told them I was sixteen years old, out of school, and needed a job. The clerk told me they were not hiring "inside help," but suggested I report to the yard tomorrow morning at six-thirty, and ask for 'Wild Bill'. "If he likes you, he'll hire you as his helper on the truck."

Next morning at six-thirty, I was there and a short, stocky guy was waiting. His feet stuck out sideways and he walked like a duck. Smiling, he asked, "Are you John Lundon?"

"Yes" I replied.

"I'm Wild Bill. My truck is ready, so let's go."

That was it. In a half-hour we were in Essex, a suburb of Baltimore. We worked Bill's route until six o'clock, and Bill was very kind to me. He bought me lunch, soft drinks, iced-tea and lemonade, none of which were Royal Crown products. I was neatly dressed when I reported to work but, oh-boy, was I a dirty merchant by quitting time. That night I slept like a baby and the next morning we were at it again. I was so excited about this job that not even the fatigue dampened my enthusiasm. In fact, I was so excited that I didn't know what I was getting paid. Or when. Again, that day we worked until six o'clock.

That evening I told Larry Barely, Georgie Emerson and Joey Campo about the wonderful jobs available over at Royal Crown. The next morning we all met there at six-thirty, and all three were hired. I didn't mind the heavy work, or the hours, because I was now a "working man." Besides, Bill promised, "We only work a half-day on Wednesdays." That Wednesday I got off the truck at four o'clock!

Overall, I was happy. I loaded cases of soft drink onto a hand-truck and carted them into the store. Soft drink cases were made of wood, contained twenty-four bottles, and weighed about forty pounds. After completing the delivery, I retrieved the empty bottles and loaded them on the truck. The empties were dirty, sticky and often covered with bugs. I soon learned not to wear my good clothes on this job.

After several weeks, the blush was fading from this bloom. Bill now "allowed" me to do just about all the work, except drive the truck. I was often embarrassed when we serviced a soda stand and a gaggle of pretty girls would stare at me, all filthy dirty in ragged clothes. Bill was also something of a bullshitter. He'd say things like "Next week we'll bring bathing suits and go swimming at a shore stop." Maybe he was sincere at the time, but when you tell a kid you're going to do something, you should do it!

Finally, I got paid—eighteen bucks for the week. I heard, somewhere, that the driver decided your pay. If that was true, I decided "Screw you!" Larry, Georgie and Joey Campo had quit their jobs as "assistants" in less than a week. After a month, I told Bill I had to go work for my father, and quit. He told me he was genuinely sorry to see me leave. I believe he was, too. He hadn't worked a lick in thirty days.

Sports

Doc Busch organized the Tenth Ward baseball club in 1951. Old Doc Busch, as he was known, was a bootleg dentist. Where most folks would have a sofa in their living-room, Doc had a dentist's chair. Everyone thought he was a real dentist until, one day, the police pulled up and confiscated his chair. However, just taking Doc Busch's chair away was a wasted exercise since business went on as usual at old Doc's.

I was nine years old when my mother sent me to Doc Busch to have a tooth pulled. How brave I was! I sat up in his big chair while Doc grabbed a seltzer bottle and sprayed my tooth. Then he put a cloth over my chest and proceeded to extract my back molar with a pair of pliers. I screamed bloody murder and escaped out the door with Doc in hot pursuit. He caught up with me, calmed me down, and promised me a job working as a delivery and cleanup boy if I would let him finish. I relented but, oh my god, what pain! True to his word, however, he put me on the payroll. I learned he did more than yank teeth.

Doc operated a false tooth distributorship out of a secret showroom, just off the living room. On the third floor of his house, he had a dental lab where he made partial plates, bridges, etc. He took impressions of people's mouths in the living room, then cast and molded teeth upstairs. Many of Doc's patients were high officials, including cops with gold badges on their blue uniforms. The prison doctor was Doc's personal physician and would visit often to check on Doc, or just bull shit with him. With all the clout old Doc had, it's no wonder he was seldom harassed by the law—and never arrested.

Doc had remedies and answers for almost everything. He constantly preached: "If you get in a fight with a nigger, don't waste your energy hitting them on the head. Kick 'em in the shins." In fact his advice for any combat situation was "A kick in the shins." Darn, it wasn't until I was fourteen that I learned shins were not your nuts!

Doc told me stories of his childhood. One was about playing baseball with the "Baltimore Boys," where his best friend was a boy named George Herman "The Babe" Ruth. Doc filled me with so many stories about his baseball exploits that I figured he might agree to manage our neighborhood team. When I approached him about it one afternoon, he readily agreed.

What a bunch of stout-hearted, positive-thinking losers we were! We were, absolutely, the worst ragtag team ever. We had no uniforms, and the few gloves we had were ridiculous. Stevie Fazzio said he had enough gloves to outfit the team and, it turned out, he was not bull-shitting this time. Somebody gave him some gloves that looked like construction work gloves with padding stuffed inside; I think they were last used by Honus Wagner. Plus, we had caps that matched. Well, almost matched. They were Army fatigue caps we purchased from a war surplus store. Thomas Eugene "Moe" Thompson was our team captain. Why? Because Moe said he was!

Moe was two years older than the rest of us, and totally stuck on himself. Moe would get tongue-tied when he got to talking too much, which is why we encouraged him to do it. It was hilarious, his trying to pull a word from the roof of his mouth, his face red in exasperation. Today, I guess, a bunch of pasty-face types would go into apoplexy over our fun with Moe, but hey, there really was no harm in it.

He had the idea that he was quite the entertainer, too. Thought he could sing. I would see Moe coming down Biddle Street, his arms swinging to and fro, his voice raised several octaves, singing out "Bobby to her miter brook, tis her poor me miter wain dwop." Translated: Babble to her mister brook, kiss her for me mister rain drop. From a song titled, "Please Mister Sun." (That's what he was singing!)

I met Moe when I was seven years old. At the time, I was lying on the ground on Chase Street, with some kid I did not know on top of me, pounding me in the face. Suddenly, this kid with blond hair and a very square chin pulled him off me. He hit my assailant in the stomach and demanded, "Never, ever, touch him again." Then he extended his hand to me. "Hi, I'm Moe. Want to be in my gang?"

"Sure." I answered. I mean, the guy just saved my life. Moe came home with me, and my mom made us lunch.

Now Moe would be leading our ball team. The problem was, most of us had no respect for his leadership ability. We all thought Mike Campo was more capable, but no, old Doc Busch, being the South Baltimore hardhead, believed "the strongest should be in charge."

In order to be sanctioned by the Department of Recreation, and thus scheduled use of fields and game umpires, you had to be within age and weight limits for your league. Many of us lied about our age and weight. Some even weighed in twice, once as ourselves and a second time as someone else. That way we had "ringers" we could put on our roster if we needed them. I say again, what a motley bunch we were.

We would all pile into Doc Busch's station wagon—I still do not know how we did it—and ride to our game. Once, when we were heading out to the West Baltimore area to play a game, we were stopped by a motorcycle cop. The cop said Doc had too many kids in the car. This caused old Doc to deposit half of us on the sidewalk with a promise to return and pick us up. Doc pulled off and circled the block and with the cop still in view he pulled up for us to re-enter the car. The cop came over and old Doc said he just wanted to give us some money to get a coke while we waited for his return. He gave us a five dollar bill and we headed across the street to a fruit stand on Baltimore and Hilton Streets. At first we were somewhat dismayed as to what to do in a fruit stand. This one had an outside stand, too.

Larry got into some bullshit conversation with the clerk about matters. He asked if they had fresh matters? The unsuspecting clerk asked, "What's a matter?" Larry quickly replied, "Nothing! What's a matter with you, you fucking punk?" The clerk retreated to the back of the store.

Holding the money Doc gave us, Big Jake asked if he could have a bunch of bananas and some oranges, The place was crowded and another clerk, possibly the owner, waited on him. Larry stuffed a bag with various fruits and he left for the other side of the street. To this day, I don't believe he paid anything for the stuffed bag of fruit.

While we waited for the Doc to return, Garbage Pants Knoop threw some half-eaten fruit back across the street at the younger clerk when he came out to wait on a customer. This was very brave of him, since Doc just pulled up to get us.

We played six different teams and lost every game we played. If our pitcher walked a man, it was as good as a home run. The walked batter would steal second on the next pitch, take third when the catcher threw the ball into center field attempting to throw him out, and come home when the center fielder fell down trying to pick up the ball. We lost by scores like 23-14. (We could hit like hell, just couldn't field or pitch).

I recall our first game was a shambles. We arrived on the field in our home style uniforms. Boy did we look great. Clean white T-shirts fatigue caps and all. Today, we will make history. We will play Capital. They can't play ball like us, old Doc said so. When we arrived on the field, we saw this bunch of guys fully clad in red and white uniforms. With bright shiny bats and gloves that looked really professional. This can't be the Capital team, from a distance they looked like a team that was going to play the Yankees. Moe walked over to them and made a hasty retreat all the way back to us saying, "Dats dem, em guys is da capital team. We can beat-em." Looking at me he said, "Jackie, we'll murder em, dey won't want to get der uniforms dirty." The game was a shutout. We were telling everyone back home it was a shutout, and let it go at that. The only thing is, we didn't tell them we were the ones shutout.

The next game, we paid Big Bob to help with the driving, and therefore we took a few extra guys in case there was a fight. Fight? Sure, we weren't going to let the next team beat us or make fun of us. We again met a well-dressed team, in fact every team we played was uniformed and had lots of fans, (parents and family) with them to cheer them on. We were somewhat different since we didn't have any fans. The next few games we did gain some respect as a team that tried, or possibly the kids we were playing were told by their parents to be nice. There is always someone who has to screw up. We soon met one. I got a single and Larry was the first-base coach. The first baseman tried to intimidate me by making fun of my uniform and Larry sucker punched him. The first baseman fell to the ground and I began to steal second. This caused some confusion in the game to say the least.

In near to our last game played only two parents were present to cheer on the team. When they left after the final inning which we lost, we got into a brawl with the other team and guess who won the fight. We started early the next year and decided to sponsor the team ourselves. I had a talent for speaking to people, so I came up with this mother of an idea. I wasn't sure just what a "Notary Public" was, but we had one on our block. He always wore a dark pinstripe suit and black shoes in winter, and a white suit and shoes during summer. I can picture him now, walking confidently in his white suit and shoes, a pinned collar bar and neat necktie. When he walked by, all the grownups would greet him and bid him good day. That was respect. He had a small sign near the entrance to his house proclaiming "NOTARY PUBLIC." I was really impressed at being in the very presence of this man. A man of his stature could probably talk to people in the supreme court or even the better business bureau. I just knew he could help if he wanted to.

I went to his home and told him we were seeking funds for our ball team, and his being a notary public could help us, if he wanted to, in our effort. He was receptive and penned a letter in ornate script, which he then offered for my approval:

> *To Whom It May Concern:*
> *This will introduce Jack Lundon, a fine*
> *young man of our own neighborhood,*
> *Jack is collecting funds to uniform our*
> *neighborhood's very own ball club. I think*
> *it is a good idea and a very worthwhile*
> *cause. I have contributed in sponsorship*
> *and will be very pleased to see your name*
> *on the list of contributors too!*
> *Signed,*
> *Your friend, Carlos Sica*

He then embossed a place near his signature. Holy shit!

Was I ever impressed. I took the letter to all the restaurants, grocery stores, bars, and barber shops. Plus I went door-to-door throughout the neighborhood. A few guys walked with me for insurance. I tapped every source in the area, and I got enough money to get us outfitted.

Unfortunately, I trusted Moe's estimate of uniform prices, and he was off by fifty-percent. Stupid me. If I asked Moe "Where's Philadelphia?" he would answer something stupid like, "Over the shore somewhere," and I had trusted him as a financier? Now I was in a hell of a predicament. I promised each retailer that his name would appear on the back of a uniform for each ten-dollar donation. Moe said the names would cost a dollar each when, in fact, the charge was $3.50. We went downtown trying to find a lower price, but were unsuccessful.

Moe and I were angry with each other and argued all the way back. I would be too embarrassed to show my face near any of my benefactors, and Moe was mad at me for, well for my being mad at him. We sat down on some steps "discussing" whose blame it was. An older guy, whose steps we were perched on, was listening from inside the house and came out to introduce himself. His name was Johnnie Allis, and he wound up solving my problem with the uniforms. He asked me how much money I had and how many names I needed. I told him, and would you believe it—Johnnie Allis said he had connections, and would get it done. He did, too. Johnnie Allis became our team manager. We fired Moe as team captain and gave the job to Mike Campo. Things were looking good for the coming season, and when I went to bed at night I could visualize the newspaper stories that would chronicle our heroics.

Unfortunately, by the time of our first game I had developed water on the knee and was out for the season. I recommended that the kid I had beaten out at second base get my uniform. His mother came over to pick it up and said how she was sorry I could not play, and how happy her son was. Good for him, but I was deeply disappointed. In the end, the team had a repeat of last season, and never won a game. They won a few fights after the games, though.

My consolation, even today, for never getting to play ball in a real uniform is the sure knowledge that had I played, we would have been undefeated!

My Family

It was wonderful growing up in my neighborhood. The Tenth Ward was, once, a desirable place to live. It was close to downtown and the markets. There were gin mills on every other corner, neighborhood bakeries, at least four local drugstores, several hardware stores, a group of restaurants and two movie theaters! On each corner, less than two blocks apart, were grocery stores all this was within a few city blocks, approximately one square mile, of my house. It is hard to imagine a single neighborhood supporting that variety of business.

We moved into the Tenth Ward in 1944 when the neighborhood was an "all white" section of Baltimore City. By 1958 most of the residents were black. The new inhabitants were not poorer than the former, but the neighborhood became littered and less attractive. I used to joke about my neighborhood being so poor it was cleared to make way for a slum.

We had riches beyond the value of money. We had a home. There was much love in that old creepy, cold, three-story house we lived in. My mother made it a home, and the watchful eyes of my brothers made it safe and secure. I never really knew we were poor, and frankly never gave it a thought the whole time we lived there. That's the way it's supposed to be. Of course, we didn't have television reporters showcasing our poverty and misery on TV every night, and telling us how shabbily society was treating us.

After my sister left home, I took orders from all three of my brothers. My sister left home to marry her boyfriend, Jack, just after she turned seventeen. My biggest brother in size was Jim. I grew up thinking "Jim" meant "Big." Jim was strong, extremely handsome, smart, and had a knowledge of, and ability with, tools of all types. Jim joined the Navy just after Pearl Harbor at the age of sixteen. During the war his ship was engaged in several sea battles, and he had a chest filled with ribbons and stars when he finally returned home. I was so proud of his service to our country, and was quick to boast of it to anyone willing to listen. After the war Jim returned to school graduated, and went into civil engineering.

Jim was fond of me, his kid brother. He kept a close eye on me and made sure I was provided for. He took me places even when he was with a girlfriend. Twelve years my senior, he was to me an adult confidant. He taught me to drive a car when I was only thirteen and allowed me to smoke cigarettes in his presence!

Next in line is Vaughn who was rowdy and an excellent street fighter. His reputation for street fighting kept me protected for years, even while he was serving an Army tour in Germany. Vaughn was in his prime, lady-wise, and considered caring for little brother to be something of a nuisance. Still, he did watch over me while Mom worked, and probably saved my life once.

I had a problem of going into convulsions whenever I was sick, and my temperature went over 102 degrees. This first occurred in 1942 while mom was at work. Vaughn carried me to St. Joseph's Hospital from our home, several blocks away. He almost dropped me in his attempt to get me to the hospital before I could bite off my tongue. His big smile was the first thing I saw when I awoke in a hospital bed.

Vaughn quit school and went to work at Montgomery Ward's Distribution Center until he joined the Army and went overseas. I recall his bringing me a small present almost every payday. He was a hard worker and did his share to help our family survive.

I missed him very much when he went overseas, but boy, what pride I had for him! Vaughn sent pictures of himself in uniform, with the Great Seal of the Tank Destroyers, and Armored Division and European Theater patches prominently displayed. Just looking at him made me feel like running out and joining up.

Vaughn was very handsome, and I guess he had his pick of the ladies. There were two in our neighborhood who tried to catch him, unsuccessfully. I remember Johnnie Spencecola's sister coming over, ostensibly to see my sister, but really wanting to see Vaughn. Vaughn would slip out the back door to escape her.

He was sports minded and played football with the pride of the Tenth Ward, the Irish A.C.'s. I still hear people talk about how really beefy that team was. In the service he distinguished himself playing basketball for the Army's championship team in Europe. Odd, the smallest brother became the greatest gladiator.

When he came home from the Army, he was more serious than I remembered. He was set on furthering his education, and worked days while attending college at night. Once, when I was playing hooky and stepped out the side door of the old Howard Theater, I walked right into him while he was unloading his Coke truck. The Howard was located in the middle of downtown. How was I to know Vaughn's service route was, too. He gave me the lecture of my life that evening.

Vaughn was often in the right spot at the right time during family emergencies. Once, when I was very young, I heard my mother open the door to our back porch. Vaughn had been staying out late, so she took his door key away, forcing him to come home before she locked up. This night, Vaughn was late and my mother heard him trying to raise the back window. She opened the porch door to summon him into the house, then heard Vaughn yell, from two doors down, "I'm over here, Mom. That's a burglar." The would-be thief took off down the alley. Who knows what might have happened if Vaughn had not startled the burglar. I consider myself very lucky to have been born into a large family where a loved one was always at home to share life with you.

My oldest brother, Leroy, had several nicknames: Sam, Slim, Roy and, my favorite, June. That's short for Junior. He was fourteen years older than I, and had my full respect, the kind generally reserved for a father. June made sure the family stayed together. His first and every thought was for the family, and he was our primary breadwinner. I believe he never married because he did not want to share his affection for my mother with a wife. June was a ladies man, though. He had an enormous wardrobe and was a fun-loving guy. With an armful of jokes, he could cheer you up when you were down. June had great empathy, and he often turned my sunny side up.

I was about nine years old and was summoned in for Thanksgiving dinner when my mom told me to wash my hands. I did and when I returned to the table she said, "I told you to wash your hands, they are dirty." I looked and saw the backs were dirty, but I washed the insides. Aggravated at my mother, I said, "Fuck you!" The silence that came over the room was more quiet than three in the morning. You could have heard a pin drop. I knew I must have said something really wrong. I immediately ran from the table and out the front door. I was across the Biddle Street Bridge, down the hill, over the rails and up another hill when I was tackled by brother June. He looked me in the eyes and with his consoling gaze asked me what I said to Mom. "I said fuck you!"

"Do you know what it means?"

"Yes, it means fuck you."

"Do you know what a fuck is?"

"No."

With that we returned home and as I went to wash my hands again June assured my mother I didn't know what I was saying.

June studied music and was accomplished enough to sing with an orchestra. Before the war he would sing around town at various spots. He wanted to become a full-time professional singer, and once he was invited to sing at The Steel Pier in Atlantic City. He turned it down because of his obligation to the family. When I was an infant, June would carry me around and sing me to sleep before putting me in my dresser-drawer bed. I could write forever of the love and devotion I have for my brothers.

One story, engraved in my memory, happened when I was twelve years old. June and I were downtown shopping; he was buying me a trench coat. After we made the purchase and headed back to his car, I stopped to look in a shoe store window. My brother asked me, "What are you looking at?"

"Those blue suede shoes. Aren't they real gone?"

"Are you kidding? You mean to tell me you really like those things?"

Quickly, I explained they were the "in" thing with the gang. A few days later, when I came in from school, Mom said, "Look on the chair in the dining room. Your brother left a package for you." I raced into the dining room, and on the chair was a shoe box. Hurriedly, I opened it and literally cried with joy. It was the very pair of blue suede shoes I had seen in the shoe store window.

June was absent for much of World War ll. He joined the Navy and served in England as a radioman/side gunner on a Navy plane. The plane was a B-25, named "The Heavenly Body." Once in the early morning over the Irish Sea on a Fourth of July, June noticed a ship below them shooting off what appeared to be rockets. They were exploding very close on port side. Notifying the pilot that the ship below was celebrating Independence day, the skipper relayed back to June that it was a German ship and they weren't celebrating the Fourth of July.

Sís

I was nine years old when I found out my sister's name is Shirley because we always called her Sis. During the war years, Sis tended to me while my mom worked in a war plant. My being the baby of the family was just as hard on Sis as it was on me. I was tied to her apron strings, and she was obligated to take me everywhere she went, or that I needed to go. She held her hand over my eyes so I couldn't peek whenever we were in dressing rooms like the one at Clifton Park Swimming Pool where the girls and ladies changed.

I was so attached to Sis that I worried about something happening to her when I wasn't around to protect her. Once I dreamed that some people dragged her into an alley. That's all I remember, but talk about a nightmare!

I was very protective of her and could not stand her boyfriends. Yes, I was jealous, and fearful of anyone mistreating her. Sis is six years older than I, but I thought of her as my ward. Still do.

After Hymie Glick told me all about sex, my dislike for the boys hanging around Sis increased tenfold. Some of them thought the quickest way to Sis was through me so I received harmonicas, comic books, movies and bowling nights out from her would-be suitors. I took them all, but still hated them for what I knew they wanted to do with Sis.

As I write about her, I'm reminded of two characters who tried sparking her. One was the eldest Runk boy, Gene. Talk about a total waste of a human being. Gene was twenty-two and would have stolen Christ off the cross if he wasn't nailed down. When I was ten, Gene bribed me with a bottle of beer to let him into the house. He and Sis were sitting on the sofa, talking, when Mom walked in. After listening surreptitiously to Gene's talk, she burst in the room and demanded he leave. Mom explained he had a filthy mouth. "He's a Runk," I explained, "from up the street." Mom said, "If he's a sample of that bunch, look out!"

Once, Gene was down at the railroad where he stuffed a large gray cat into a burlap sack, then he set it on fire. It was a horrifying sight and left a lasting impression on me. His stooge, "Kookie," was with him, and was every bit as sadistic as Gene. One day Kookie climbed atop some rail cars and contacted high tension wires. I felt no sorrow when I heard he was found electrocuted on top of a boxcar! Gene continued to be involved in several dirty doings, and eventually was incarcerated for breaking and entering, among other things. While on parole he climbed into a truck that had a partial cover over its back. The truck was filled with crates of oranges. Gene laid low inside and awaited an opportunity for the truck to stop. It did, but the stop was at a point where he could not exit. It was at the entrance to the State Penn on Madison Street. The truck started moving again but this time went inside the yard of The Big House, and Gene was history.

The other would be red-hot-lover was a half-witted guy by the name of Buddy. He slobbered when he talked and smelled like stale smoke. I didn't like him one bit so I manufactured a story about him. I told Vaughn, Buddy was bragging he was going to get Sis. Vaughn made short history of him. My poor sister didn't have a chance to experience life as many do today.

Mom

Throughout this book I have mentioned my mother. Always faithful in minding the security of our family. A reader might ask, "What about your father? You must have had a father." I did. It was my father who gave me the opportunity of becoming a man loyal to my mother and to discover things mostly on my own. I owe my father relationship to my oldest brother, who took the burden of our family on his shoulders. His shoulders were extremely broad for he was not only raising himself but his siblings too. I was introduced to my father in a manner that may be different than most introductions to fathers.

It was in a hospital and it was my birthday, only it was not the day I was born. It was March 11, 1944. It was my sixth birthday. My father and mother lived in marriage for seventeen years, long enough to have five kids. One baby boy died. They divorced and got together afterwards and that is where I came in. I never had any trouble with that part of life, because I never knew about it until maturity. When I did learn of it, it was from someone who must have thought it would cause me a problem. To their amazement I held no bitterness toward my mom and dad for my being born. In fact I'm glad they got together. If you enjoy my adventures, you will be glad they got together, too.

I was six years old and awoke in Saint Joseph's Hospital with pneumonia. This was my third bout with the killing germs. My mother summoned my father, I was in a comatose state and he came immediately to Baltimore. That is when I first saw this huge man. He looked very familiar, almost duplicating the features of my brother June. I was somewhat joyed by this first encounter. However, I was disappointed to see he was not my brother. My mother spoke, "Jackie, this man is your father." My father then asked how I was doing as he grasped my ankle through the blanket. All I could say was I wanted to go home and began to cry. My father commanded me not to cry and assured me I would be home in a few days. Leaving me a package of games he and my mother then left the hospital ward.

My mom was a hero. She should have been English, she had all the qualities of royalty. Having two of her sons off in the North Atlantic fighting the Nazis, and working nights at a war material plant near the inner harbor weren't enough. To add to the aggravation we were constantly being frightened by the evening air raids and air raid blackouts. I don't know if she was ever truly happy.

A woman of mostly German descent born in Petersburg, West Virginia, my mother was a beautiful woman possessing a deep Mediterranean complexion with jet black hair and Germanic blue eyes. She was seven years older than my father, which may have contributed to their marriage breaking up. Perhaps my dad was too young to be wed and accepted the responsibility before his time.

Mom was trained as a nurse with the sisters of Mercy in the early 1900s. She was 45 years old when I was born. I never knew anything about my dad other than he was a lieutenant with the Fire Department in Cumberland, Maryland, and had spent a lot of money on rotten women. My mom never taught me to hate the mention of my father. She often told me my talents were natural to me duplicated from my father. When I became a man, I was proud to know of my father. If I wasn't his son, when he died why did he have so many pictures of me among his personal belongings?

My Elevator Stealing Days

We used to steal elevators. No, we didn't dismantle and heist them. We would locate an elevator, preferably one that had an operator, coax him off, and hijack it. One day we were walking through a downtown alley when a large door opened. It was a freight elevator and the guys who got off failed to close the outer door. All that was stopping us from taking a little ride was a wooden grated door, which we soon raised. After turning the brass swivel handle, away we went. As the elevator slowly ascended, we passed floors filled with sewing machines with hundreds of women busy at work behind them. Then came a floor that smelled like burning fish (it was the ink and alcohol used in a printing plant). As we arrived at one floor, a man started to lift the wooden door and realized the elevator was in use. He merely asked us how long we'd be using it, and requested we close the door tight when we got off. The elevator wouldn't move if the door was ajar, so we left the door all the way open when we left. We were real shits.

Freight elevators though, were nowhere near as much fun as apartment house elevators. For one thing, freight elevators posed the danger of annoying guys too big for us to handle, and young enough to beat the shit out of us. Apartment house and department store elevators were carnivals.

A favorite target was an apartment building on Cathedral and Tyson Streets. It's a large red-bricked building that still exists. The building was a "flatiron" (slice-of-pie shaped) and had several entrances. An old colored guy who smoked a pipe was the attendant. He was a nice old guy because he never called the cops on us. At least, I don't think he did. We called him Smoky Joe and, while he was old, he had enough "leg" to pose a threat. On warm evenings he sat outside the building near the elevator entrance. When we felt Smoky was relaxed or distracted we'd race from the side of the building and burst into the lobby elevator. (We never felt we were doing anything wrong, except, maybe, trespassing). The thrill of "violating," and the risk of being caught was a siren's song to us. I can still feel the thrill of racing past Smoky Joe, so scared that the piss was about to explode inside. Then, hopping into the waiting elevator and praying that the door would close before that maniac could grab me!

Did I wonder what would happen if he caught me? Did I fear Smoky Joe beating hell out of me? Would he, enraged, kill and discard my broken body in a dark alley? Nope, never entered my mind. I was immortal! I was eternal! I was too dumb to know better. Smoky, alerted, would give chase and holler, "You little sons-'m-bitches, I'm calling the poleeces on you." We wanted him to chase us. When he did, we would suddenly appear at another entrance down the street and taunt him, boasting that we were going to steal his elevator. Smoky would run into the building only to find us behind the elevator's glass-door, ready to engage. Once, Stevie did a sort of dance for the old guy while yelling through the glass door, "Kiss my ass you black bastard!"

Once the elevator was engaged, the door could not be opened. We'd stop it in the middle of the floor and ring the emergency bell. Smoky Joe would be furious with us. Through the glass door we could see him cursing and stomping. We'd go up a flight and open the door and wait until he came roaring through the stairwell door. Then, hooting and hollering, we'd pop up another floor.

Sometimes we'd run down the hall with him in hot pursuit, then down the stairwell and enter the elevator on the next floor. Or we'd take the elevator to the top floor and back down to the bottom. This was our Six-Flags-Over-Baltimore! One night when we were leaving this, our very favorite of all buildings, I shouted, "Thanks a lot for the ride!" and waved to him. He shook his fists and yelled "Stay the hell away from my building!" In a perverse way, I think old Joe had as much fun as we did.

The Big Swindle

"Help Wanted Boys 14 and older," the newspaper advertisement began. I called Floon, my then best buddy, and told him about the wonderful opportunity awaiting us. "All we have to do," I told Floon, was report to a "Mr. Ritter" in a certain building in the 400 block of North Charles Street. The ad gave no job description, offered no clue as to salary, so my imagination could, and did, run amok. I saw myself wearing a suit, making a hundred bucks a week. Oh, the things I would do with all that dough! Floon and I went to meet Mr. Ritter.

When we entered Mr. Ritter's office, we were greeted by a receptionist that made us forget why we were there. She was built like a brick shithouse, and was gorgeous to look at! In my mind's eye I could see her naked; she looked like the Vargas girls in Esquire Magazine. She had an aroma like the cosmetic counter at Read's Drug store. My mind started to wander and I began to stutter. "Wa, wa, we're here about the ad," I mumbled. "Oh good!" she responded, "Do you fellas play baseball?"

HUH?

She directed us to a display of baseball equipment that occupied one whole wall. It was crammed with baseball equipment—gloves, bats, catcher's equipment, everything! "So that's it," I thought. "Mr. Ritter wants kids who know baseball to sell this stuff! We sat down waiting for Mr. Ritter with our thoughts divided between our forthcoming job and how long before we could fuck this nice lady. Meanwhile, she got up from her desk five times (I counted) and jiggled to the water cooler. I went "fantasy land." I saw myself walking through the door, clad in a nice suit, carrying a briefcase filled with orders for baseball equipment, with the receptionist racing to the door to greet me, her arms embracing me as her huge breasts pushed into my face . . .

Suddenly, the door opened and Mr. Ritter appeared, "You boys ready to make a lot of money and prizes?" We stood up in unison, wide-eyed and without an answer. Mr. Ritter took us into his office and explained the art of selling magazines. We would receive a dollar for each subscription we obtained and, he assured us, most customers took two or three subscriptions.

What was the baseball display about?

Mr. Ritter waxed eloquently about the glorious opportunity we had and, as we left, order pads in hand, the receptionist called out, "Do real good so I can see you guys again."

We began banging on doors as soon as we got back to the neighborhood. We sold fourteen subscriptions, for fourteen dollars profit, and decided we had enough money for the next few weekends. We hurried back to the office. As we entered Mr. Ritter's office, my blond angel, the girl of my dreams who wanted to see me again, inquired "How can I help you?"

"Don't you remember us? We work here." Jeez, her face was blank!

"Is Mr. Ritter in?"

"Maybe I can help you" she smiled, "and, please, call me Charlotte."

"Okay, uh. Charlotte. We have our subscriptions and want to turn them in."

"Oh good, I can take them. While I tabulate your sales, why don't you boys pick out the prizes you want to receive for your points?"

"Prizes? What prizes? We want money."

"Didn't Mr. Ritter tell you? You pick out the prizes you want, and when the subscriptions are paid, you'll be notified to come in for your prizes."

I suggested that we did not want "prizes," and were not leaving any subscriptions with her. She summoned Mr. Ritter who came out and asked for the subscriptions. He "wanted to look them over." Surrendering the forms to him, Mr. Ritter fanned through the stack, then, with heartiest congratulations, steered us over to the baseball display. After we again objected, Mr. Ritter relented and said we could take one baseball glove (in good faith) until he had time to verify the subscriptions. Floon, halfheartedly, was ready to take a glove and be done with it.

"Mr. Ritter," I interrupted, "the signatures and telephone numbers on the subscriptions were written by the persons who took out the subscriptions. To sign a name not belonging to you is criminal and punishable by fine and imprisonment. If you don't believe me, you can call my father, Lt. Lundon of the Baltimore City Police at central station, downtown. As a matter of fact, he's on duty now. Can I use your phone to call him?"

"That won't be necessary." Stammered Mr. Ritter, "I'm sure your father is very proud of you. You're nice boys. What prizes did you have your hearts set on?"

"The money, a buck for every subscription is all we want."

"Very well, I'll have my wife pay you." Mr. Ritter turned to Charlotte and said, "Pay the boys, dear." While Charlotte handed us our money, Mr. Ritter explained, "We have reached our quota and will not be needing any more sales people this year. Thanks so very much for helping us.

Jones Resort

If you thirsted for adventure in the great outdoors, you traveled Falls Road to Maryland Avenue. You were now in the "country." Falls Road, but for a few coal yards and some railroad track, was undeveloped. The "mighty" Jones Falls, a small stream running parallel to the railroad tracks, was not more than fifty feet wide, and had a maximum depth of ten feet. The stream originated north of Baltimore and was used as a storm drain for the communities it traveled through. Sewage was also dumped into the Falls at various points, which accounted for all the dreck floating on the surface.

For us, though, the Jones Falls was a source of legend—and plain old bullshit, depending on who was talking. For instance, Dave Startus told of finding Indian arrowheads in a cave along the stream, and embellished his tale with an account of settlers, savaged and scalped by ferocious Indians.

Dave was a skinny kid with brown hair and penetrating green eyes that shone when he was telling a tale. He was short in stature, but he wasn't short on tales. Excepting that he didn't sing, you could call him the "Tenth Ward Troubadour."

Here's another of Dave's tales: He was fishing the Falls when a huge fish hit his line, which got tangled around his leg, and pulled him in. His leather jacket became so waterlogged it pulled him under the water into a great whirlpool. A farmer near the water's edge jumped in and saved him. We believed every word. Dave could entertain us with his stories for a whole afternoon. It's a tribute to him that we, who otherwise would interrupt anyone else with " . . . That's nothing, I can top that," never interrupted Dave's tales. He was a great bullshitter.

I recall Dave talking me into soaking a nose inhaler in a glass of water. The resulting concoction, he promised, would make me ten times stronger. I would also be immune from pain and thus, not feel the blows from my opponent. I chugged down the vile potion as Dave watched slack-jawed. Immediately, I became so scared and sick that I went home, and was in bed by four-thirty. Mom suspected something was wrong and listened to my "last confession." We were not even Catholic! (Many of the guys were, though. I was ready to try anything). I was so scared that I was going to die! Mom took me to the Mercy Hospital Emergency Room where an intern examined me. When I told him what I had done, he shook his head and told mom to take me home and have a nice dinner.

Dave lived on Warden Street and was my classmate in P.S. No. 32

from grades three through six. When you really got to know Dave, it was easy to like him. I think his family was poorer than most in our neighborhood, but he never complained. And, of course, he was entertaining.

Dave and his sisters had a special audience with Santa every year, about a week before Christmas. This was an annual event at the Fifth Regiment Armory. Dave told me he was a member of the Stocking Club, a special group of Santa's own special kids. Santa wanted to make sure they were taken care of first. Santa Claus never did come to Dave's house.

When our class was going on a field trip, and funds from home were required, Dave stayed behind with other kids who hadn't forked over. If being left out of so many activities bothered him, he never let it show. In fact, he would say, "Are you really going on that trip? Hey, you'll have more fun not going."

He always went home for lunch where, he told me, he had cereal. Occasionally he would say he wasn't hungry and would spend the lunch hour throwing a tennis ball against a ledge of a house on Barclay Street. After I told my mom about Dave's lunch habits, he began eating lunch with me. When mom, who was 56 years old, took a job in a sewing factory, she arranged to have a neighbor prepare lunch for us.

From junior high school on, Dave and I were separated. I saw him once and he was wearing an Army uniform and said he was on "good-behavior" leave from reform school. I don't know why he landed there but Mom said he would be better taken care of. Dave gave me some gifts that I really treasured, until I lost them, a Nazi arm band and a Nazi belt buckle. They were treasures his dad brought home from the war. I remember thinking at the time, "Dave's dad had gone off to save the world from oppression, and here he was, a conquering hero, living like a dog."

Larry Barely referred to the Jones Falls as Jones Resort or Jones Beach. Those who heard us talking about our trip to Jones Resort were, no doubt, impressed. The best time to swim at Jones Resort was just after a rain storm. The water was, or seemed, cleaner. Another bonus with an after-storm swim was the many balls—tennis, rubber, and the like—we found floating down the stream. We gathered them up and used them in our games.

There was a cavern on the side opposite from where we swam. On this particular summer afternoon there were two Negro men and a Negro woman, a very well-built woman, I might add. They were nude and just inside the cavern. Their clothes neatly piled on a ledge and they weren't swimming. They were actually hiding, but not completely out of sight.

Let's see, it was the two Rizzo boys, Little Jimmy, Stevie Fazzio and me. We tried to make ourselves unnoticed so as to watch the trio. Just then we hit on a brilliant idea. The three cavern people couldn't get to us unless they swam and I don't believe swimming was in their program. We had with us a small net that we would use to gather floating balls. Suddenly, the net and ball idea was furthest from our minds. We would use the net to catapult floating turds at the cavern people. Stevie was beside himself. He was laughing so hard after throwing or winging (if you prefer) about five turds gathered in one swoop, he lost his balance and fell into the Falls. I don't know who was laughing more, the cavern people or us. Of course Stevie failed to see any humor at this time.

When swimming at Jones Resort, you came as you were when you were born. There was no reason for formality. No swimsuit, no rules. Boy, were we ahead of our time-we had a nude beach!

Once, while most of us were skinny dipping, a small group of colored kids appeared on the bank. They commenced to steal our clothes and tried to make their escape on our bicycles. They should have gone on foot. Standing near our bikes were the non-swimmers among us. At first, our guys were startled as badly as those coloreds were to see them. One thief snatched a bicycle and headed for the open road, then slipped and tumbled down the side of the bank. With a few of our guys in hot pursuit, he righted the bike and tried to ride it across the top of the dam. Everyone froze and watched as he maneuvered the bike along this slippery trail. Then he fell, bike and all, into the upper portion of the dam, which was a stagnant cesspool. He swam to the other side, which was Druid Hill Park, and made good his escape. The bicycle lay at the bottom, in the green slime. We stood there contemplating the turds floating on the water when Freckles Jarvis realized it was his bike that was deep-sixed.

Freckles was a real piece of work. He once threw Larry's cigarette lighter off the Biddle Street Bridge after lighting a firecracker. He kept the firecracker. He slid down into the slime and out of sight. The seconds seemed like minutes, and we began to worry when Freckles emerged and, in a loud voice, exclaimed, "I can't move it. It's stuck in some tree branches." After dragging his slime-covered self onto the bank, he asked to use my bike. Half an hour later he returned with a city fire truck right behind him. The firemen, using a grappling hook on a rope, fished the entangled bicycle out of the water. While all this was going on, those of us who had been swimming started searching for our clothes. I found everything but my T-shirt, but a few of the guys only had their shoes. We laughed it up about Johnnie Spencecola and Phil having to walk home bare-assed before Dave biked home and returned with some pants for them.

A new guy, making his first visit to the Jones Falls Resort, once asked Johnnie Spencecola, "How do you swim in this type of stream?" Johnnie answered, "I always swim near the little falls by the crossover. The water is deeper there and you can see to dodge the turds." Ah, the good life.

Capers

Seventeen of us, led by Pete Dickerson, decided to sack Gay Street, and I don't mean working as bag boys. Gay Street was a shopping district and home to the popular Belair Market of East Baltimore. Pete's idea was simple. If we swarmed a store, the owner could only watch some of us while the rest would load up. All of us owned Army field jackets and or paratrooper fatigue pants back then. This was because they were cheaply had at any military surplus store and our parents had no money to fritter on clothes. Both jacket and pants featured large pockets, and lots of them, which were ideal for concealing booty. Our fearless leader, Pete Dickerson, was a lot older than the rest of us. A short time later he was the first guy in our gang to enlist in the Marines. He went to Korea and returned two months later in a coffin.

There were two things we needed to be concerned about and we only anticipated one of them. The market was in an area populated almost entirely by the colored. During the daylight hours this was no problem since the market drew large crowds from all over the city. At night, though, a pack of white kids would stick out like a sore thumb. On the other hand, we knew most of the colored kids in that section, having played ball against and with them several times. We cleared a field for playing ball on railroad property (The site is now covered by the Jones Falls Expressway.) Then we pragmatically allowed the colored guys use of our ball field rather than fight them. Most of them were good guys and we had, I believe, less racial tension in our old neighborhood than exists in the new version.

That the stores would be closed when we arrived had not been anticipated. It was a Wednesday, I think, and the stores closed early that night. We found just a single food store open, and drew so much attention that the manager threw us out as quickly as we entered. For all our great plans, we may as well have gone to church. Returning to our haven in the Ash Tunnel, we discovered that one guy had managed to swipe a large can of sardines in tomato sauce. Nobody wanted it despite it being our only booty. We set fire to some old Christmas trees, watched them burn and went home.

My participation in the aborted Gay Street raid to the contrary, other than some soda and a few comic books, I rarely stole anything. I'd been caught shoplifting when I was eleven and the experience had a salutary effect on me. A group of us had seen a movie at the Times Theater (now the Charles) when someone suggested we emulate Major Mosby and stage some raids. Each of us was to select a store we would run into and grab whatever we could, preferably candy, and make a quick escape. My target was the drugstore near the theater. Others were to race through the train station and hit the candy and cigar counters, or the drugstore near the Mount Royal Park. We were to meet under the Biddle Street Bridge and divvy up the loot.

No sooner had I entered the drugstore when I saw the candy counter blocked by a clerk. I turned to the cigar counter and, quick as a wink, grabbed a handful of loose cigars and dropped them into my umbrella. I turned for the door and was grabbed by some fat prick of a customer who had observed my larceny.

"What did you put in the umbrella, kid?"

"Nothing, sir!" I cried, "Let me go! I won't ever do it again!"

I was trying to empty my umbrella of evidence, but the fat man took my arm and manhandled me over to the pharmacist's counter. I was whimpering like a lamb led to slaughter. The druggist, a calm man, asked me, "Why did you do this son?" There were no tears, but my chest was heaving with dry sobs as I testified. "Please mister, I swear I didn't do it, please, I won't never do it again I promise to God, please don't tell my mother." Throughout my plea bargaining, my lardass captor was suggesting they break every bone in my body. After weighing both our positions, I suppose, the druggist landed on my side.

"Son," he began, "I'm going to let you go this time. But, if I ever catch you stealing in my store again, I WILL call the police. Do you understand that?"

Six years later, I related this story to my mother. "Jack," she said, "I think it would be nice if you went back and thanked that man." My intention was to do just that, but I procrastinated until it was too late. The drugstore was closed many years ago and I lost my opportunity to thank him.

T.V. Star

In 1953, WBAL television station originated a teen dance show. The first M.C. was a local disc jockey from radio. (The show would change M.C. several times before settling on Teen Canteen). This show was my passport to fame and popularity. In the Tenth Ward, anyway.

I wrote, asking for tickets, and they arrived in less than a week. When I arrived at the studio on North Charles street, the lobby was packed with kids wanting to be on the show. A guard asked for a show of hands from those who had tickets, and a collective moan was heard since most did not. After the ticketless rabble was cleared, he briefed us about proper television dance etiquette (no ass grabbing, please). I was so nervous, I went to the toilet where I combed and re-combed my hair and postured in front of the floor-length mirror every way possible. When I emerged, nobody was there. It was obvious the crowd was inside, but the doors to the studio were closed and a red warning light was on. I slowly opened the door and squeezed in. The host was on a stage overlooking the crowded dance floor.

We were assigned a dance partner before the show, and mine was a girl from Brooklyn Park named Ramona. She was hot stuff, dressed in a fluffy pink sweater and a puffed out gray skirt decorated with a pink poodle dog. I grabbed Ramona and started dancing. During commercial breaks, Ramona's friends would tell her how great we looked, which was no surprise to me since I was a great dancer. Hearing the compliments, though, certainly bolstered my ego, so more and more I would guide Ramona in front of the floor camera. Soon, the M.C. announced a jitterbug contest. He would tap dancers on the shoulder until just one couple was remaining. I was very confident about at least lasting to near the end, if not winning outright.

The contest started and the M.C. walked the floor, tapping the unworthy on the shoulder, sending them to the sideline. Soon, there were two couples left and we were one of them. I was crushing my opponent when my cuff link got caught in Ramona's hair during a particularly snazzy move. As she was swinging under my arm, her head yanked back and she fell right on her ass, pulling me with her. Ramona was screaming bloody murder and the crowd was laughing so hard they couldn't hear her.

I was sorry for our loss, but enjoyed myself so much I wanted to be a guest again. That week I dreamed up a plan to get into the show without a ticket. I asked two of my buddies if they would like to join me, neglecting to mention I didn't have tickets. We caught a taxi and went to the studio. The guard was going through his drill when I announced I had to go to the men's room and insisted that my pals join me. One of my pals Georgie Emerson, didn't want to miss anything so I messed up his pompadour. No respectable drape would be seen on TV with his "D.A." messed up, so he followed me into the men's room. I still didn't tell them there were no tickets. Instead I made sure they went into the studio ahead of me. If they were stopped, I could bolt. Nobody asked for tickets as we filed into the studio, and once in, nobody cared.

Georgie asked about the tickets, suggesting we could use them next time, provided they weren't dated. I said they were dated and let it go at that. I knew if I let on how we got in, the place would be overwhelmed by freeloaders. I began attending the show two or three times a month, on my own. I was on television so much that people I didn't know would say hello to me on the street or at school. Even the teachers commented that they enjoyed my dancing on television. I was sick for a two-week period and when I returned, the camera operators asked where I'd been.

When my homeroom teacher asked if I could get tickets for the class, I naturally replied, "No problem." That afternoon I asked the show's host if he would get the 25 tickets for me. He thought for a moment and said, "No, the show is booked solid through the season." Then he added, "Hey, how is it you're on so often?" I told him that I was part of the show and he looked at me with a "Do I look that stupid?" face. So I told him the truth. He laughed and said to keep it to myself. The next week his secretary handed me an envelope with 25 tickets to the show. Nobody was a bigger hero than I was during this period of my life. I mean, TV star! Public benefactor!

On one show, the Saxman himself, Earl Bostick, was a guest on the show. By now I could walk into the studio as soon as I arrived, which was usually a half-hour before the show. This day, Mr. Bostick was on the set when I arrived and we talked for ten minutes or so. What a thrill! It was an even bigger thrill when, the next day at the Famous Ballroom where he was a guest star, he saw me and said from the bandstand, "Well, hello, Jackie."

The Fight

One spring day in 1953, Mom came home in an agitated state. After putting away her groceries, she turned to me. "I just came from Resnick's. Someone gave Sonny Bonn a terrible beating. Both of his eyes are black and someone said you did that to him!"

I had.

From the time I was ten years old, Sonny bullied and embarrassed me whenever he could. He was a big kid whom I disliked to the point of hatred! I daydreamed about slugging him, but never mustered enough courage to do it. Larry Barely could see what was going on and was offended that I could allow this to continue. Although "Barely" is not Italian-sounding, he was a true Dago -a real prince- and so was his temper. I greatly admired Larry, though, for his sense of value and fair play. Everything came down to "respect" for Larry and it bothered him that I was letting Sonny push me around.

Three years earlier, when I was twelve years old, something had happened that caused me to crawl into myself. It began when Georgie Emerson got into an argument with Johnnie Spencecola in front of my house. The argument involved Johnnie's sister Emma and Georgie's brother Billy, who were married for a short time. Georgie was getting the best of Johnnie in a battle of "badmouth," but Johnnie was particularly annoyed when I laughed at every zinger. After one particularly cutting putdown, I let out a guffaw and Johnnie turned and called me a queer. I gave him a mouth full of my fist! Though Johnnie was bigger than I was, he was wearing a pair of Union Ball Bearing Roller Skates, which put him at something of a disadvantage. According to the laws of physics, it was a six-foot punch because that's how far Johnnie rolled backward. Recovering, he charged—well, rolled—at me with a cry of rage.

My mother, who was congenitally hard of hearing, heard the commotion and came flying out of the house. Then she did the unpardonable. She stepped in and broke up the fight, slapping my face in the process. "You get right in the house!" she demanded. Now it was Johnnie's turn to laugh. I turned and ran into the house, mortified and without honor. She had slapped me, for God's sake. That was one of the few things that could make me cry, and she did it in front of my friends. When she turned on Johnnie, he responded by cursing both me and her. Seeing me watching out the window, he pointed and yelled, "Queer!"

There were two violations of our neighborhood code that could never go unpunished. One was calling someone a son-of-a-bitch; the other was calling him a queer. I jumped through the open window and pounced on Johnnie. His feet went forward while the rest went backward. Kneeling on his chest, I began pummeling his face with my closed fists.

Again, Mom broke us apart and demanded I return to the house. I was so enraged that tears poured down my cheeks. I found it impossible to utter an intelligible oath at him. Instead, I yelled, "Yoooaa gobitin monee flish battern," or something like it. I was totally destroyed.

Over the next few months, I became a twelve-year-old recluse—afraid of being seen anywhere in the neighborhood. Still attending sixth grade at P.S. No. 32, I would make a beeline to and from school to avoid my former pals. I believed that everyone was against me. In my paranoia, I imagined buses rerouted past my house to facilitate the passengers' name-calling. They say that being paranoid doesn't mean you don't have enemies, and I did. Why, even Garbage Pants Knoop was calling me names. He'd yell "Jackie Fag!" and I'd just walk away.

I had few friends that year. Reading and a few hobbies became my only interests. I confided in no one about my loss of self-esteem, and pretty soon the guys quit coming over altogether. Oddly, I had no hatred for Johnnie and was sorry I hadn't gone out the next day and either finished the fight or made peace. Johnnie and I had been friends since I was seven. In recalling all my relations with this skinny kid of about five-foot-five with coal black hair and an extremely long hook nose, I have to laugh about the time he and I found a manila envelope in some trash. It was filled with checks, canceled paychecks from a pajama company payroll. We didn't know for sure just what they were all about, but we soon learned. Now, you must understand, Johnnie was a little older than I and by virtue of age should have been a little bit smarter, but he wasn't. We both attended P.S. No. 32. I was in a graded class and Johnnie was in a class that had no grades. In fact, it had children from age six to fourteen. It was called the opportunity class. I guess it was for slow learners.

Anyway, Johnnie's parents were Italian immigrants and didn't speak English very well. Johnnie's dad would give his wife his paycheck and she would send Johnnie to Resnick's to pay off their store tab while getting the check cashed. This was a regular weekly chore. When we found these checks the first thing, Johnnie remarked, "We're rich!" Off to Resnick's we went to get some cash.

Now, old man Resnick was a Russian immigrant who also had a language problem. He didn't speak English very well either, so... welcome to the neighborhood. Even the natives here spoke something other than proper English. Johnnie gave old Mr. Resnick a check for thirty-two dollars and the old man gave Johnnie thirty-two dollars in exchange. I went in and handed the old man a check for an additional thirty dollars, at which time he called his son to the front of the store and all hell broke loose.

I ran out of the place with my stack of checks and Johnnie must have figured I queered the deal because he started running, too. You would have thought young Resnick was playing halfback for the Baltimore Colts. He ran like hell around to the Spencecolas' house to try to retrieve the thirty-two dollars, but he was too late. We watched him go down Brentwood Avenue toward Johnnie's house. Johnnie decided we weren't interested in what young Resnick may have on his mind. After all, we found the checks and "finders keepers" rules applied. We were going to divide up the money and enjoy a feast at Mamie Schrek's with "fried arsters" and everything. We even invited several friends to join us along the way. I'll just say that when Johnnie got home, he was grounded for the next month.

Following the fight with Johnnie, illustrates how low I sank. I took the most shit from new kids who weren't aware of my pre-scuffle-with-Johnnie stature. I went nowhere without being harassed by them. Before the fight with Johnnie I was a fairly respected kid. After that fight I lost respect, which took me three years to regain with the fighting of Sonny. One, of the new kids, a punk we called Big Jake (a name given by mommy, no doubt), was incessant in his verbal attacks. He didn't look like a tough guy. Big Jake was slim, with reddish-blond hair that hung in his eyes. Compounding his geek look were red horn-rimmed glasses and buck teeth. He did, however, stand in good with the Italian bunch, a group whose respect I felt I had lost.

I was trying not to make waves, but one day Big Jake was feeling his oats and forced a confrontation with his name-calling. I told him to stop. He said he wanted to knock the shit out of me, and followed me home, tormenting me the entire way. By now I was ready to fight, but I was afraid the punk would try to knife me (one of my biggest fears). I asked Big Jake what I had to do to get him off my back, and he replied, "Write a note that says 'Big Jake can beat me up,' sign and date it." I wrote the note and was extremely sorry afterward. That punk must have shown the note to every guy in the neighborhood because my situation really worsened.

Eventually, I managed to pass from primary school into junior high school and took solace in a book on the art of boxing. I filled a duffel bag with clothes and used it as a punching bag. I'd pound that thing until I was gasping for breath and sweating like a hog. In a short while, I considered myself a "boxer." As a result, I began to constantly get into fights at school, fights that I won. I demanded satisfaction for every imagined slight (someone bumping me in the hall or looking at me the wrong way). There was no waiting period between argument and fight, either. The "Johnnie Spencecola experience" had taken a real toll on me. My new motto was, "He who turns and runs away, worries like hell the rest of the day!" I also learned to avoid any fights where good old Mom could intercede. . . . The fighting continues . . .

Lundon the Lionhearted

I had a real dislike for bully boys and class clowns. It seemed the two, bullying and disrespect, went together. When I started at Lafayette Junior High School (P.S.No. 79), I was without my friends and was a little apprehensive. Very few from my neighborhood attended Lafayette, and those that did were not my kind. At the outset I understood that we "freshies" were subject to various forms of indoctrination (like having your face held under toilet water) at the hands of upperclassmen-Hugo Footley among them. I was a little intimidated and scared, but resolved not to eat toilet turds or otherwise be pushed around.

Lafayette Junior High School drew from the nearby Jewish community, an area that was going quickly to slum just as the Tenth Ward was. Somehow I chummed up with them and it was quite an experience. They were, for the most part, very sheltered and were scared out of their wits by the roughneck hillbilly bully types that populated Lafayette. I affected an air of bravado around them and they seemed to take comfort in my streetwise attitude. But boy, oh boy, I didn't like this school. This was just after the time my mother "saved me" from Johnnie Spencecola and I really didn't have my heart in it. My reason for choice of junior high school was simple: The neighborhood crowd wasn't attending this school.

While trying to regain my self-esteem, I broke loose. I thought I had to. I had a lot of anger inside me and felt sorry for myself. Suddenly one day I came out of my shell. I was standing in line with some of my Jewish friends when three Linden Avenue thugs came up. The smallest one grabbed my friend, Sheldon Rosenfeld, by the nose and squeezed it, telling him he'd better buy the thug lunch. Finding the tallest thug, who was no bigger than me, I reached out and grabbed him by the hair. Pulling his head down, I socked him in the nose. Then I reached for the smallest one, who was so startled he started running for his life. The third one was sputtering that he wasn't with those guys.

The Jew boys were laughing and telling me what a good guy I was, giving me the moniker "good goya." The rest of that year I tried to stay out of trouble. I did have a few fights, but I was quick to throw the first punch and soon had a reputation as someone it was best not to screw with.

The next year at P.S. No. 79 was hard on me. The Jewish kids had laid another title on me the year before and it stuck into year two: "Big Guy, protector of the freshies." I felt like a Jesuit protecting the pope. There were a couple of thugs in the schoolyard that liked to shake down the little Jews for lunch money, whereupon of course, "Big Guy, protector of the freshies" was summoned. I fought the bastards and kicked their asses, and was brought to Mr. Donnenberg's detention room for my trouble. Mr. Donnenberg complemented me for my taking up for the little guys and said he respected me for it. However, he added that he would not tolerate fighting and any recurrence would result in my suspension. I was scratching my head, trying to figure out whether I had been complemented or not. Later, my homeroom teacher, who was also my math teacher, pulled me aside. "Lundon," she said, "I was going over the recommendations for the honor roll and had to pass you over because of your recent conduct. I want you to know that makes me very sad. Why can't you keep your hands to yourself?"

Despite being known by every teacher, the principal and vice principal as a potential troublemaker, I had little trouble with them. One of my teachers, a sweet young thing whom I fantasized boning, even asked me to help her move. I was excused from school for the day and her husband paid me to carry boxes and the like. I took a pair of her panties and showed it to the guys, The panties were light green and had the day of the week embroidered on the lower right side. I claimed I had taken it as a trophy. I know that some of them believed me. I was in class on a Friday morning and one of my buddies said aloud, "Lundon, it's Friday and you know how you love Fridays." Then he started giggling. The teacher looked like she just ran into a truck and looked right into my eyes. In fact, I believe she looked inside of me. I slapped the wisecracker at lunch and he promised never to mouth off like that again. Of course that only modified and strengthened my claim.

When it came to being serious in school, my favorite subjects (in order) were art, history and math. The rest of the subjects bored the crap out of me, especially the subjects that seemed to be on a self-taught basis, like science. The teacher would have an assignment written and you would read and write. Oral demonstrations were not in the offering. Getting back to art, I excelled. I often drew sailing vessels or warships or tugs or anything that could float. Desert scenes with mountains were also among my favorites. One day, a blonde-haired girl with some fine physical attractions caught my mind's eye and I reproduced her on paper. We were doing watercoloring and I drew her for my subject. A drawing of her as a semi-nude. I hesitated to turn it in, but the art teacher collected it up, turned to me and said, "This is magnificent." It hung on display for weeks. My mom questioned my brother Jim what he thought of it and he said, "That's art mom, art."

On a spring afternoon in 1953, Mom sent me to Resnick's grocery for bread and milk. She disliked shopping at Resnick's in person after a big spat she had with Mr. Resnick about padding her bill and would send me when it was convenient. Her distrust of the Resnicks undoubtedly colored my attitude toward them, but I believe they were innocent of any intentional wrongdoing in this instance. Stevie Fazzio, who lived over the store, would regularly run down and pick up things for his mother. As I mentioned earlier, Stevie and I were always being mistaken for each other, and I think that's what happened here. When Stevie said "charge it" for his groceries, Resnick would mistake him for me, and debit Mom's bill. Honest mistake, but Mom was outraged over her inflated bill, and that led to the confrontation. She called Resnick a thief; Resnick called her a deadbeat. "I'll never shop here again," she swore when leaving the store. Well, Resnick's was too convenient, so she sent me whenever she needed a bag of sugar or quart of milk. Eventually the mistake in identity was discovered and Resnick apologized to Mom and things went back to the way they were. What bothered me was the way they treated me after this incident. Whenever I entered the store, the Resnicks would break into Yiddish and laugh while looking at me. I could only imagine what they were saying. Each time their storeroom was broken into, or a window was broken, Mrs. Resnick would ask me, "Did you do that?" I'd proclaim innocence and the Resnicks would break into their Yiddish prattle. It drove me nuts, and really pissed me off.

When I happened to tell one of my brother's girlfriends about this treatment, she had the solution. She was Jewish and taught me to say, phonetically, "Gay cocken de ofen yom," which translated, means "Go take a shit in the ocean." I could hardly wait for the Resnicks to start on me with their Yiddish shit again, which they did my next time in. They jabbered on while I paid for my purchase. As I got to the door I turned and yelled, "Gay cocken de ofen yom!" I thought their eyes would pop out! Calmly, I left their store and that was the last time they spoke Yiddish in front of me.

Anyway, this spring afternoon I was in the store when the head clerk, Arnold, asked me how I felt after Sonny pounded the crap out of me the night before. "Who said that?" I demanded. "Did Sonny tell you that?" Pissed off, I was leaving the store when, who do I bump into but Sonny.

"Did you tell Arnold you beat me up last night?" I demanded.

Defiant, he yelled right back, "No! But don't you think I can't!"

Putting my purchase on the ground, I took the proper boxer's stance, right out of the book. I challenged, "No, I know you can't beat me, punk. If you want me to prove it, let's rumble!" Sonny stood there, shocked by this sudden turn, then finally recovered and said, "Okay, I'll meet you down the Fallsway Park at seven o'clock when I get off work. I don't want your blood on my good clothes!"

I went home to an early supper, but was so nervous I couldn't sit still. Today, I experience the same feeling before talking before a group. I didn't realize at the time, but I was experiencing a burst of adrenaline that filled me with an energy that, if controlled, allowed a weaker combatant to win over huge odds.

On the way to the fight I was greeted by many of the same kids who had, only recently, been tormenting me. When it came to me or Sonny though, it was no contest about whom they wanted to prevail, even if they gave me little chance for success. By the time I got to the park, there were at least seventy-five people there, and the crowd was growing. Unbeknownst to me, the word had passed quickly throughout the neighborhood of the compelling fight and a chance to gamble on the odds. I was not the one expected to win, but I'm sure most were hoping I would.

Mike Campo had advised, "When you get ready to fight, start to take off your shirt then say, 'I don't need to take this off to beat you!'" Oddly enough, when Sonny arrived and when we were squaring off, he used those very words on me.

"Oh yeah," I responded, "Go ahead and take off your shirt. It'll be bloody if you don't. I'll be pounding your head in before your shirt hits the ground."

Sonny took his shirt off and gave it to his pal, that prick Hugo Footley. I was getting into my boxer's stance, fully aware of all the boasting I'd done about being a "trained boxer." I started to move my arms in a jab and protect manner when Sonny swung and missed. I remained calm, constantly looking for openings, and found he was wide open. I was able to land a punch pretty much at will. I played with him for awhile, enjoying myself immensely. There, dancing around him on the park grass, I imagined myself imitating a great fighter. I was Argentine Firpo, the Wild Bull of the Pampas, a fighter I once read about.

Finally, I tore into him. While repeating my left jabs with lightning speed, I suddenly let him have it from the shoulder, a hard right to the head! Blood splattered from his left eye. "This fight's over," I thought, and let my guard down. Sonny hit me and knocked me straight back on my butt. Getting back up, I again began to circle him. Then suddenly, with all the strength I could muster, I attacked. I put my right shoulder punch into his left eye, and when he spun around, I connected with another right shoulder punch to his right eye. The combination was perfect. Blood was flowing, profusely, down his face.

Sonny yelled out to Hugo, "Footley? Where are you? I can't see you!" I wasn't going to fall for that trick a second time and remained in a boxing stance. Suddenly, Hugo jumped in front of me with fists up, indicating it was now his turn. Jesus Christ! With the realization I had beat Sonny came a release' that left me limp. Now I had to go again? Just then Big Bob Emerson, of all people, got in front of me and asked Hugo, "You wanna go a few? Do 'em with me." Wow, maybe Big Bob never figured out who switched papers on him. It turned out Big Bob had just made a bundle off the fight and was worried a beating at the hands of Hugo would give his clients a chance to renege. There was no way Hugo would go toe to toe with Big Bob, so that was the end of things.

That fight was the best thing to happen to me. It took a long time recovering my self-respect, but I had it back now and was the neighborhood hero for some time after. Larry Barely gave me a pat on the back. It was a great feeling, knowing I had pleased him and was again his goomba. Another great thing about "The Fight" was a lot of money was wagered that night, and the good people at Resnick's lost a bundle. *And more fights ....*

I Break Bad

After my fight with Sonny, I was a firecracker with a short fuse. I planned no vengeance on those who had harassed me, including Big Jake, but I wasn't going to tolerate any more crap from them either. It was fall, and we were playing football in the field along the Fallsway, the same field I beat Sonny up on five months earlier. Big Jake caught a pass, and I was about to tackle him when he said, "You tackle me and I'm busting you in the mouth." I immediately took a boxer's stance and responded, "I been wishing for you to smart off like that. Now, I'm going to beat your ass to a pulp!"

Big Jake jumped five feet backward and cried, "Don't come near me because I'm going to kick you. I saw you fight and I can't fight so leave me alone."

Oh, thank you sweet Jesus. "Do you have that note in your wallet from last year? I know you carry it with you." Big Jake reached into his hip pocket, opened his wallet and pulled out a piece of yellow legal paper and handed it to me. As I took it, I swung a hard left near his head, but pulled up short. He screamed. I laughed and so did my pals. Big Jake smiled and said, "I really thought you was gonna hit me." After that, Big Jake couldn't suck up to me enough. If I mentioned a fight he'd volunteer, "I'll back you up Jackie." He probably would too, but if I lost, who in hell would protect him?

The Battle of Drunken Bill

It was during this time that Bill Christy got the handle "Drunken Bill." A new guy named Bill Christy moved to Biddle Street, just across the street and down two houses from my own. He was from Johnstown, Pennsylvania. He was a swell enough guy and moreover his dad had a car and allowed Bill to drive it. Bill was a few years older and a sharp dresser. He wore blue suede shoes with peg pants and sported a square back haircut combed in a D.A. His curly light brown hair hung over his eyes making him look older than he was. Bill was an amateur boxer possessing a terrific build and had well-developed arms. He was a cool cat.

When school was out, Bill got me a job at Air Ways Contractors where he worked. Air Ways was a small air-conditioning firm located twelve miles away on Belair Road, but still within the city. I lied about my age telling the foreman I was eighteen years old. I lied so I could work without a permit. Bill worked in the field as an installation helper and I worked in the assembly and fabrication shop. Talk about a liability. I'm quite sure the bookkeeper noticed the results of my employment before anyone else did. I tried my best, but I had no skills for the job I was assigned to do. What the heck was I doing in this place anyway?

The standard wage was seventy-five cents an hour, but this job paid a dollar an hour. That was excellent pay and I was lucky to get hired. During the short time I worked there, I got a feel for the machinery and how it worked. Unlike the sheet metal shop at Lafayette Junior High School which was little more than a hobby shop, this place was the real thing. I was using a 100-ton forming press, spot welders and machines that could chew you up. This was man's work!

One day, I was given permission to make a call using the phone in the plant foreman's office. When I picked up the receiver to dial, however, someone was talking. I waited, then tried again but they were still talking. I soon got tired of waiting and yelled into the receiver, "GET THE HELL OFF THE FUCKING LINE." "Why," I wondered, "does a busy company like Air Ways have a party line?" I soon found out they didn't have a party line and my phone privileges were revoked.

I began disliking my job at Air Ways. I was bored, primarily because there was nobody my age to talk to. One morning, while waiting for a bus to take me to work, I let two buses pass by before finally boarding one. I rode the bus because Bill had already quit his job and was working with his dad on a construction job. So when my boss asked me if I had any friends looking for work, I eagerly volunteered Georgie Emerson. The next day I brought Georgie in and the boss hired him. Johnnie Spencecola and Freckles Jarvis had tagged along, hoping they would be hired as well. The boss saw them hanging around and asked me if "all these guys are eighteen?" I naturally lied in the affirmative and they got hired, too.

Bill Christy and I soon drifted apart and Bill befriended a guy from Preston Street named Joe Clifton. Joe wore his dress pants high up, over his waist, so we called him High Pockets. I had nothing against Joe, other than his sarcastic lip. He was loud and talked from the side of his mouth.

I walked out onto the Biddle Street Bridge where Bill and Joe were sitting. As I approached, Bill asked if I wanted to get some booze with them. I said, "No, thanks." Some guys would go out of their way to get booze, but I never had that problem. Being tall, I could get served in a few bars, but I had a pact with Mom. If I didn't drink with the crowd, I could have a few beers at home when I wanted. That was very wise of her, because I never found it exciting to go out with the gang and drink like a nut. So when Bill asked me if I wanted to go with them to get some booze, I wasn't being a prude, I was just saying "No thanks." I guess Joe didn't take it that way because he said, "Don't ask that shitass to go with us."

"Hey, Joe, you aren't talking about me are you?" I asked him.

"Na, jus talkin' bout your mama."

I walked slowly over to Joe and he got up from the concrete rail and put his guard up, saying to Bill, "Watch me put this shitass away." I put my guard up and started dancing around in front of Joe saying, "Let's go, big mouth." He swung and missed. I connected and Joe bent over, holding his mouth in both hands. Joe must have figured Bill would back him up and he did. Bill now, was up and in a beautiful boxing position in front of me and blocking Joe. Joe was now really out of the picture. Bill was ready for a boxing match, but I wasn't. I was going to street fight this son of a bitch. I sucker punched him in the stomach and again in the head. He thought I was just going to stand and exchange nasty remarks with my guard up. When you're about to fight two guys at a time no rules applied. You just give all you can and any which way you can.

From half a block away Garbage Pants Knoop yelled, "Fight!" Suddenly, twenty or so people had gathered, including none other than my mother. Bill was back to standing erect, blood streaming from his nostrils, his fists clenched and on guard. Joe was laying on the ground in a pool of vomit holding his stomach. My mother shouted, "Stop that fighting! Jack Lundon, get back to the house!" I thought, "Oh, no. Not again." Now, yelling at Bill she cried, "Leave him alone you big bully!" Bill responded by calling her a bitch! Calling my mom a bitch was his death warrant. I ran straight into Bill, no jabbing, no sparring, no dancing, just straight slugging. I went for his head.

I had sparred with him before, and he was good, but now I was better.

Bill backpedaled away from me and I thought, "My God! I'm beating him up. He's backing away. I'm doing it." I was in command of the fight, but could sense my mother closing in when Bill suddenly dropped his hands and I signed his right eye four times. He backed up, imploring, "No more, I'm too drunk to fight!" Turning, I put my hands up in the air, looked at Mom and said, "Stop. It's over. I won."

We walked back down to the steps of our house, and she asked "What was that all about? I was afraid those two would beat you up."

Meanwhile the guys were gathered at our steps, laughing about Bill having been "too drunk to fight," because he wasn't. Garbage Pants came up to me with his hand balled into a fist like he was holding a microphone, and said in his best announcer's voice, "We're here with the champ. Who you gonna fight next champ, now that drunken Bill is over the hill?"

And that's how Bill Christy came to be called Drunken Bill, a name he may still carry.

Things were swell for awhile. I had my job at Airways and making big bucks thanks to Drunken Bill and I had three friends to talk with during breaks, and was getting good with some of the more sophisticated machine work. Now that Johnnie Spencecola had a paying job, he decided to buy a car and we went along. He bought from the first place we stopped, a used car lot on Belair Road at Sinclair Lane. The place reminded me of a coal yard. Anyway, Johnnie bought a brown 1947 Pontiac. What a piece of shit it was. He pulled to a stop at the first red light out of the lot and the front bumper fell off. We all, save Johnnie Spencecola, laughed our asses off.

"Jesus Christ, Spencecola," Georgie said, while helping load the bumper into the trunk, "take this shit-heap back and get your money. I know a guy wants to sell a cherry '49 Ford for almost nothing."

"I can't," replied Johnnie, "the guy said he'd give me his best price only if I bought it 'as is'."

Later, we were washing the car and the chrome trim fell off the side I was washing. Like I said, a real piece of shit, but I don't think any of us will ever have as much fun as we did with Johnnie Spencecola's Pontiac. We'd each pitch in 35 cents for gas and drive out to Harley's Sandwich Shop for a Polish ham sub. We also had a ride to work each morning.

One Friday night we drove over to the YMCA dance and noticed a few of the guys were wearing really neat clothes. "Hey man," one explained, "there's a clothing store on Baltimore Street that'll let you buy anything you want, 'Hollywood style.' You just gotta have a job and pay two bucks a week."

"Hollywood style" was a term we used meaning buying on credit. Hey, we all had jobs, so the next morning we drove downtown to the men's store on Baltimore Street. Just as we were told, after filling out our applications we were extended credit. We went nuts, buying right up to our limit. Man, life was good.

Lest the reader thinks we were all hardened criminals, this is why I finally quit my job at Air Ways. One afternoon, a cop car pulled up behind the plant. I don't know why, but it made me nervous as hell. From that moment on, I waited for the cops to return and arrest us all for lying about our age! On payday, I quit.

The Industrial Building was located just a few blocks from home. Among its tenants were garment factories, printers, an ink company, several novelty firms and a shoe factory. Since I quit my job at Air Ways, I needed a job. I canvassed the Industrial Building looking for work and landed one as stock boy in a garment factory. After working there for half an hour, I decided it was a rotten job and quit. Again, I started canvassing and I was good at it.

The next day I landed a job at a printing engraver's firm as a messenger boy, despite their need for a licensed driver. Hey, major problem at first. I was only fifteen and you had to be sixteen to get licensed. "No sweat," I told them, "I'm getting my brother's car in October for my nineteenth birthday present, and I'll be learning to drive right after."

My mother told me, "The devil threw Tom Pepper out of hell for lying," so I guess I will not worry about going there. Anyway, they hired me but I wasn't there two days when the company next door hired me for a nickel more an hour. I recommended a friend, Joey Campo, as a replacement for my old job. Joey was fifteen years old when I told him about the job on Tuesday, eighteen on Wednesday when he applied. He was hired and never did return to school.

I worked at my new job for three weeks. They paid me on a Thursday and I took off "sick" the next day. Now, deep down, I saw myself as an entertainer. One night while watching a comedian on TV who played a guitar while telling jokes, I got an idea. The guy did not really play the guitar he just used it as a prop. I decided to buy some tricks from a magic shop on Howard Street and create an act. My schtick would be to tell jokes while screwing up the magic tricks. (Much later, I saw someone doing this same schtick).

Floon went with me and while walking down Howard Street, we ran into my boss. I didn't have to wait until the end of August to quit that job. When school began, I felt there was no way I'd learn more than I had over the summer. I did feel bad about lying about my age to all my employers and constantly feared being found out. However, if you wanted to work, it was necessary. I also felt bad that the clothing store that extended us credit ended up eating our accounts.

Larry Barely

When I was eight I was on my way home from school. I was just crossing the Guilford Avenue Bridge when a goofy-looking colored guy jumped out from behind the girders. I say goofy because he looked abnormal, and he spoke that way, too.

"Where da hell you find you goin'?" he demanded.

Scared shitless, I answered, "I had to stay after school and I'm going home. I live just a couple of blocks on the other side of the bridge. My name is Jack. What's your name?"

He was holding a metal airplane exactly like one I had at home, except his had a broken wing.

"You gotch any muni?"

"No," I answered, and nervously added, "But I sure would like to have that neat airplane you have there. I have some money at home in my piggy bank. Would you take five dollars for it?"

"You ain't got no fi' dolla for this," he challenged while holding the airplane in my face.

"Maybe. I know I have a lot of change."

"Jewry. You mama gotch any jewry?"

"Oh, yes, lots."

"You mama home?"

"No, just my baby brother and he's sick. I have to get home and give him his medicine because my mom works and I'm the man of the house because my father was shot down over France fighting the Germans." I was scared, and I was rambling on, but I couldn't resist that lie. "I goin letchu hab dis here toe, but I wants to see sum jewry first."

"Okay. But only take a few pieces. I don't want to get my mom mad at me."

Hurrying together, we crossed the bridge. I didn't know whether to make a break, or trust that Vaughn would be at home. "No," I decided, "If I try to run from this moron, he'll kill me." My mother was at work and Sis would be no match for this guy. "Oh shit, please Vaughn, be there," I prayed. As we approached my house, I saw my brother pass by his bedroom window. My "friend" saw him too and asked "Is it dat you house, one wif da guy in it?"

"Yes he's my brother and is home from prison for killing a man. Please don't let him see you or he won't let me trade with you. Wait here and I'll bring our mom's jewelry box and you can take your pick."

I raced up the stairs where Vaughn started yelling at me for being late. "Vaughn," I cried, "That nigger is making me give him mom's jewelry!" Vaughn was down the stairs in three strides. He grabbed a kitchen knife and flew out the front door. That guy took off and, my God, could he run. Vaughn couldn't catch him, couldn't even come close. After that I took the long way home, avoiding the area altogether.

Now, seven years later, I was walking near the Guilford Avenue Bridge, minding my own business, when approximately ten colored guys confronted me. One of them, who was wearing a red scarf to protect his "process" hairdo, addressed me. "Hey, you. You Larry Barely?" I guessed that, either all white guys look alike to him or, since he didn't know me from Larry, he was not Larry's friend. "Hell, no." I replied. "He's the cocksucker that beat me up last week, the son-of-a-bitch! I could have taken him but he had two other guys with him." Red scarf looked over to his buddies, then said, "I'm Frankie Love and I want to see him for beating up on one of my guys. You see him, you tell him the Spoon Gang wants his ass."

"He's a bully," I groveled, "I hope you find him. Do you know where he lives?"

"Nope."

"Give me your phone number and I'll call you with his address." God, I was being helpful. Of course, if he had given me his phone number I would have given it to Larry. Instead though, he asked for my phone number, so I said the number for radio station WITH, a station that I was familiar with since I use to call the Buddy Dean morning radio show. I did tell him my real name. They left me standing there, in one piece. All I could think of was, what a tough guy Larry was to have all these guys after him.

Larry Barely lived next door to a lightweight boxer, "Two-Toes" Tony Gallio. By virtue of that alone he was accorded a certain respect, as though he absorbed Gallio's talent through osmosis. But Larry was a fight enthusiast, and he did get some tips from Tony. No matter, everyone readily believed that Larry was a professionally-trained fighter. When he walked, he strutted. You could distinguish his gait from blocks away. He was headstrong and cocky as well, which was enough to scare off most guys. Larry's lineage was Northern Italian, he had light brown hair and blue eyes, just the opposite of Johnnie Spencecola, who was Sicilian. It was Larry I tried to emulate after the Sonny Bonn fight. I was thrilled to be his friend.

Larry used a ploy to set someone up for his sucker punch, which was perfect. I never really saw Larry in a balls-out fight, but I did see him make short work of a protagonist quite a few times. He put great stock in getting respect, and his perception of the respect being shown at any given time would change, according to his mood. Larry found himself in many "situations." All fights began with a ritualistic name-calling and threat-hurling

("You cocksucker! Cross that line and you're dead"). While his opponent was getting his tongue warmed up, Larry would casually rub a mole on his cheek while clenching his fist. Suddenly, he would release a hard right, straight from the shoulder. That was all it took any time I was a witness.

I stood on the corner of Biddle Street and Brentwood Avenue telling Mike Campo about how tough Larry was, what with the Spoon Gang after him and all, when Larry appeared, from out of nowhere. His shirt was torn down one side and his face was bloodied.

"What the hell happened to you?" I asked.

"Some niggers."

"Niggers?" Damn, I thought to myself, the Spoon Gang must have found him.

"Yeah, three of them."

"Where?"

"Aw, forget it. They were broads."

"Huh?"

"Three nigger broads. One of them asked me for a cigarette. I offered her one and she took the whole pack. When I reached for the cigs, one of the other two hit me with a milk bottle and then the third one starts ripping my clothes." "Did you hit 'em?"

"Hell, no. They was Amazons! I took off running."

"No shit?"

"Hey, man, don't tell nobody."

The Infamous Four Dot Gang

From The Evening Sun, Baltimore, April 14, 1953

"'ZIP' Gun Making in Schools Denied"

"Reports of the manufacture of deadly weapons in the city's vocational schools are without foundation and are "damaging to the public school system" the Assistant Superintendent in charge of vocational schools said today. He would look into reports that youths have been manufacturing "Zip" guns capable of shooting .22-caliber cartridges.

Police said the guns were made with equipment in an East Baltimore vocational school. The Asst. Superintendent said he did not believe there was any truth in the report. Vocational classes are small, he said, ranging from 20 to 25 boys. Any illegal use of machine tools would be quickly detected by an instructor, he added. A 14-year-old boy was charged with possession of one of the guns in a complaint filed yesterday in Juvenile Court. A Police spokesman of the Central District said another partially completed gun had also been recovered.

The Asst. Superintendent of vocational schools also said today he planned to discuss the incidents with the Principal of Samuel Gompers General Vocational School at North Avenue and Broadway. The Principal said he had received a complaint about two months ago after a policeman reported seeing a youth with a "zip" gun on a street car. The boy had told the policeman he made the gun in class under the pretense that he was using it for a lamp stand. The principal said subsequent investigations had failed to yield any more information."

"Police Test Gun"

"The gun seized by police was tested at police headquarters. It looked like a toy consisting of a piece of wood fashioned in the shape of a gun, a short length of metal tubing, some rubber bands and the hammer from a cap pistol. Tests showed that a bullet fired from the gun penetrated a piece of 1-inch wood at a 14-inch range. The user always suffered powder burns from the discharge of the weapon, police said. And many of the boys questioned had such burns. Each of the teenagers involved was said to belong to the "FOUR DOT" Gang, which runs in the area around Greenmount and Preston Street."

When that story came out in the daily paper on April 14, it was all over for our gang. Our parents were ready to lock us in the cellar. That was our hangout and my school.

What surprised me then, and still concerns me today about news accounts is the degree to which they can stray from the truth. The Four Dot Gang incident is a good example.

Jack Robinson was a new guy in the neighborhood. He lived on Guilford Avenue, just across the Biddle Street Bridge. Just as so many did during that period, the Robinsons moved here from West Virginia to find a better life.

Jack was in trouble with the law before for breaking and entering, and would eventually be incarcerated by his adopted city. He hung with three guys from the neighborhood who shared his values. Soon after his arrival, he and his goons visited a tattoo parlor on Baltimore's famous "Block." While one of them was getting tattooed, the others stole an artist's tattoo machine. At home they set about using it, but could not get it to start, which is why we got involved. Mike Campo was attending Poly-Technical High School and was really a smart guy, and everyone knew it. Jack approached Mike to ask whether he could help them get the tattoo machine working. After looking at it, Mike suggested that a transformer, similar to the kind used with model railroad sets, was needed. Who had a model railroad set? I did.

Intrigued with seeing a tattoo machine in action, I gladly supplied my transformer. We assembled in Robinson's apartment where Mike quickly got the thing running, and then figured out how it worked. He demonstrated by putting a small dot on his hand. Immediately, others were imploring "Do me . . . give me a dot." Mike began a frenzy of "dotting" and soon he and most of the others wore four tattooed dots. They were placed on the web of flesh between thumb and forefinger and, although small, were quite visible. My mother was death on tattoos and I refused as did Stevie Fazzio. Warren Grimm, on the other hand, not only got the dots but took the gun and was tattooing his arm as though doodling on a piece of paper. He eventually had quite a few designs done by a professional to complement a police record several inches thick. Anyway, excepting me and Stevie, the whole gang ended with dots on their hands.

Later, Moe asked, "Hey Jackie, where can I get some goat's milk?"

"Why goat's milk?" "Robinson told me, if you don't like the tattoo, you can rub it with goat's milk and it will come off. My dad is really pissed at me. So?"

In the spring of 1953 there were several news stories concerning zip guns. One story concerned a man who summoned the police saying he had been shot. After investigating, the police determined he accidentally shot himself while making a zip gun in his basement.

That story, added to the one about a group being questioned near my neighborhood, helped to fuel other rumors. There were a few zip guns made by almost every boy in our gang. They were made with the best of intentions—A challenge to accomplish if that can be applied to a gun.

Again Jackie Robinson designed and made the first one. I remember he burned the hell out of his hand when he fired it.

For the most part, the gun was more of a danger to the person firing it. There was only one incident where I saw a zip gun fired and that was when Jackie burned his hand. Most made the guns just to see if he could.

The story being handed to the police was because some little kids got into trouble and the local cop on the beat was an opportunist. He had been trying to become a sergeant ever since the day he got out of the academy. He didn't last long on the force. But he was always after our crowd.

When this story surfaced in the newspaper, the whole neighborhood was enraged. The location of the gang was indicated as being on Preston Street and Greenmount Avenue. The officer, in a rush to solve the case, combined a few gangs as the bad guys and, of course, drew honors for a job well done. He was a respected police officer, but he lost our respect.

Once he gained the admiration of the neighborhood for trying to save a child from a burning building and in that he was a hero. Another time he picked a fight with one of the Solon brothers. He laid down his badge and night stick and when the Solon brother was about to take him on, he re-mounted his badge. Finally, there was the time he enlisted our gang to help nab a group of black youths who were robbing the truck corral at the Royal Crown Cola Company.

One evening, the gang was engaged in carving our initials in the new fence at the top of the Biddle Street Bridge. From out of nowhere came the cop a.k.a. John Law. "You're all under arrest! Don't move."

"All bullshit!"

"Which one of you said that?"

"I said it," exclaimed Mike.

"Hey you guys, it's about time we made a pact. I don't want to arrest you for destruction of property. But you don't leave me any choice. You guys want to be my deputy?"

"Like how?" "Like what?" "What do we have to do?"

Within minutes we were lined up behind the billboards on Preston Street observing a large group of Negro kids unloading soft drinks from the Royal Crown Cola delivery trucks. What a terrible thing to do! John Law said, "Sneak around the hill and engage the thieves." He said he only wanted to catch three of them and pointed out the three. "The rest don't matter," he said.

Mike Campo caught the first, and it was kind of funny. When the cop blew his whistle, he yelled, "Freeze." Negroes started running in every direction. So did we. I didn't know whether to run, catch, or hide. Soft drinks were falling all over the ground and a few were being tossed. I caught one on the top of my head. No sooner did I get hit, than one of that bunch clobbered me in the face with his fist. It was so dark from where I was standing I could not see the black guys. I'm sure they could see me in the light of the moon. Luckily no one was injured seriously. Mike reached out and caught one black kid by his shirt and said, "Come here nig." The black kid stopped. Mike felt like a hero. Big deal. This kid he caught was one on the cop's list.

Freckles Jarvis and Vernon Solon were directing the few black kids on the railroad to place their loot in the tunnel and to escape up the other side of the hill. It was like a "Get out of jail free" card. The cop, in his attempt to make a flying tackle of the largest, fell over the side of the hill. His would-be captive got away. With only one in custody, the one Mike caught, John Law walked him to the call box. We returned to the bridge and the fence we had carved up. When the cop left, we retrieved the loot and stored it in the hollow sidewalk of the bridge.

The next time I saw John Law, he was a uniformed guard at a teenage dance. I don't know the reason he was no longer a policeman.

The following story appeared in the Baltimore News-Post newspapers on April 15, 1953 which in brief stated:

"Zip Gun" Boy's Dad Blasts Environment

The irate father of the "zip-gun" boy on Wednesday told the judge, "The Baltimore environment was responsible for the youngsters' behavior, and said furthermore that the environment was the worst he'd ever seen."

This explosion followed the judge's action in sending two boys, one twelve and the other thirteen, to Maryland Training School as delinquents after they were found to have thrown bottles and rocks through a restaurant window.

The twelve-year-old is the brother of the designer of the "ZIP-GUN" which fires .22 bullets. The judge declared it to be a "deadly weapon." Nevertheless, he permitted the "Zip-Gun" builder, fourteen, to go home in his father's custody pending further investigation. He also permitted an eight-year-old, said to be the fourth member of the "Zip-Gun" Gang, to be taken home after lecturing the youngster's parents about seeing to it that their son attends Sunday school and day school. The Zip-Gun is made of wood, a metal tube, a firing pin and some elastic tape. Whoever fires it, police said, gets a powder burn. A patrolman discovered it while investigating a "gang" charged with molesting a restaurant at Greenmount Avenue and Preston Street and police found a bullet fired from it would penetrate a one inch piece of wood. The designer in juvenile court, denied making the gun at one of the vocational schools, and said he put it together in his basement. He said he had fired it only at targets, as had the eight-year-old, who had powder burns on his hand.

When this new edition came out as follow up the next day in the News-Post, we were able to cover ourselves with our parents. We simply told them it wasn't us that they read about. That story really upset the gang as we didn't have any eight-year-old hanging around with us. I was fifteen years old and, possibly, the youngest member of the pack. Also, we didn't take on such a deed as breaking windows. That went out when we were about ten years old. That story gave us a bad reputation and our parents were easily convinced it wasn't true. The cop on the beat made an investigation and tied the two unconnected stories together for sensationalism. We did deny the story as a group of little kids spread a rumor that they were part of our gang. There was a possibility the little boys in the newspaper story were Robinson's kid brother and his friends. Thinking back now, that possibility seems a reality.

Soon punks all over the city were saying they were in the Four Dot Gang. Only thing was, they didn't live in the area of the story. This story only harmed our reputation with grownups not with our peers.

We and no one else were the "Four Dot Gang."

The Moonlight Cruise

On a Saturday night during the summer of 1953 the smart place to be was aboard the S.S. Bay Belle. Berthed in Fells Point, at the foot of Broadway, the Bay Belle was an old excursion boat. She was about the size of a ferry boat and was fitted with three decks. The middle deck contained a bandstand and huge dance floor. You could buy soft drinks (and beer if you passed for 21), potato chips, there. The top, or observation deck, was used to "makeout."

On this particular Saturday evening, Big Bob offered us a lift in his "Blue Beetle"—for a quarter apiece. This showed how big a heart he had, since gasoline only cost seventeen cents a gallon, but there was dignity in arriving in a car. A bunch of us piled into the "Blue Beetle," a '47 Plymouth coupe painted baby blue, while others opted for a taxi. Tonight we would cruise the Chesapeake Bay to the sounds of Bill Haley and the Comets. We were excited because cruises on the Belle were great fun, and your chance of getting laid was excellent.

Even as the Belle slipped her mooring, we were having a swell time dancing. Most guys, myself included, arranged to meet a young lady on board. This was pretty much how we dated then. Boys would arrange to meet their "dates" some- place, thus avoiding the formality of meeting a skeptical father and the cost of an admission. We had just cleared the harbor when a commotion erupted below on the bar deck. Next thing, we felt the Belle slowing until, finally, we were dead in the water. Two guys, sloshed on beer, had bet one another on who could swim to Sparrows Point the fastest. The Harbor Police fished them out of the water and placed them back on board. They spent the remainder of the cruise in a makeshift brig.

Larry Barely had managed to get served at the beer bar, and eventually became loud and boisterous too. Screwed with liquid courage and feeling a foot taller than he was, Larry picked a fight with a very large adult male. Asked to leave the bar deck, he later confronted the man on the dance floor. Larry cold- cocked the guy, who then proceeded to clobber Larry. He picked Larry up and was carrying him toward the rail, apparently intent on chucking him over the side. Was Larry apologizing? Was he telling the man it was all a big mistake? No. On his way to being deep-sixed Larry was mouthing off. "You cocksucker," he yelled. "Your ass is grass. We get off this boat I got ten guys gonna rip your fuckin' ass off!" Fortunately, or maybe unfortunately, a security guard intervened and locked him up in a cabin near the engine room for the duration. He deserved it, too.

Meanwhile, the guy's friends—adult friends—had gathered on the dance floor. They talked about "making sure that punk," referring to Larry, "got it when he got off the ship." Now this was a group of very tough-looking guys, and they started giving us the hairy eyeball. We decided to split up when the ship docked and rejoin at Broadway and Eastern Avenue.

As I left the ship, a couple of "Bakery Boys," as we called the gang who hung out at the bakery, yelled to me from a taxi, "You going to the Ward?" Not wanting to hang around any longer than necessary, I jumped into the cab. I told them about Larry's altercation and they claimed to know the men I was talking about. "You don't wanna mess with them guys," one admonished. I got a ride to Eager and Greenmount and walked the rest of the way home.

The next day, each of us told a bullshit story about, "Fighting my way off the ship." And, in a few cases, "All the way home." I went on at least ten cruises that summer and, if I described each, very little would change in the retelling of this one. Still, those cruises are among my fondest memories.

The Good Bad Guys

Winner of the Most Mischievous Family Award, Western Ward Division, was the Solons. At one time every kid in our crowd was trained in the hell-raising arts by the Solon brothers: Donald, Norman, Kippie, Gerald, Vernon and Gilbert. Bad as they were, and they were bad, I never disliked them like the other hoodlums in the Ward. I can remember Vernon, the next youngest saying, "Jack, I'm a no-good son-of-a-bitch, a real rotten bastard, but you like me don't you? Why? Because, I'm a nice guy." He was right. I did like him. I liked the whole family. They were poor as church mice, but talk about magnetic personalities! There was a real mystery to this family. They loved opera music. They liked the popular stuff of the day, I mean like rhythm and blues and the new stuff known as rock and roll. But they loved opera; Mario Lansa and David Whitfield were among their favorite vocalists. These few facts about the Solons lead me to believe there is a difference between stupid and being poor.

But they, all of them wore a sign: DANGER! STAY AWAY. Still, before long, the Solon magic would work and you'd find yourself in trouble because you succumbed to it. Thank God I pretty much avoided them.

My mother openly considered asking the Solons if she could foster Vernon when we were both about eight years old. Thank God she didn't. I told my mother what I thought to be a very amusing story about the Solons Christmas. This Christmas Day Kippie, the most aggressive Solon, was home on early release from reform school. He found Gilbert, the youngest, sobbing to himself in a corner. Gilbert had a severe learning disorder and would probably be termed dyslexic today. Dyslexic, or whatever, Gilbert could identify any song on the popular charts, including artist and record label. Anyway, Gilbert was crying because Santa Claus had not left the JC Higgins bicycle he promised when Gilbert saw him at Sears. Kippie addressed the family at the dinner table. "What's wrong with you guys?" he addressed his brothers. "Santa made a mistake and gave Gilbert's bike to some other kid. Have you forgotten how to steal it back?"

The Solons' were endowed with great nerve, if not brains, and loved to fight and steal. Going into their house was like visiting Butch Cassidy's Hole-in-the-Wall Gang. It was exciting. You never knew what new contraband they would pull from beneath a bed, or what tale of conquest would issue forth. The fact was, they were pirates, and were convinced someone was riding around on Gilbert's bike!

They went to the Guilford Avenue Bridge and waited for a bicycle to come along. They did not wait long before a hapless colored boy rode by on a newish- looking bike. They took it from him and took it home to Gilbert. Problem solved.

After telling my mother about this, she explained the horror of it, moving me to the point where I actually cried. To assuage the guilt and sorrow I felt for the poor colored boy, I rationalized him to be the very culprit who had recently hit me in the head with a thrown railroad spike. This tactic only allowed me to shuffle it into my memory so it still turns up periodically.

There was one other piece of poetry I neglected to mention, Mr. Solon was a guard at the Maryland Penitentiary located across the street from the Solon's home.

Big Screen TV and In Color, Yet?

To the south of Biddle Street were streets that are non existing today, but like I said earlier in this book, we always could manage to find persons worse off economically. The Solons and the neighbors intermingled of those few blocks were a collection of worse offs.

I had a subscription to Popular Science magazine and my brother was receiving Popular Mechanics; so when I learned Hughy Footley a neighbor to the Solons had a giant screen fourteen inch color television, I was flabbergasted. It was true that the Footleys had one of the first TVs in the neighborhood. And yes, there was such a thing as color TV.

I had seen it in my magazines—but they were much too expensive for the Footley's. One thing for sure, if he had one I wanted to see it. I started fishing around, trying to see if I could finagle an invitation through one of Hughy's friends.

I approached Freckles Jarvis, a Footley neighbor, and inquired about my chances and Freckles could hardly contain himself. While telling me about his visit next door to see the color television with a big fourteen inch screen, Freckles began laughing so hard I thought he was going to be sick. The Footleys had placed a magnifying glass, about fourteen inches square, in front of a ten inch screen. In addition, they taped pieces of red, green and blue cellophane over the screen to make the color. Hugo Footley should have been a used car salesman but I understand he became a collector for a finance company after leaving school. What a waste of a fertile mind.

I Got Beat Up, Punchy?

When thinking back on all the fights I got into as a kid, it's a wonder I didn't become punchy. Perhaps I did. I believe what saved me from serious injury was that I did have many fights and learned to defend myself. The culture of the times was such that it was not uncommon for parents to buy boxing gloves for their sons, much like parents now buy soccer shin guards. We used them, too.

There were many evenings when we would have boxing matches under the alley light behind Biddle Street and Brentwood Avenue. No one ever got angry about settling an argument with the gloves. It was a way of establishing a pack hierarchy and settling differences. Grownups would watch from their yards and were ready to step in if someone got a nosebleed or the cursing got too loud. Boys boxing at the tender age of eight were not uncommon. During inclement weather we used my cellar.

I only remember being beat up once. That was at school by a boy named Jerry Grumbel. I was in the school basement playing Tarzan—jumping up and swinging on water pipes—something we all enjoyed doing. I took a good jump and was swinging on the pipes when I got the idea of walking from pipe to pipe. The pipe I was transferring to was scalding hot; I let go and fell to the floor, landing on my hand and spraining my right wrist. As we were leaving for class, an emissary told me Jerry wanted to meet after school. "For what," I asked, knowing full well what "meeting after school" meant in schoolboy parlance. I had no idea what affront had prompted this challenge. (I learned later that his older brother was instigating Jerry into fighting me to "make his bones," or get a reputation).

After school I walked onto the yard and found him waiting for me. When I got close enough to speak to him, he pushed me. Of course, my first action was to respond with a push of my own. I asked, "What the fuck is going on?" and Jerry's brother yelled, "Beat him up. Hit him! Beat him up!" I looked at the brother.

"Hey, man, can't we settle this some other time? What'd I do to you?"

"You got smart with me last week and I couldn't hit you so my brother Jerry will."

"Look, I'm sorry. Okay?" My wrist was killing me and I did not want to fight anyone.

"Hit him, Jerry!"

"Hey, I have a sprained wrist."

"Where's your bandage? Coward!" With that remark, Jerry tore into me. Every time I hit him I thought my arm was going to break off. After a few minutes, which seemed like hours, I was down flat on my back.

"You had enough?" Jerry asked.

"Yes."

"Don't let him up until you have both of your fists bloody." That from Jerry's brother, who was lathered up more than Jerry. At that point a teacher broke up the fight.

That was a bad incident, but if I wanted to avenge it, I would eventually have to fight his brothers repeatedly. Jerry wasn't at fault. It was his brother. I was twelve years old when that happened.

About five years later, Tony Vespi and I were in a sandwich shop and there was Jerry standing at the counter looking very cocky. Tony looked at me and said, "Hey, Jackie, you okay? You look like you're ready to kill somebody." Jerry turned, looked at me for a split second, and left the store quickly.

"Hey, where'd that guy go?" the clerk asked.

"Who? Jerry?"

"That guy was just standin' here."

"Yeah, Jerry."

"Can you catch him? Catch that guy. He left his sandwich!"

"No problem, I know him. I also know where he's going. What's in the bag?"

"No shit, you know him?"

"Yeah, he's one of my best friends, I sent him here for my sandwich. What's in the bag?"

"Two Polish hams."

"Two Polish ham subs, right? They paid for?"

"Yes."

"Did he give you even change or a bill?"

"He gave me a five-dollar bill."

"The lying bastard. He told us he didn't have any money. That's why we gave him even change. How much are sodas?"

"Fifteen, twenty-five and thirty-five cents."

"Here's a buck. Give us two large sodas, Cokes."

Turning to Tony Vespi, I said, "Here, Tony, carry our subs. I'll carry the sodas."

"Thanks a lot, fellas."

"Hey, don' mention it."

In the car Tony looked at me and said, "When you gonna tell me what the hell is going on?"

"You like Polish subs?"

"Hell, yes."

"Then don' worry 'bout it. Just eat your sub."

Trouble Returns

Once again Warren Grimm returned following a release from reform school. Being an "ex-con" had given Warren standing among the slimier elements. He came back a tough guy, minus a few teeth, eager to apply newly acquired talents. After watching Warren Grimm I am cynical about boy's "training" schools. The only thing he got training in was a proper criminal behavior.

Within days of his return, Grimm was again hanging out with the Hollywood bunch and dressing like a gangster. He owned several topcoats, as many as fifteen suits with shirts, ties and shoes to match. Where in the hell does a stock clerk, which was his profession, get money to buy a banker's wardrobe? Soon, however, his actions became too much for even the Hollywood gang and they quit hanging out with him. They were replaced with the Solon Brothers, a mean bunch. I was at a dance when the Solon brothers egged Grimm into fighting a guy from the lower end of Calvert Street. That started a small gang war in which I was the principal casualty. My frequent partner at neighborhood dances was Doris Grimm, Warren's sister. She may have been sweet on me, I don't know, but she was just a very reliable dance partner to me. Friends of the guy Grimm had beaten up told him that the best way to get back at Grimm was by kicking his sister's boyfriend's ass. That would be my ass. A week later I was shooting pool in a hall on Bolton Street, two miles away from the safety of my neighborhood. Someone said, "Billy's out front, and he wants to see you." I walked out the door to see who Billy was when one guy blocked the door and two others grabbed and held me. Grimm's victim started pounding me with his fists and cussing Grimm. Later, my guys were all for ambushing the whole lot and kicking the shit out of them, but I said, "Aw, fuck it. The guy's a pussy and I didn't feel a thing." A month later our ball team was playing in Clifton Park. Guess who played for our opponent? Yeppur, the very same son of a bitch, "Billy" who beat me up while I was held. During his team's fielding practice before the game, we stood along the foul line and let him know who he was playing against. He was scared shitless and played that way. I left after the game. Later, Garbage Pants told me, "Jackie, we beat the crap outta dat guy. You just don't mess with wunna our guys."

I stayed away from all gatherings where Grimm was present after that. He graduated to a level of bad ass past the Solon brothers and was running with Little Louie Petri, a truly vicious punk, and Larry Barely, the guy I once admired who had turned bad. When these three were together, it was best to stay out of their way. Barely and Louie were shaking down little kids. Barely allegedly had one boy snatching ladies purses as repayment for a loan made at a Shylock interest rate. The kid got caught and did a stretch in the reformatory for his troubles.

Larry Barely soon disappeared for a few years, doing a stretch in a federal prison for armed robbery. It wasn't long before Grimm joined him on the same charge. While posing as hitch hikers, they had been robbing travelers along the Baltimore-Washington Parkway at gunpoint. Little Louie was not implicated and he settled down, although far short of becoming a good guy.

Oysters

Across the street lived two families related to each other. They were from Virginia and West Virginia and moved in just after World War II. The McCarthys were from Virginia and the Freymans were from West Virginia. The boys, Everett Freyman and Billie Gene and Jimmy McCarthy were cousins. Despite sharing a common gene pool, Everett was nothing like his cousins, who were brutish. Everett was more congenial in his demeanor and we were friendly from the start.

We were classmates in primary school and during our early teens we became bonded buddies, sharing our innermost thoughts and secrets. He lived with two sisters, his mother and a stepfather. It was certain Everett would leave home when he came of age because he had lost all respect for his stepfather. His mother was a good woman if somewhat ignorant. This sensitive emotion was due mostly to her poor education. She thought, "What I don't know, my husband does." If, between the two of them they didn't know, then no one else could know either. You know what I mean?

There were times when the phrases they used caused me to laugh. Once Everett's mom, disgusted with his running around with me, told him to go in the house and read a book and get some knowledge. There were other times when I would long to bust his stepfather in the mouth. He would brutally correct Everett for the most minor thing, such as being two minutes late. I didn't know what a razor strap was until I saw one used on Everett as he retreated into his house.

Everett's stepfather was a bus company mechanic who married Everett's mother during the war years. He gave her children his name and was a good provider. He was just too severe a disciplinarian. They had a television set before anyone else on the block and Everett had an air rifle, which he used in the basement range his stepfather set up for him.

Still, Everett lived a very sheltered life. His mother kept a watchful eye on him. There was a picture in their house of her tending bar in some gin mill. I guess that might account for her very protective nature. I recall she was a good looking, well-built woman. I noticed this due to my sex education from Hymie Glick. What she saw in her husband must have been security because he was short and very fat. The cartoon Dick Tracy featured a character known as "Pearshape." Mentally, I compared her husband to Pearshape. You could have knocked me down with a feather when I heard Mr. McCarthy refer to Mr. Freyman as Mr. Pearshape.

Everett was not allowed to fight, or at least that's what he told me. Come to think of it, I didn't know anyone who was actually allowed to fight. Being meek and having bright red hair was in no way an advantage to Everett. As time went on, I taught Everett the art of fisticuffs and for a while I even made him a legend. Having a natural ability for promoting things at an early age, I made up this imaginary character and gave him the name Blackjack. I told stories about this character to guys at school mainly because I didn't have any real heroic stories to compare with the ones my peers were telling. Sooner or later, I was going to have to produce him.

Everett got a job in a grocery store on Cathedral Street and was earning his own money. Therefore, it was not a problem for him to cough up enough money to purchase a double-breasted topcoat when the time he needed one arrived. I showed him how to make a weapon out of a newspaper and instructed him never to walk around without it. Together we made blackjacks, which I designed but let him have the credit for. When the time came for me to produce a character known as Blackjack, I planned to present Everett.

Everett had been lifting weights since he was twelve years old. His muscles were overdeveloped and I had already made him a boxing candidate. Too bad he was a sucker for a right hook. Every time we'd spar, I'd finish him with a hard right to the jaw. Sometimes he'd get red-faced and teary eyed from anger, but we were friends and never got mad enough at each other to want to fight.

The grocery store in which he worked was not in our neighborhood. It was a real old-time store, the kind you would see in a western movie, cracker barrel and all. A cat went with the store, too. The store was located in a rehab area. Most of the residents were upscale, artists and fags. Everett would tell me about one guy in particular who wanted to feel his muscles, later he realized the old fag was into free feels. He also mentioned the guy would ask for "Pussy in The Can," explaining it was his way of asking for canned cat food. One day when his boss was away, Everett asked me to come to work with him as his helper. The proprietor trusted Everett to the point of allowing him to run the place, thus affording himself a day off. It was the first week of summer vacation from school and I hadn't placed myself in a job, so I went to work with Everett. I couldn't believe my eyes. Within a few hours Everett had split the till with his employer. It was no secret, he always had money. He gave me an extra five dollar bill straight from the register, as if it belonged to him.

I showed Everett a car I wanted. He just got his license, so we went to look at my prospective auto. A baby blue convertible. Boy was I pissed when he bought it with his stepfather the next day. When he drove it out of the showroom into the heavy traffic of Mt. Royal Avenue, he smashed into a truck. All Everett's fault, too!

A few months before our venture to eat oysters, Everett called me to come over to his house. He had something urgent to show me. When I entered his house, he informed his mother he wanted his turn at having the basement to himself and not to let his sisters come down. His mother told him to be careful with that air gun. Down to the basement we went. Along the way Everett kept saying, "Wait 'til I show you." "Show me what?" "Just wait. You'll see."

We entered the basement and Everett handed me his air-rifle loaded with BBs, saying, "Here, shoot some targets!" Meanwhile, with a "girlie" comic book in hand, he disappeared behind the furnace saying, "Wait until I show you what I can do." Since that time, I also learned to do this wonderful thing he showed me. I will tell you how later in this story.

Everett was a good-hearted fellow. I remember when he asked me to join him in an extremely fashionable restaurant on North Charles Street. He said we could go there and eat oysters and he would pay. I had never eaten raw oysters on the half shell, although I had eaten them fried in a sandwich.

When we got to the restaurant, the waitress, the clientele and the decor of the place set me back. I did nothing but stare at all the finery. We must have made their day! I believe every waitress in the place came to our table for some reason. They were all friendly. One waitress, when informed we were there for the oysters, removed us from the dining room to a small private room. We were both thirteen. As a matter of fact, I was one day older than Everett. You may be wondering why we were there for the oysters. The reason was Everett had learned that oysters were an extremely potent aphrodisiac!

You see, there was this "thing" we were learning to do. I didn't need "girlie" comic books. Besides, the lady next door had some very exciting benefits to purvey. She was, as the story goes, a former girlfriend of a famous gangster of the '30s. She was a Romanian woman with an accent who had come from Chicago. The benefit she had for being a neighbor was her daughter, a tall redhead who was a burlesque queen.

Our rented house had a third-floor porch in the rear that was great for a kid who was into spying. Our first-floor kitchen porch was covered with morning-glories and an excellent source for spying. The beautiful redheaded daughter would go out on their porch in her robe where she'd stand and comb her extremely long hair. She would stare at herself in a mirror she had set up on their porch. The back of her porch was hidden from view except on the western side, which just happened to be in direct view of my porch. While spying on her with much delight, her robe fell open but she just continued combing her glistening tresses while I imagined she was aware of my watching her.

We ate at least seven dozen oysters and sat and talked about everything imaginable. The waitress brought Everett the bill, which he gracefully paid and left a generous tip. The bill was at least ten dollars. When Everett paid the waitress, he handed her a shiny half dollar saying it was just for her. Everett was sure this new thing we learned to do would need a reload.

What's for Nothing?

Would it be at all possible for a person today to identify with the life-style we had in the Tenth Ward? Yes, I think so. You'd have to look hard for those red-blooded gutsy people. You see, we didn't know we were any different than anyone else. We weren't a bunch of complainers looking for a handout or wanting someone else to take care of us. We didn't blame anyone else for our problems because we didn't know we had any problems. The idea of being poor never crossed our minds. For the most part, we thought of ourselves as rich and any wished-for item was achievable.

In school we read stories about poor people. Our teacher at P.S. No.32 asked what we would do if we were suddenly rich. The most popular response was we would take care of the poor. I think we were an extremely healthy lot.

What was the reason kids in our neighborhood lied so? They weren't really liars—dreamers was more like it.

My mom rented a three-story house on Biddle Street and furnished it with used furniture. Where did she get her money? Mom was a swing shift worker in the war plant. By the time World War II was over, she had furnished the whole house, all eight rooms. She rented the third floor out as an apartment. Two of the three bedrooms on the second floor were rented to maids of a local hotel. We managed to squeeze into the rest of the house very comfortably.

I never realized I was poor until I was about eighteen years old. I guess the reason was no one had told me. What gave me my drive was I never thought of myself as being inferior. My mom afforded me a life-style in this poverty-stricken society that was several cuts above the rest. Thus, I would feel sorry for the less fortunate and could understand when my pal Stevie would tell us he had a duplicate of everything anyone else had and better. Then there was Jessie, who would tell how he spent weekends in the comfort of his parents and kid brother and sister. His dad would take them to the beach or an amusement park. Fact was, his old man left home years before and was never heard from again.

What the hell was wrong with this kind of lie? They weren't beggars looking for sympathy. As I said earlier, we never made fun of those less fortunate but we sure had a lot of fun teasing each other.

I'll never forget my first one-button roll. I made it myself. A one-button roll was a sort of "zoot suit" with only one button. My older brother was discarding his blue double-breasted suit when I retrieved it. I cut off all the buttons and sewed two buttons back-to-back, then placed them in the one button hole that was sewn into the suit jacket. Boy, didn't I think this was the cat's ass? No one, I mean no one, made fun of the way I looked! That was until I got around to Aida Potato's restaurant. It was really the Brentwood Lunchroom, but Big Bob hung the name Aida Potato on the lunchroom and it stuck.

The restaurant was okay, I guess. I never ate anything there other than a hot roast beef sandwich, which I remember as outstanding. The big thing we really went for was a dish of French fries with beef gravy on them. You could get that dish for free. Just ask Miss Aida if she needed any potatoes peeled. There were a few pinball machines and a juke box which possibly accounted for the income of the place. What I enjoyed was the fact you could hang out there, nursing a soda and never be asked to leave. Aida's clientele was mainly from the Industrial Building across the street and the post office garage next door.

By the time I arrived at Aida's, I had already been in street contact with at least seven of my buddies. We were en route to Aida's and everyone was commenting on my good-looking new homemade sports coat. However, some did mention it was a little large. Since it was a former double-breasted coat and no alterations or allowance had been made for the excess material, I could easily have another person or two fit into my "new" home-made suit.

My entourage and I arrived at our destination and sat down to order when someone in the restaurant made a comment about my coat. Soon everyone was making comments. Actually, it was somewhat hilarious. Everyone was laughing about my "new" coat and I can still hear Mike Campo . . . "Hey fellas, look at Jackie's new coat. He made it himself." By now, even I was laughing. Nobody was hurt, except maybe me because now I would have to save to buy one. I remember Floon saying, "Hey, Jackie, look at Tommie's new socks. Don't they look great? They're mine. He doesn't have any!" For the most part no one became upset.

A bunch of us were down at the YMCA on Cathedral and Franklin Streets when a couple of guys went in to steal the elevator. On the elevator was a rolling tray of chocolate pudding. All thoughts of stealing the elevator were discarded for the pudding. Suddenly, the tray was rolling out onto Cathedral Street and just as quickly, cops were coming from everywhere. Ronnie Fonni ducked into a doorway and brazenly emerged leaning against the entrance. A cop came over and asked Ronnie what he was doing there.

"Hey, I live here!"

"Are you Doctor Floon's boy?"

"Yes."

Henceforth, Ronnie Fonni became Floon. We had many nicknames in our gang. Tommy Knoop was "Spanky" as he did look very much like a large "Spanky" from our gang comics. Big Jake had a very pointed nose and wore glasses reminding us of "Ollie Owl" from the comic book. A boy with a face full of freckles who could never whisper was Freckles Jarvis the "loudspeaker." A girl from Warden Street had the cruelest of nicknames, "Bucket Head." Her friends didn't call her that, but those who did were making fun of her. Nicknames are usually friendly and in some way only used among friends. I wasn't aware that some of the names we used were anything but nicknames. When I was with someone who would call to another person by their nickname, I took for granted that was what their friends liked to be called. That was until I called a Negro from Gay Street, "Bootlip." Needless to say he wasn't amused.

Making the Most of No Place to Go

If you lived in the inner city at that time, you were very much aware there weren't any places for youth recreation, especially places that were free of charge. Certainly nothing like today. I hear kids today saying, "There is nothing to do. No place to go." That tells me a lot is taken for granted. We used to schedule ourselves to a selection of entertainment. For instance on Monday nights, the big stores on Howard and Lexington Streets were open. That meant the downtown shopping district would be alive with thousands of shoppers. Downtown Baltimore in the '50s was unique. Freddie Walker's Music Store would be open and there we could get a private sound booth and listen to the latest records. We might even buy one.

Wednesday was the big night at the Enoch Pratt Free Library. The top floor had a planetarium and the lectures were great! Great, that was, until we were asked to leave. Somewhere in the fourth or fifth week we discovered shooting paper wads or metal paper clips from rubber bands added to the "effects" of the Universe. They looked a lot like shooting stars! Obviously, the lecturer didn't find it amusing, which was why we ventured across the street to the Y.M.C.A.

While I ponder my thoughts, I am reminded of the day we hooked into the Times Theater on Charles Street. A very popular theater, the Times featured two motion pictures daily and was open until four. If you went on a Tuesday evening, you would catch the changing of the features and see four motion pictures for the price of two. There we were, about seventeen of us going to the movies. That particular night we must have had good reason to be all dressed up, for dressed up we were. I had on my gray double-breasted topcoat so it must have been winter. We would really dress up in the winter. No dungarees for us. Only sharkskin or gabardines.

If we didn't have to pay to enter the theater, we would have extra money for hot dogs with chili when we came out at midnight. We played odd-man-out to see who would have their way paid in by the gang. Once in, they would open the fire doors for the rest of the gang to enter. Stevie and I were the chosen ones. I was to sit near the screen in front and Brave Stevie would open the fire door. No way he was doing it alone. In our "Sunday best," we went down to the front seats where we slid down to the floor and crawled to the blackout curtain that concealed the fire door. We had to open the fire door very carefully, being sure not to make any noise. Success! The fire door was opened. Now we had some seventeen guys in their "Sunday best" crawling in the aisles of the theater.

We were all to spread out and take seats in separate parts of the theater. Stevie, Tony Meatball and I went for seats in the center of the theater. However, each guy who sneaked in wanted to sit with the next guy. It was very obvious the theater was filled in the center within seconds. This was noticed by the usher, who came down asking to see our ticket stubs. Larry broke bad with him and told the usher to get back where he belonged. That didn't do the trick. While he was en route to get the manager, most of the gang scattered but Stevie and I stayed to present our ticket stubs. Satisfied with this and not seeing anyone else, the manager asked us to be quiet and enjoy the movies. Within minutes the gang was back together. This time some had brought popcorn and other refreshments.

Suddenly, from nowhere, four uniformed cops appeared. Two at each aisle waiting to escort us out of the theater. Today that would be called police brutality. The cops lined us up in front of the famous Chesapeake Restaurant and gave us quite a lecture. One of them exclaimed, "I'll bet you guys are from that teenage snake pit on Greenmount Avenue and Chase Street." He was right! Two of the older guys from the neighborhood had just opened a hamburger shop there. The cops should have let us stay in the theater as we were only going to present them with a most complex problem. By the time we got to Charles and Preston Street we had split into two groups. Since we were now hanging out on Charles Street in addition to the old neighborhood, our number had increased. A lot more action was to be found. This night one group would walk to Biddle Street via St. Paul Street while the other group walked up Charles Street toward Biddle Street. When we met, a gang fight would take place but it was only make-believe. On this very busy street someone threw a milk bottle, which drew a lot of attention. We began shouting, cursing, more shouting and then the contact of phony fighting. It was so real people started running and yelling "Call the police!" To add to the reality, I did accidentally connect with Johnnie Spencecola's nose. Within minutes it was over.

V.I.P. Treatment

When I started going out on dates, I discovered a new method to get into theaters. Matter of fact, it had an air of dignity about it. I only did this a few times as it took extremely steady nerves. Early in the day, I would call a theater in the rural area inquiring as to the manager's name and who or which corporation owned the theater. Armed with this information, I would select a theater where I wished to take my date.

Silent Sam and I, with two very nice young ladies, found ourselves in the midst of downtown one Saturday evening. We had selected a theater and I went to a telephone booth where I could call the theater of our choice. I asked for the manager as he or she was always available. It would be more to my liking if the manager were not available to come to the phone. That way, the message would have to be transferred. The conversation would go something like this:

"This is Lew Ennis, assistant manager of the White Way Theater. A couple friends of mine are downtown and would like to see your feature. Can I get a couple of Okays for them at the door?" Once inside the theater, Silent Sam wonderingly asked, "How did we get in? What's the story?" I replied in my usual slang, "Don' worry 'bout it." Naturally, I had discovered a key that unlocked a world of entertainment. I got the idea from an old movie where the star asked a box office clerk if there were passes there for him. The first time I tried it, the receiver of my call informed me they were known as Okays, not passes.

Me Lie About My Age? Never!

When I was thirteen, I wanted money so badly, I went downtown right after school to a Walgreen dime store and applied for a part-time job as a stock boy. The manager hired me. I was to start in a few days but I needed a work permit. Incidentally, I told the manager I was sixteen. I was so excited I had a job that I found it hard to sleep that night. The next day I put my birth certificate under the eraser and with the aid of our old typewriter changed the "38" in 1938 to "35" making me "officially" sixteen years old. Armed with my birth certificate, I headed to the Child Labor Bureau on St. Paul Street, a walking distance of at least two miles. In those days youths didn't have automobiles available to them like today's kids do. You rode the streetcar or you walked. Arriving at the bureau, I presented my birth certificate and was told the certificate had been altered. The date had been erased and typed over. "Gosh. It has?" That lady should have given me an "E" for effort. They already had a record on me because that was where I got my permit to sell newspapers the year before. The next day, a boy at school told me he was an usher in a theater on Howard Street and they didn't ask him to get a work permit. I didn't know if he was lying or not but I was determined to get a job! So, I went downtown and canvassed a few theaters. I found the same confrontation would apply. You must have a work permit or you don't work. Hence, no permit, no job.

At one theater I tried, the gentleman wanted to hold my hand and told me what a nice boy I was. He continued to hold my hand and told me he would like me to come back. He said he would talk to the manager for me. He was such a nice man. I told him how old I really was and that I needed a job. I hoped the honesty approach would do the trick. However, I also believed this nice guy was a fag. He asked me to come back again when I had time to watch a movie.

"Sure. May I bring some friends?"

"That would be fine." He also said if he wasn't in, to see the nice lady he introduced to me.

Days later, I showed up and went inside. I saw the lady and told her I was there with my friends. She told the doorman it was all right for us to enter. "This boy and his buddies are friends of Mr. Hollywood." You should have seen the doorman's face when twenty-seven of us walked through that door. We were about thirty minutes into the feature when the "Old Fag" came in and said we would have to leave.

Georgie Emerson and Joey Campo were telling me of a great movie they saw at the Aurora Theater and were exploding with excitement over the way they got in. They got in for nothing by sneaking through an open window in the back of the theater. In passing by the theater they said, "We noticed this opened window and peered in. Seeing it was a restroom and part of the theater, we got the idea to climb in. Once in, we discovers we're in the ladies room. This window was over a covey hole."

"You mean a toilet stall?"

"Yeah, a stall thing. We climbs in real quiet like and that's when we finds we're in the ladies room."

"Then what happened?"

"Nothing, we opened the door real quiet like, and goes in the movies. You wanna go with us next time?"

"Hell, no! Some people just don't got no class."

Working My Way Through School

At sixteen I worked in a pharmacy on Charles Street. It was the perfect job for any schoolboy. I worked four to ten Monday through Friday and from noon until ten on Saturdays. The pay was twenty dollars a week or fifty cents an hour. I didn't complain because I enjoyed this job. What made it great for me? At that time it was the money. However, I was getting an education that I would learn to appreciate later in life. First of all, I was learning about retailing and communicating with the public.

There wasn't a soda fountain as this particular pharmacy was dedicated to the serious side of life. However, it did sell perfume, magazines, candy and cigar products. When I wanted Saturday off, I would trade with the druggist's son, who worked on Sunday.

I had passing grades in school but was suspended for bad conduct in May. One day I decided to take a smoke in the toilet area, which was strictly against school regulations. I waited for the bell to ring, assured there would be no one in the toilet area. I entered with a pal of mine, and together we lit up. Now we would need an excuse to enter class late. No sweat, my pal was sick and throwing up his lunch and I stayed with him to see if he needed help. This was an excellent excuse, we always had an answer for everything. As we headed out of the toilet, a kid came out of nowhere suggesting we may need a late pass. He had a pack of them and asking our names, he scribbled a signature that resembled a teacher's. Reason we were late? Change in excuses, we helped the teacher move some boxes. We headed for our homeroom and in the hallway stood a couple of my eightball classmates. One suggested that upon entering the room I yell "Yea, Rowdies!" It would send the homeroom teacher up the wall. I thought my homeroom teacher was a really neat guy as he put up with all our crap. We used to ask him "If we quit school and joined the U.S. Army, would we have a better chance in combat than in the Navy?" This question was asked of him so many times in a hundred different ways. Being an ex-Marine and a Flying Leatherneck, it would send him into a lecture session that almost always screwed up a coming test. That particular teacher was fond of me and since I was wearing white bucks, khaki pants and a regimental tie, he wouldn't get too upset and the class would get a good laugh. Anyway, we figured he would just tell us to shut up, sit down and pay attention.

When I ran in the room and belted out my last hurrah, I looked and the class wasn't laughing. I turned to see the school principal sitting in my homeroom teacher's place. We may have not been in so much trouble, but my buddy gave the principal our fake late passes. By mutual agreement we were out of school for the duration of spring. I was now working in the drugstore in the evenings and looking for employment during the day.

A chemist came into the pharmacy in June and enlisted me as a laboratory technician for his business. He was president of a chemical corporation. I discussed this opportunity with the druggists and they had two schools of thought to offer. First, I should stay on at the drugstore and finish school. Second, if I wasn't going to return to school, then this might be an excellent opportunity. My own thought was to take the job. The drugstore and school could wait. Besides, if the job didn't pan out by September, I would be able to re-enter school then. Here's the catch. I had to know the metric system to be accepted for the new job.

I struck up a conversation with a rather nice looking blonde-haired guy who came into the drugstore every evening. On most occasions he got a pint of chocolate ice cream and a Seven-Up. We got into a conversation over the soft drink and ice cream combination. He said he made an ice cream float and enjoyed it while he was working. He worked evenings at the radio station upstairs. During the day, he taught science at a high school in Towson. I enlisted his help with the metric system and learned more from him on this subject than I possibly could have in school. I gave my notice and left the drugstore for the job with the chemical company.

The job was the pits. For one, it was on the county line on the opposite side of the city so I had to arrange for transportation. If I wanted to ride with the chemist, I had to be at his apartment by six-thirty in the morning. The job was eight to five, but because he worked late, it was seven at night before we got to his apartment and then I had to walk the six or so blocks home. The hours and travel were not to my liking and the job was really as a clean-up boy. I'm sure the job could have worked into something better if I had given it a chance.

The few technicians employed there were very nice guys. There was one guy who was not as educated as the others, for most were college graduates. This particular guy was only a high school grad and thought his shit didn't stink. I believe he resented the college educated technicians and with my being the local high school dropout, it gave him a superior feeling. Now he wasn't fooling around with your average dropout.

I already had as much or more experience dealing with people then this jerk did even if he was given a few extra brain cells. Therefore, I steered clear of him and made friends with all of his superiors. I even went out of my way to be friendly with his supervisor. Sometimes his supervisor would give me a ride all the way home. Looking back over this technician who used to try to intimidate me, I think fondly on the incident.

The chemist would have the technician go to a restaurant and get us a sandwich. Man, this guy really hated to do that. He would come to me, wherever I was in the plant, and ask, "What are you going to have for lunch?"

Once, he made a comment referring to why he should be doing my job. I thought of about ten different things to say to this guy, but I also thought about my big mouth and how it had gotten me into trouble at school. I was given a nickname as the "Chemist's fair-haired boy."

With the dislikes overwhelming the likes of the job, I quit. I quit without notice. The chemist's assistant came to my house to see if there was anything wrong. I was really ashamed of not confronting the chemist and being a man about quitting. But isn't that what quitters do? Quit?

I was back at the drugstore in a month and besides, the drugstore now felt like home. The ice cream float guy was surprised to see me back. He thought I made a good decision to try to get back in school.

Boy, when I found out about the job this ice cream float guy had at the radio station upstairs I couldn't believe my ears. He was Jack Dawson the evening disc jockey of the radio station and I was really impressed. He invited me to come up and see the station after closing the drugstore one night. That began a relationship that lasted for a very long time. I would spend about an hour every evening talking and learning about the disc jockey business. I was sure to become a disc jockey and I now wanted to become a radio "Personality."

I talked to the school counselor and managed to get back in school. He told me if I kept a good conduct record, I was sure to get out of the vocational school and into the Polytechnical High School by the winter semester. With the help of my brother Jim my drafting grade was excellent. Jim bought me a complete drafting set consisting of board, Tee Square and everything I needed to draw.

I started to be an all round student, I bought a tutorial book on English so as to learn to speak properly and I saved enough money to purchase a tape recorder. I was on my way. Evenings after work at the drug store I would go up to the radio station and stack records for Jack. I was even helping him with his career as he was getting requests from all over via my big mouth at school. I told everybody I knew to listen to his show and they did. Even some of my teachers had requests played on the air.

History by Jack

From our earliest beginnings we were a creative lot and when we played we put our all into it. If it were a job to do or an objective of any sort we were not quitters. In fact we would look for the ultimate in almost everything even when we played cowboy on the railroad. We would race along a slow-moving freight train and pretend to rob it by hopping on and riding for several blocks or until being summoned off. We had no fear of getting hurt. We thought of ourselves as immortal. We would climb the high walls of the railroad tunnels, walk the steel girders of the trestle bridges on St. Paul Street and Calvert Street as well as the street car trestle on Guilford Avenue. We used to play follow the leader, a most popular game until Billy McCarthy plunged some fifty feet from the billboard at the Biddle Street Bridge and landed on the ground near the railroad tracks. The fall didn't kill him, but it did leave him crippled for life. We were all saddened by Billy's fall. Billy stayed in the hospital for months and when he came home, he was a very bitter kid, I guess his bitterness was understandable.

The years of being nine, ten and eleven seemed to pass so quickly and suddenly, I was a student transferring from Grammar School Number 32. My daytime chums had split with some going to Clifton Park Junior High School while a few attended Lafayette Junior High School Number 79 with me.

Clifton was a beautiful school with a rolling grassy knoll surrounding it and only two trolley car rides away. I can't help recalling the memory of a girl I went to school with so many years before. She was a petite pretty girl and had a crush on me from the fourth grade. I gave her a wallet for a Christmas present back then. Her first year at Clifton was the last year of her life. She was run over by a steel- wheeled street car while racing across the tracks that ran through Clifton Park in front of her school. She was to meet her father who came that day to pick her up. If only she had attended Lafayette instead of Clifton. Lafayette was a run-down school on Park Avenue and Dolphin Street and much closer to where she lived. In fact the school made the news when I attended it. No, not because of me. The city had condemned the building, although it was to remain open for many years afterward.

While writing, I'm reminded of Thanksgiving Day in 1951. I won the opportunity to be on the radio for three hours in the afternoon. I was to be Lee Case's kid brother for the day. Lee Case hosted a local radio show that was informal and swing music. I learned later many of the teachers listened to the show. It also helped with my popularity with the kids at school. After Mr. Case introduced me, one of his first comments was about my school and the fact it was open even though the city had condemned it. I agreed it should be condemned and went on to tell just how dirty it really was. I came out of the station and was waiting for a bus when three hoodlums forced me to hand over my money—all of a dollar and a half. I arrived home about an hour and a half late to find my mother worried over the fact something may have happened.

I never played hooky until my pal Floon came to Lafayette. He was asked to leave St. Johns and was enrolled by a police officer. The officer was his oldest brother Joe, but Floon never let on to anyone it was his brother. Floon let them wonder what he had done to deserve a police escort and of course he gained notoriety as a bad-ass from the get go. Floon lived two blocks from my house. We shared a lot of laughs, perhaps too many for our own good. I remember when he brought his pet white rat to school and it got away. We would hear stories for months to come about a giant albino rat that was terrifying the janitorial staff. Now that Floon was a classmate we started to also share non-school activities as well.

I wasn't big into fishing and stuff. I hadn't gotten too much experience at it, but I could appreciate a nice fish when I saw one. Floon and I went fishing at the Jones Falls and Floon caught what he said was, "A big fucking bass fish. Maybe one of the biggest." A real trophy, I talked him to letting me have it, to take home. My mom made me give it back to Floon. She said, "Get that mud carp out of this house immediately!" So much for a carp masquerading as a bass.

During the time Floon and I became classmates, I was invited to attend the open house of a technical vocational high school on Broadway. I somehow believe I was given the invite to separate Floon and me. I guess it was because we were cutting classes to go to radio giveaway shows in the afternoons at North Avenue Market. It all started when Floon said he wanted a submarine sandwich for lunch. The closest place to get one was at the market. While there, we took part in a live radio broadcast, forming a new habit for the afternoons and we eventually stayed away from school the entire day. The school wrote my mother a letter telling her I had not attended school for two weeks and demanded an answer as to why. Playing hooky became a bore and I was glad I got caught. The old Howard Street Theater was where we would spend the morning hours until going up to the market for the broadcast. The Howard opened the door at nine. By the time you watched a movie, the news and a cartoon it was lunchtime and that even became a boring thing. What was so strange was no one seemed disturbed that the theater was filled with so many school-aged movie goers.

Floon and I parted company in the daylight hours as I was now accepted as a student in the vocational school. I believe my boredom ended about that time, I became enthusiastic about school and the greatest part was the mornings. Almost every day, I would walk two miles to this school. I didn't mind it because I would stop on North Avenue and Harford Road at a pharmacy and have a coke with the cutest girl ever. A girl named Marie. She was part of a clique of young ladies that was attending St. Paul's Commercial High School on North Caroline Street. Both schools were in the next few blocks, mine and hers. I never let on that I was absolutely nuts about her. I constantly thought about her and would imagine myself in her company when I wasn't. You see, I thought it was cool not to show your emotions and besides, I had a reputation of being a cool cat to keep. I had never really kissed a girl and couldn't have gotten the nerve up if invited to do so. The rule of life is, "The squeaky gear gets the grease." In love, "Faint heart never won fair lady."

What fun I had at this combination gym and reform school on North Avenue, as it was better known. I remember a guy setting next to me in class, he jumped out a window when the principal and two uniformed policeman entered our room.

You had to be cool and "play the role" as we called it to keep from being beaten up. On his first day in this school, my buddy Tony Vespi punched out a punk at his locker. The punk demanded Tony's lunch money. When Tony entered the classroom, the teacher asked his name and Tony was suspended. In those days you didn't rat out your enemy, instead you got even in different ways.

I played the role of an amateur prize fighter to keep most of the hard-boiled punks from banging on me. I mean this place had them, too. They would mill around looking for a weakling to pick on. That was when they would be in their glory.

Changing classes, I was walking down a flight of stairs in a single-file line. In the opposite direction came some guys on their way to who knows where. They started to taunt the group in my line and one of the loud laughing punks reached out at me and put something in my face. What? I don't know but it had an extremely foul odor. He was laughing aloud with some of his buddies about what he had just done and they were in approval and laughing, too. I broke out of line and wrestled him to the bottom of the steps. I then commenced to beat the living hell out of him. Later on I felt somewhat guilty that I had taken advantage of a situation, but I established myself, that justified my deed. That was all I needed and the rest of the school term went easy for me.

Vernon Solon was a freshman at this school and kept close contact with me during lunchtime on the campus. Both Tony Meatball and Vespi plus a few others from our neighborhood were attending this school, but our classes were at different schedules. However, we were within earshot if trouble ensued and needed us as a pack.

I was reminded of my problems while attending Lafayette Junior High and was not about to make the same mistakes of being a goof off or of taking the part of the underdog. Well almost. One morning I witnessed a scene, it goes like this: I was taking a smoke on the south side of the school in an area that allowed smoking. In an instant a little guy weighing no more than ninety pounds walked up to another guy, who must have weighed at least two hundred pounds. On contact, the little guy slugged the big one a hard right in his face, cursing him and the big guy withdrew up against the building while the little guy commenced to pound on him. I didn't know what the heck that was all about and the first bell of school rang and I headed for my Homeroom.

The next morning the same thing happened, this time with the big guy handing a pack of cigarettes to the little guy while, retreating away to the little guy's curses. In no way could I honestly allow this to happen in my presence. I was naturally drawn in. I just happened over to the big guy as the little guy crossed the alley to disappear into a small store.

The store was a convenience store serving the kids attending the school. It was operated by blacks and contained a jukebox, two pinball machines and sold soft drinks, cigarettes and cookies. No milk, bread or anything else. Their stock was limited only to the real necessities of life. That is if you're a teenager. When I approached the big guy, I had only pity for him. I asked, "Hey big boy, what was that all about?"

"Aw, nothing. He just likes to kid around."

"Kid around? What are you a fucking nut? That guy did that to you yesterday and again this morning. I want to know!"

"You're not on the student body are you?"

"Man are you a real lame? I'm no student whatever. So you gonna tell me or what?"

"Well okay, he's been doing this since school started. Last year near to end of term, he and a couple other guys jumped me and every day, I mean every day after that they took turns beating on me." He continued, "I didn't want to come here this year but I had no other choice." Pausing he drew a breath and in a low tone of voice he said, "I was giving him fifty cents a day to leave me alone."

"So why is he picking on you now?"

"He said I have to give him a pack of Pall Malls and fifty cents a day. He said the cost of living has gone up."

I asked the big guy his name and he answered, "Buddy Pearson."

"Buddy," I asked, "You ever see me before?"

"Yes, you're Jack Lundon from Tenth Ward. Heck, just about everybody knows you."

"Buddy, why don't you just hit that little punk?"

"I can't fight, I don't know how."

"Neither does that punk, that is why he picks you for a punching bag."

"If he finds out I told you about this he'll want to kill me."

"Make a fist. Roll your hand into a ball like you're going to pound on a desk, but instead of pounding down, reach straight out. Here, hit the palm of my hand." With that the big guy punched straight out at me and the force liked to move my whole body.

"Buddy I'm going to be right here tomorrow morning and you're going to punch that punk as soon as he gets close to you. If you don't do as I say, I'm going to kick the living hell out of you myself."

"Suppose he beats me up?"

"Believe me, he won't. You've got to learn to take a chance on yourself. Look, If he even so much as hits you back, I will cross the alley like gang busters and beat the hell out of him. We got a deal?"

Stammering Buddy answers. "Wa. . . wa, ye. . . ah we got a deal, hell yes we got a deal."

I felt pretty good and very positive about the whole idea. If I get in trouble for this at least my mom will understand. The next morning I made sure I was at the school early. My concern was Buddy may not show up. For once in my life, I kept it quiet about what I had done. My incentive for keeping hush about this act was simple and in two parts. One, I didn't want to become the protector of a bunch of thankless characters. Two, I really wanted to see justice done and I was confident of my judgment.

It was judgment time, and I was at ringside for what was about to happen. Buddy has just shown up. He crossed at the corner where me and some of my chums grasped our last few puffs of smoke before the show. Only thing now was to see if the punk showed up. I told Buddy to stay as far away from me as possible and not to let on until the punk got up to his face. "Don't say a word. Just act like you're itching your jaw and throw a punch as hard as you can into the punks face."

This is what happened:

From a half block away the punk was making threats to the big guy. Obviously to gain some respect and admiration from whoever may be watching. I thought to myself, "This guy has the markings of a real potential Bully." He continued cursing Buddy as he got close to Buddy's face. Buddy looked like he was about to throw up. " Oh come on. Don't chicken out," was all I could think.

BAM! Buddy hit the punk and I wasn't sure whether the punk would be getting up or not. Holy shit, he did get up. He screamed and ran into the side door of the school. Buddy was looking at his fist examining it as if he never saw it before.

"Hey Ma, look what I just found, my Hand!"

Let Me Out of Here!

I came to this school to take a business course that included typewriting, adding machines, etc. Within two weeks I was ready to quit. I mean Quitsville here I come. I didn't like the course or classmates. My homeroom was packed full with sissies and for the most part actual fags. I wasn't sure about fags, but this group was disgusting. In the showers they would stare. The feminine type would giggle and smile at you as if you were something strange. There was this one big guy that looked really tough to me, and in the boys' lavatory he asked me if he could bite me on my!#%$#@!. I didn't know what to think, I wanted out. I begged the counselor, who was also the assistant principal to let me take another class. He suggested sheet metal shop, considering my experience the past summer in a real sheet metal shop, I quickly replied with "No thanks!" I told him of my desire to follow my brother and become an engineer. This got me into a drafting class. The homeroom for the drafting class was full and I was assigned to take my homeroom with the sheet metal class. The sheet metal class was more my style anyway. It was filled to capacity with the eightballs of the school, also the biggest guys. It was the jock class, too! They may not of had much brain but they made up for it in brawn. They had the best contact sports teams in the city. The class football team was known as the Rowdies. I attended classes and began to show improvement. In addition, I was attaining an 85 plus average.

I gained so much confidence in myself with the improvements to the new me and having Marie as a secret love, I used to sit in history class with my hand raised always ready to answer questions. In reality I was day dreaming of Marie and would I ever let her know how I felt. I found the more I volunteered, the less I would be called on for answers. History has always been my "big shtick" even when I was a child. I gave up reading comic books at ten and fell in love with the blood-and-guts adventures of our forefathers. All wars, the American Revolution, Civil and both World Wars, I loved them all. Therefore, I was not easily stumped for an answer.

I guess it all started when I met Pop an old man I adopted when I was nine years old. He was to become one of the encouraging factors for this love of history. Pop was a plumber and lived in a plumber's shop on the Guilford Avenue side of the Fallsway. Pop had this special talent for making puzzles out of heavy wire and was generous enough to make every one of us boys a slingshot out of bucket handles. They were the best slingshots ever. They could knock a pigeon off the Chase Street Bridge with one marble in the wink of an eye.

I was about eleven years old and in the fifth grade and had missed a lot of school due to sickness. My teacher, Miss Column, told me she would probably have to fail me if I didn't bring my grades up. A test was to be held in a few days. The test would be on the history of the American Revolution. I conveyed this to Pop who gave me a book that I kept until I left home at eighteen. It was a complete history of Early America containing some 500 pages in a red clothbound book. I went home and retired early that day. I read that book deep into the night and for the next few nights to come. When the test took place, I was outstanding. Miss Column asked me to stay after school and talk to her about the test. She knew I didn't cheat because no one had as many right answers as I. She asked me how I knew so much about the subject and I explained to her about my friend, Pop.

Now, almost five years later I'm faced with a like predicament. I had formed this terrible habit of raising my hand, one day I was called on to answer a question, most obviously, no one else in class could answer. I sat there with my hand raised. The teacher's lips were moving but I couldn't hear her. I was, for the most part, daydreaming about Marie, we were embraced and I was about to give her the kiss of a lifetime.

"Okay, Jack, tell them the answer!"

I stood up and paused. "What was the question, again?" I couldn't quite make out what she was saying, it all sounded like gibberish to me. I did make out the name George Washington and Trenton. I had to do something. This was my favorite teacher and I couldn't let her down. I decided to speak in gibberish. A language that is garbled and doesn't mean anything, although it sounds like it does. I said, "It was apparent that the northregis of the free to scram on would be forever Blyth so Washington for poor and sat nut to Trenton in favor of spilack. Rather, than cherrie the magantow for Burgeons."

With that I sat down. Miss Krause had the darnedest look on her face. Many of the students were quick to declare they couldn't hear me so Miss Krause asked me to repeat my answer and as near to what I said, I tried. She looked at the class. "Does everyone agree with Jack?" Then she gave the answer and stated, "Doesn't that somewhat agree with your answer, Jack?"

I replied, "Very much so! And I would like to add that many have seen the wonderful painting of the crossing of the Delaware? Washington standing up in the boat holding a flag? Our country didn't have a true stars and stripes flag at that time, in place of the stars was the cross of Saint George. We were defying the British in every way possible. In fact the reason General Washington stood up in the boat is, if he sat down in the boat, he would have had to row."

This brought a smile from the teacher and my brownie points went through the roof. Danny Funk, also known as Funk the punk, a pal of mine in school, whispered, "What the hell did you say? You didn't say anything did you? Lundon, you've got to teach me some of that crap."

I enjoyed the time I attended Samuel Gompers Technical Vocational School No. 298, known to others as the Teenage Gym on North Avenue. While attending that school, I turned sixteen and got the job in the drugstore on Charles Street. I wasn't a lazy kid. I worked in the drugstore forty hours a week while attending school. From the money I earned, I liked to dress up and enjoy the recreation. I managed to give my mom Six dollars a week, but I also managed to borrow it back during the week. I got a fair education by working in the drugstore, which brings me to another paradox.

I had to prepare a book report for English class and was unaccustomed to doing homework. So, like other things, I was ready to take on this challenge. I did have the respect of most of my teachers and they had mine.

In the Tenth Ward, we had an old drunk named Gallagher. From whence he came or went, I will never know. What I do know is when we boys would see him, the fun would begin. Gallagher would ask us for money of which we hadn't any, of course, and someone would shout, "Look, Gallagher, Germans! There are Germans down the street." With those words would come a hardy yell of "Charge" from Gallagher. Away we would all go, running toward a make-believe German Army. I still don't know what that was all about. Was Gallagher patronizing us? Or was he reliving something? I used to wonder about the mystery of Gallagher and decided he could have been a real hero. With Gallagher in mind I concocted a story that was to become the winner of an A-plus.

Eisenhower was president at this time and as a character for my book report, I will include him. That should bring much attention to a normally "dull" class. I added the name of a publisher and presented my report as an autobiography of the president. I asked to give my report orally. The teacher was a nut for oral reports. When I entered class, I immediately approached the teacher and told her I had prepared my report at work and that somehow the janitor disposed of it. I tried to rewrite it, but worked overtime and didn't get home until midnight. I would appreciate it very much if I could give my report orally. Besides being a soft touch for oral reports, this teacher liked literature and dramatics. Here was my oral report given that day in late May 1955

"My report is "Ike," an autobiography on our president. Brown and Schuster Press From the Publishers Copy to be introduced in the Fall 1955. Before I start, I want to add, a salesman for the book company loaned me his copy upon learning I wanted to give my report on something not of the ordinary. World War I. Somewhere in France we find Lt. Eisenhower, an aide to General Blackjack Pershing.

Pershing sent Ike to locate the Germans. Ike took with him a very capable sergeant named Gallagher. They went too far into the French countryside where they were almost captured by the Germans. Gallagher found a farmhouse that was vacant and, being experienced, took the lieutenant under his wing to protect him. The sergeant hid Ike and himself in a wine cellar under the house for two weeks. By the time the American Expeditionary Forces arrived, Gallagher became an alcoholic. Eisenhower managed to get him an honorable discharge recommending him for a medal. Today, they're still friends. Ike entertains the former sergeant on holidays at the White House." The teacher said this was an excellent presentation and gave me an A-plus. She commented she could hardly contain herself waiting for the book to be released. I told her I couldn't get her a copy as the salesman was a little upset with me for taking so long in returning it.

* Pershing's aide was a young officer by the name of George S. Patton.

Fags

I remember standing on the Biddle Street Bridge one day when I was about ten years old. I was daydreaming when a well-dressed man came running out of the tunnels of the Fallsway. He ran under the bridge holding his head as if it weighed a ton. On second glance, I saw another man equally dressed running in hot pursuit with a group of boys at least sixteen years old. I would see similar scenes in the years to come, but what I was witnessing was tragic. Punks busting fags.

The fags were lured to the tunnels from the downtown shopping district. In the cover of the tunnels the exchange of sex for pay would take place followed by a beating and robbery. I almost became ill when I realized what I was seeing. There were those who for a few dollars would stoop so low as to sell themselves for money to fags. Because of the nature of the act, during this time in American history, the robbers wouldn't get caught. Why? Because the fags were not about to report the how and why of their being robbed. My street-wise-education was being broadened as I grew older. I was becoming more aware of life and it's cruelties. By the time I reached fifteen some things began to make sense. Most of the crowd being senior to me, I was being educated rapidly. I would hear stories in the gang about the twisted experiences of the male prostitute. Sometimes, they would joke about it and I do recall many of them telling their stories and admitting to robbery and beatings. Larry and Louie were both male prostitutes and I remember once when I saw Louie hurrying to meet a fag he referred to him as "A ten dollar customer." I asked him if he had any thoughts of robbing the fag and his reply was, "No! This is a business, you don't beat on your customers."

One Sunday evening prior to Larry being sent to prison. I was walking out to the bridge and saw about ten of my buddies gathered as if readying for something. They were all talking about going to some guy's apartment and listening to hi-fi. What the hell's hi-fi? And who the hell is Gene Bork? What will going to his apartment have to do with making Larry and Louie pissed off? These questions were soon answered.

Across the Fallsway was an affluent neighborhood. You have, no doubt, heard the expression "across the tracks?" This was "across the tracks." Since this section of town was separated by the Biddle Street Bridge, it was like a great wall of separation between two peoples. In the 200 block of East Biddle Street is an address that for some years was the former home of the lady known throughout the world as the Duchess of Windsor. Across the street in the same block was the former home of Gertrude Stein, the poet who wrote, "A rose is a rose is a rose is a rose." Other than the location, it really has nothing to do with this story.

We ventured across the bridge to the apartment of Gene Bork. On first encounter you could have bought me for a penny. When Stevie knocked on the door of Bork's apartment, Louie answered the door and questioned Stevie as to what was going on? Stevie explained it was cold out and he had brought the guys as promised.

Larry sat in the living room and this loud sound of music was coming from a record player. My questions were now being answered and in order.

Hi-fi was a way of amplifying music in high fidelity from Bork's record player.

Gene Bork was a well-to-do-gay-blade.

Larry and Louie wanted to keep the gang away from what they regarded as private property. Our being there would evidently piss them off.

We were, in turn, introduced to our host, Gene Bork. Upon introduction, Bork said to me, "You live at 325." I had no idea why this tall, thin, limp-wristed man would know my address. Was he a spy for the FBI or what? Here I was some fifteen years old and introduced to a person of questionable character and he knows me! What was going to happen? Nothing! This guy's apartment liked to knocked my socks off. It was beautifully decorated and the rooms were large. He had as much room in his apartment as we had in our whole house. We all enjoyed similar visits to Gene's place. Although he never confessed to being a homosexual-sex-seeking-fag, he made it known he was very lonely and very gay. I certainly was confused and wasn't sure what gay was, but I was soon to find out.

Bork was far from being an ugly person. His manner was extremely polite. He was probably around twenty-seven and you couldn't help feeling sorry for him as he seemed out of place within himself. He had auburn hair and a fair complexion with a sprinkling of freckles. The freckles seemed to fade away from the area of his eyes giving him a rather commanding masculine look. But then add his feminine movements and you can easily understand why I became confused about this man. Bork would invite a few of us to come over and listen to the hi-fi. For the most part, I really enjoyed the music, but when the crowd dwindled to just one or two, Bork would allow us to have some wine.

On one occasion, after I had a few drinks of wine, Bork was going to show me how to really relax. He started massaging the calves of my legs, which I had elevated on a footstool. I asked him if he was going to try to get funny with me. He explained he was not a cocksucker, but was merely passionate. He said he was very passionate about me. He went on to explain he had these feelings for several in our gang. I told him he was a queer. He immediately dismissed this as being untrue. He said, "I'm very lonely and I would enjoy a relationship with you and several others in the crowd, but I don't do the oral thing."

"Why not?"

" Because I'm not a queer, I'm just very gay."

Looking him in the eye I said, "Try something funny with me and your gonna get the shit knocked out of you."

With tears in his eyes as he spoke, "I don't want you to stop coming over Jack. I have a crush on you and I promise I won't try to hurt you. In fact I will help you with some facts of life I believe to be very important, music. I will help you to better understand music with a sense of appreciation. I'm very lonely. My family has disowned me and your pals only want me for my money and wine. Please be my friend. That is all I ask."

I sat and listened to him as he went on to explain the mental anguish of his childhood. He went on to tell me more about his current life and that he had a girlfriend. I asked him if he screwed her and he said he did. He also said she was in love with him and understood he was gay. This was still confusing to me as I still believed the horse shit Hymie Glick told me about fags and stuff when I was nine years old. I felt so sorry for this guy almost to a point that I wanted to protect him and in other thoughts I wanted to run from him.

I would go to see Gene at least once a week to talk. He was educated and could carry on a conversation at a much more elevated level than that of my gang pals. Plus, he always had snack foods and wine. He never made any advances toward me as I made it clear to him I would be his friend if he didn't try any funny shit. Gene must have respected me as he never got funny with me. I believe I was fond of him in a strange sort of way. I did enjoy the music and his conversations and realized even gay people were people, too.

Little Louie Shakedown Artist

Louie Petri, Larry Barely and Warren Grimm were in to a number of escapades that never warranted being remembered, but I can get glimpses in my memory of their combined dirty deeds of muggings. Together they would step to no ends in crime. Their raids included mugging, breaking and entering, hijacking of trucks and hot cars. Eventually and in separate incidents they were caught. Grimm was the first to be separated from this band of three after trying to rob the Loyola Bank. He entered the bank gun in hand, but concealed by a brown paper bag. He handed the teller a deposit slip that read, "Give me all your money." The teller was one fresh-out-of-training. She told Grimm she would have to see her manager. That being said, Grimm made a mad dash out of the place. He stumbled into the arms of an off duty, but uniformed police officer. With hands in the air Grimm surrendered. He would have been released on a lesser charge but it turned out he fit the description of a wanted for armed robbery suspect' and was proven to be just that. Charged with attempted armed robbery of a federal institution, it was further learned he was a wanted man in another state. Grimm was actually hiding out while in the company of Larry and Louie. He escaped the would be jailers while in route from the court to the big house.

Larry was arrested for armed robbery on the Baltimore-Washington parkway. The parkway being Federal Property meant his being incarcerated at a federal institution. Somehow Louie escaped being involved in either of Grimms or Larrys escapades. Neither of the two made knowledge of Louie being involved, but he was. He was waiting as the get-away-driver on the bank job with Grimm.

Larry departed from the neighborhood for about two years, and Grimm was already an escaped convict touring the lower U.S. He was now wanted for escaping the law in Florida, West Virginia and of course Maryland, too. Louie sought the friendship of the gang. None of our crowd really ever alienated anyone, that is unless you were a rat. You could be rotten to the core, but if you didn't squeal on the gang members and were not dishonest to the gang you would have nothing to fear. On the other hand, if you were any of the above, consider yourself as grass and the gang as lawnmowers.

Louie, as I had mentioned did quiet down and became a barrel of laughs. I guess because of his dominating personality most were afraid not to laugh and after awhile his antics did become entertaining. Louie Petrie was a good fella but dabbled a bit in protection. If you had cash, he was always ready to try and coax you out of it. He was also known throughout the neighborhood as Little Louie. He got his name because he was no more than five feet tall. Louie would comb his hair in a pompadour to raise his height an extra two inches. He was somewhat stocky with a fair complexion and a pug nose, which made him a candidate for a Leo Gorcy look alike. He was the type you didn't want to mess with. I remember he was, at times, looking for an easy way out and a quick easy score.

Once, when he was without a job and honest funds, Louie gave me an order to fill at the drugstore where I worked. He told me to get cigarettes and toiletries such as shaving cream, cologne, etc. Furthermore, he told me I would do this thing for him since he was my friend. What if I didn't? Well, he was prepared to cut off my balls. I didn't figure he'd go that far, but I was afraid of what might happen in a fight.

I couldn't erase the fact that I was an excellent fighter. It was humiliating to think I was being forced to do some cheap underhanded deed, stealing from my employer. The next day I kept drifting mentally into reliving those moments of small glory when I was in charge. If only I wasn't so afraid of Louie things would be different. After all, he wasn't as much a threat as Billy Spitler. I fought Spitler and he was a rapist and that's just short of being a murderer. I proved to myself some years before I could stand up to bullies with Drunken Bill, Resnick's Sonny and Big Jake, not to mention an amateur boxer I kicked the hell out of in a street fight. I promised never to brag about that as it would damage his career. Louie was not nearly the size of these guys.

Then there was the time I had to make my defense on Charles Street months before when on three occasions I was challenged or egged into a fight defending Mervy, a girl named Julie and Tony Meatball. All my fights were fair and some were confined to The Flying Saucer Restaurant's men's room. There I could beat up and then wash up. It was also a convenient place to use after the fights I had in Mount Royal Park. But a fight with Louie, a guy who was known to have broken legs for money and extortion. What the hell have I gotten into?

Searching for solace I drifted into my earlier most frightening fight. Once I was told a guy was looking to fight me. I asked what it was all about and the reply was some guy told Mervy his pointed pennyweight shoes were for queers. Mervy told him they were great for dancing, but not satisfied with that, the guy said only queers wore them. Mervy exclaimed, "Jack Lundon wears them!" The guy told Mervy I was a queer. Mervy told the guy he wouldn't dare say that to my face. There is more to this incident that comes to my mind but while I reflect, let me tell you about a very nice girl who was staying at a charity home for women and girls. I liked this particular girl first as a girlfriend and later looked on her as a kid sister. Because she may read this I'll call her Mary Ellen. I took Mary Ellen on a date and then home to meet my mom. We sat on the sofa and listened to the radio's Top 40's and necked. After several days of this, she became very serious. I must add she was stacked like a movie star and quite pretty. Here I am being very respectful to her when, wanting to be honest with me, she begins to tell a most horrifying story. The story caused me to like her less as a girlfriend and more as someone to be pitied. I was quite upset and angry that she had been used and me being a virgin, I didn't want used furniture. I realized things happen and it was best to accept things that can't be changed, but who the hell was I to pass judgment on her. That's when I became her protector and big brother.

She told me she had this date with a redheaded guy who picked her up in his car. He was accompanied by two other guys who were to meet their dates en route to who knew where. They took her to a wooded area and attempted to rape her, but instead settled for her performing oral sex. They threatened her with her life. I felt sorry for her when she told me this story and, being only sixteen myself, couldn't give her much advice. I grew very distant from her within minutes and felt a deep hatred growing within me for those creeps. Life holds many mysteries.

Guess who the punk was that wanted to fight me. Billy Spitler, the very same punk that Mary Ellen said, tried to rape her. Yes sir, another mystery of life unfolds. Fortunately, my buddies, Blackjack, Mervy and a host of friends were with me when I met up with this punk and three of his friends. We convened at the Mount Royal Park where a fair fight was called. Every time this guy knocked me down or clinched, Blackjack would stop the fight. That poor punk could probably have torn me up, but rules are rules and a fair fight was agreed on. What reason would Spitler have to try some shit with me and my army of friends. I cut this guy's right eye wide open in the first few minutes, thereby stopping the fight. Realizing what they had done to Mary Ellen a few weeks before. I wasn't sure whether or not he would try to knife me. I never trusted him or his band of three. However, there must have been some respect for me as they never tried anything after that. They seemed to just fade away from the area. That was encouraging to think of how well I handled myself against Spitler, but it still didn't change anything with my upcoming meeting with Little Louie. No, Spitler didn't try to knife me but maybe Louie will. If I give in he may coerce me to supply all of his family with stolen goods and if caught I would end up in prison. I had no comfort in any of my former thoughts. I could only imagine myself being carved up by Louie or becoming a recluse again. There was no where to hid, mentally or otherwise.

What about Mary Ellen? I saw her not long after the Spitler fight. She told me she had a steady boyfriend and asked me where I was going. I told her I was heading up to North Avenue to see a flick. She said she couldn't go with me if I was to ask because she had a steady boyfriend. She asked me if I was hurt, and I told her I'd get over it and to keep in touch. Funny thing. I never heard from her. My thoughts were even about maybe finding her again and running away from home, Baltimore and Louie. I believe

Mary Ellen would owe me that much to accompany me. Still I must face reality. Louie is real and won't go away.

One night in the fall of 1954 Louie was waiting for me on the Biddle Street Bridge. I approached him with a large bag in my arms containing a box of ice cream, a couple of magazines and some other things I bought for my mom. From the time I awoke that morning my emotions began to flex first one way and another. I had fully intended to do something for Louie to keep him off my back. When evening came and I reported for work the reality set in. As the evening grew on, I began to get very worried. I thought about buying Louie the goods he wanted and having it taken out of my pay. The druggist on duty was the senior partner and he was the most serious of all the druggists. He most certainly would fire me if I in any way gave in to Louie's wishes. Without mentioning names, I told the druggist what I was up against. I even suggested he fire me so I wouldn't be in a position to be forced to give in. However, I needed my job. So while I was telling the druggist, I started to think that bum had a family he could sponge off or he could go out and get a job. Out of the lousy twenty bucks I earned at the drugstore for forty hour's work, I cleared about eighteen. Two bucks went for taxes and I gave my mom six dollars. Sometimes it was the other way around and I only got six dollars. The druggist asked me what I wanted to do. The choice was mine. He could let me buy the goods and take it from my pay each week or he could fire me as soon as he could replace me. Then he told me, "Jack, I'm very proud to be associated with you. You have a quality about you that is outstanding."

Being a history buff, I was reminded that I was not unique. Bullies have been doing this sort of thing forever. I made my decision to stand up to this bully and when we came face to face that night, he smilingly said, "Hey, you did it, my man." I replied, "If you like ice cream and magazines, you're welcome to what's in this bag, but if you want something from the drugstore, they are open ten to ten." With that Louie looked at me, smiled and said, "Aw, fuck it, man, I didn't think you were gonna do it anyhow!"

When I think about Louie today, I don't reflect on him with hatred. In fact, I have mixed emotions. There was the time Louie's old man let him have the use of the family limo. What a piece of shit this car was, a 1937 Chevy with a stick shift on the floor that was so old the stick shift had lost its memory. Sometimes it worked and sometimes it would jump out of gear. But we had a ball in it when Louie borrowed it.

Stevie and Louie would entertain the crowd with telephone calls to people selected at random from the Baltimore telephone book. At first it was calling people and convincing them they were part of a radio show. The caller would ask the receiver to identify a song being played over the phone via a record player and when they did identify the song they would be told to wait for the prizes that would be coming very soon by truck. Another was just to tell the person they have won a new garbage can from the local hardware store and a years supply of garbage, then hang up.

Among the more memorable ones was when Louie called a lady every ten to fifteen minutes.

During the Friday late night television movie we would harass people via the telephone. This would start about eleven o'clock. At each commercial break using the name and telephone number selected at random from the telephone book Louie would call and say, "Hello, I want to leave a message for Stevie." The receiver would at first explain the caller must have the wrong number. This would continue with all of our crowd calling the same party in different voices, asking to leave a message for Stevie. Finally, by sound of their voice, the receiver would be getting really pissed and say something like, "You have the wrong number there's no Stevie here!" and finally to, "I'm calling the police!" Then Stevie would call asking, "Hello, this is Stevie, do you have any messages for me.?" Of course we would all laugh like a bunch of loons.

The humor graduated to a more exciting phase. Louie started calling up colored night clubs listed in the yellow pages of the telephone book. We identified them by the address. It was fun calling and disguising our voices. We might ask something like, "Is Brown there?" Many times a Mr. Brown would come to the phone and be told something like, "I've got you now Brown, you mother fool you! You been playing around with my old lady! When you comes outside, I is gone to kick your black butt! I is across dah street." The phone call would then be terminated.

Once Stevie called a club and ask for a Mr. Green. This time he didn't try to make his voice sound anything but a natural white guy. The conversation went like this, "Mr. Green? This is Doctor Fazzio down at University Hospital and your girlfriend just gave birth to a nine-pound baby boy. She asked me to call you." The telephone call was terminated without any further conversation. We could only imagine this guy running out of the club and entering the hospital wondering who it was he was supposed to have knocked up.

After harassing, unless there is a better word for it, we got so brave as to ride up and down Pennsylvania Avenue on a Friday or Saturday night. The black community was alive and we for a change were behaving ourselves. We were not bothering anyone, just virgins about the night and looking for entertainment. I actually enjoyed seeing all the crowds in their high-style clothes. They projected a scene of enjoying life.

Pennsylvania Avenue, for those not familiar with Baltimore in the fifties, was the center of the black community. This one night in particular we made the mistake of going with Little Louie in the '37 heap, as the old Chevrolet became to be known as. We had just enjoyed our tour of a warm summer's night. We rode Pennsylvania Avenue with the windows down from North Avenue down to Dolphin Street. We were sitting at the red light awaiting the green to go, and Louie broke bad with a group of young blacks on the corner as the light changed. We all began to laugh when the gearshift failed and the '37 heap began to stall out. Now the black guys were laughing as we rolled the windows up. We now were facing certain death. The blacks began chucking stuff at the car and a bottle came against the glass on the drivers side. Louie must have shouted S-H-I-T a hundred times in the ten or so seconds we sat motionless. The light changed to red and the car acknowledged Louie's cry for help. We jumped the light, not waiting for green and made a two-wheeled turn onto Dolphin Street, side-swiping three parked police cars. A half a dozen vocal s-h-i-t-s and we were now dead ahead for home. We realized later, the reason the bunch on the corner didn't act on impulse and attack the car was, on that corner was the Western District Police Station.

Then there was the time Louie saw me standing on the Biddle Street Bridge. Louie and a few others were going to eat Chinese food. As they got in the taxi and were about to pull off, Louie got out of the cab and called for me to join them. "Hey, Jackie, you coming?"

"No, I'm broke!"

"Aw, come on, I got you covered." With that, a smile that could sell boats to fish came over his face.

Another time, he was going to beat the hell out of me because he blamed me for his falling down and tearing a hole in his brand new suit. For that, I paid him cash money rather than face him in a fight. Funny thing though, when Louie would threaten me with bodily harm, he would always bring up the fact that I would be fighting him and not someone like Drunken Bill. I wonder if perhaps he was more afraid of me than I was of him.

Louie had a brother who must have been his mentor. His name was Alfredo, a.k.a. Freddie the thief. I only saw this guy when I was a very small boy. He surfaced some years later by way of the news media as a kidnapper and was discovered mysteriously dead in his cell at the Fallsway Apartments.

Louie had one admirer named Georgie Emerson. With a little help I imagine Georgie could have been just like Louie. He told me, "Louie is above us."

"Hey, man, speak for yourself."

Louie, being a year or so older, was out in the full-time working world ahead of us. I remember how he made fun of school and all the dumb stuff he learned and was sure never to use. He got a job at a hotel as a handyman's apprentice, but that didn't last long. Next, he was working as a dishwasher in a prominent restaurant on Fayette Street. Little Louie really liked that job and was promoted to the pantry. He brought Georgie Emerson in as a night dishwasher and the two were constantly bragging about the high status they had now achieved. Georgie then went on to tell me about Louie blackmailing some younger guy into paying him for working at the restaurant. He was taking the larger portion of the poor guy's pay. Louie graduated from the restaurant job and went for more open criminal things adding to his male prostitution, race track touting. Touting is an art of telling a person a horse is going to win with no real knowledge of that being true. The person assumes a scheme to make a quick winning is at hand. If the horse wins, Louie returns for a payment of the very good tip. Louie also was seen to have done this in court rooms telling defendants that for fifty dollars in advance he could get a trial fixed.

The last time I saw him he had a marriage license in his hand and told me he was getting married to a girl that I went to school with. Thinking about the girl, I thought she must have gone nuts. Louie said, "This is the only girl I ever loved. I can't stand being away from her. We're getting married next week and I'll be the best husband possible."

"You working?"

"Why? You writing a book?"

Louie's demise was his extortion racket. I tuned the radio on some eight years later to hear a murder had been committed during the night. The victim, Louie Petri. A newspaper carried the story and stated briefly that Louie was shot to death in a pool room on North Charles Street in Baltimore. The killer's motive for shooting was he was being blackmailed. A trial was held and the shooter was released with little punishment.

First Black Friend

Lester Towson worked at the drugstore as a delivery driver. Lester was about twenty years old and the first Negro I was to have personal contact with. I guess what really fascinated me was his close resemblance to Sidney Poitier. There were times when I would hook school for a day and ride around with Lester in the pharmacy's delivery truck. Lester and I would exchange stories about good times and girls. We exchanged stories about politics, too. I was amazed about the stories he would tell me about the slackers who would let a woman keep them, have their kids and not marry them. He said that most neighborhoods had at least 60 percent slackers in it. I thought that was terrible, Lester did, too. He really was a swell guy.

"Mothers day," said Lester, "Was the big fun day in his neighborhood." I thought that odd instead of Christmas, but Lester soon put me wise to Mothers Day. You see Mothers Day was every month on the eleventh—the welfare checks would arrive. He said "Jackie you're really something else, a dumb cracker. He said, "I guess you don't know about, Piss Whitey Off Day either?" I don't know whether he was fooling or not, he just laughed and went on . "You live at home in a nice house protected by your mommy and daddy and have a nice job at the drugstore while you get an education. I bet you've never been laid. Have you?"

"Hey hold on Lester. That's where you're wrong. I don't have a father at home. I guess you could call me, a bastard."

Lester's face changed expressions to one of a stare and his eyes grew large and his forehead wrinkled, I had his complete attention.

I continued, "My mom and dad were divorced long before I was born and my mom never collected welfare. I work in the drugstore so I can have money to go to school and buy my clothes. I ride with you because I like you. But now I discover you're just as bad as that other nigger from Philadelphia. He works in the drugstore, stealing two packs of butts while pretending to sweep. I don't like him because he says almost the same shit you just handed me. And his crying about being from slaves. That shit happened before 1865 this is 1955. Let me tell you Mr. Towson, oppression can probably be traced to every American. This country wasn't founded by rich white crackers. It was founded by rounders, rough-and-tumble people."

"Hey hold on man, I didn't mean to piss you off. I really didn't know. Look, I'm sorry and, don't refer to me as a nigger or compare me to that nigger from Philadelphia."

Then Lester began to chuckle, which also made me chuckle. We understood each other. He asked me to tell him about my home life and that was understandable since we both were from different cultures.

I told him, "I was never taught to hate my father. I was six years old the first time I can remember seeing him." I continued to speak, pouring out my personal feelings, "When I first met him, I awoke in St. Joseph's Hospital, this large man in dark blue uniform was standing at the foot of my bed. I looked around the room and saw my mother at my bed side." Seeing Lester was extremely amused and interested, I continued on, "My mom said, hello my darling little boy, someone has come to see you, someone who would like very much to know you. Jackie dear, this is your father." My eyes started to fill and I wondered if I could continue. I told Lester, that was my first meeting with my dad. My dad reached down to my covers and patted me on my leg and with a smile that warmed my heart told me he had heard I was very sick. He was pleased to know I was going to be all right.

Tears began to run down my cheeks and I finished by saying, "Turning, he then went away, somehow I remember this as if it were just a few minutes ago. I fell off into a deep sleep. I had a severe case of pneumonia and I never saw my father again." Tears were now streaming from my eyes as I tried to speak. I guess Lester understood all too well how I felt, because he got quiet and so did I. Personally, I never made it my business to concern myself with what may have been between my mother and father. After all, I was used to a house with no father and since that was the way it was, I couldn't appreciate it any other way. Not having a husband was hard on my poor mom, but we boys tried to make up for the loss. We also strived to be successful. We had drive and a loving mother who taught us right from wrong. She was quick to correct us when we were wrong and lightening fast to defend us when we were right.

Lester and I became buddies and extended our camaraderie to getting together on a few evenings. One particular Friday night, in the company of one of his buddies, Lester picked up four of my Charles Street chums and me. We were headed for a night of boozing and cruising on the town. What a night. We headed for a liquor store and having no trouble whatsoever, we purchased a couple of cases of beer, a bottle of whiskey and a bottle of cheap wine. The wine was for Mervy. Mervy was trying to impress us with his education for the finer things. Lester was given instructions to purchase the best wine he could find for one dollar and forty-nine cents. We drove to Herring Run Park to indulge in this booze. All in all, we had a grand time. We laid in the grass under the stars of a warm summer's night and drank to our hearts' content. We told jokes and even formed a singing group. Somehow, the jokes got even funnier. We told jokes about Negroes and Lester and his friend, Jimmie McGee, told some very funny jokes about "Whitey." It was great telling jokes about ourselves and laughing together. We were forming bonds of friendship and trust. That was when I discovered the only real barrier between our two people seemed to be the color of the skin. For what we were doing and the fun we were having, there were no barriers.

Mervy was now quite drunk. As for me, I don't remember leaving the park. We drove around for awhile and Mervy started upchucking out the window of Lester's '49 Chrysler. We pulled into a gas station where Everett decided to wash Lester's car. That was a fun thing to remember. Everett also "washed" Mervy, by turning, the hose on him. Eventually, we drove to an all-night restaurant in a black section of town. There we drank hot coffee and ate doughnuts until we became somewhat sober.

Lester drove Everett and me to the Biddle Street Bridge. We walked home from there. I made it as far as the bathroom before I became ill. I no sooner entered when I got deathly sick. The next morning I heard my mother ask my older brother if he was drunk last night and threw up in the bathroom. I heard him give her an emphatic no. A few hours later she was hollering at me. My mother was informed by Everett's mother that Everett came home late, sick and smelling like a brewery. My mother was not too upset with me. She was more disturbed at Everett's mother for telling her that I had hot pants and would rather I not influence her son. Naturally, that put mom on the defensive side and ended any further conversation about the episode.

We started to draw a bit of criticism about our black friends. One in particular was when we went to Highlandtown in Lester and Jimmies company. We pulled up near a street carnival and went in on the grounds like we were celebrities, Lester, Jimmie, Everett and me. Lester was confronted by an oversized youth that answered to the name Gong. As for me it was more like Kong as in King Kong. Highlandtown in the fifties was an all white mostly Polish and Bohemian neighborhood. Highlandtown is located on the extreme east end of Baltimore. We had no idea how unwelcome our dark-skinned pals would be. We weren't far into the crowd when a blackjack was applied to Lester's head from behind and shouts of, "Niggers" were filling the air. I turned to a few and said, "He's with us," and a board connected with Everett on his head. I have no idea what the hell hit me. Anyway, I awoke on a sofa in a house on Highland Avenue. My face and head was being bathed by a girl that was a second for the best looking brunette I ever laid eyes on. She was in short-shorts that if any shorter she'd need a haircut. I started to speak, "What, where, who?"

She said, "Easy Jack."

I had a headache that felt like a goose was laying on my head and slowly slipping off. I was dizzied, too. I began to speak, "Who are you?"

"I'm a nurse and you just got the living hell beaten out of you. Were you trying to stop the fight with those Negroes? I guess you don't know a girl from this neighborhood was raped by a Negro last week and the heat of the act is still in the air."

Obviously she didn't know that I was with Lester and Jimmie. So I asked, "What happened to the nigger?"

"There were two of them, the police took one of them away in an ambulance. The other was escorted to a car parked a block away and he drove off. There was a red headed guy in the car, too, very strange." Smiling at me she began to ask some questions, but I interrupted her with, "How did you know my name?"

"Your wallet, it fell out of your pocket when my brother and a neighbor carried you in here. You live quite a way from here. Were you visiting someone?"

"Na, I just like the polish sausages and came over for some. But I'm sure glad I did. When I awoke and saw you I thought I was looking at a most beautiful picture. This room was strange and I thought you were an angel. What's your name?"

"Janet, Janet Winters"

"Janet, I'm in love with you. I don't want to leave here, ever."

"Well, Jack I love you, too. But there is just a couple of things wrong with this picture. I could fix a bed for you in my son's room but I don't think my steel worker husband will like that very much. He's asleep upstairs, but if you would like I can wake him and ask. Still I don't think he will like you as part of this picture. If you would like a ride to Biddle Street my car is outside."

"How old are you, Janet?"

"Eight years older than you Jack, You're only sixteen and to me a sweet kid."

Janet drove me home and I dreamed of her for the next few nights. In my dreams she was wonderful, but I would awake and find her gone and be love sick for the next few weeks.

Lester and I decided to cool our relationship to just being friends at work and never anticipated any further adventures. Lester and I never spoke of the carnival episode and when I left the employment of the drugstore I left my first black friend.

Happy Halloween

It's fall 1954, and surveying my ever-decreasing circle of friends, I recall most had quit school. Mike Campo knocked up his girlfriend, she and Mike both being good Catholics did the right thing and got married. Johnnie, Pauly and Moe were in the Army, soon to be joined by Stevie. Georgie, Tony and most of the crowd, having an urge to have spending money, became aggravated with the competition of school peers. The peers were from "haves," we soon found our crowd was from the "have nots." This was an unhealthy state to be in. Our general philosophy was if you can't join 'em, quit. The reality that we were from a low-income neighborhood had started to set in.

There were several places close to the neighborhood where a sixteen year old could get employed almost immediately. It was like they had a sign hanging over their buildings that proclaimed,

"Dummies Wanted, No Thinking Necessary"

Within walking distance from the Tenth Ward was Polytechnical Institute, an outstanding engineering high school located on North Avenue. Within walking distance may have been convenient, but it housed the Creme de la Creme of the city's boys. Most of our crowd were discriminated against by the preppy type that attended Poly. However, Mike, Stevie, Everett and a few others chose to become Poly boys. Just before Mike quit school to marry, we went to a football rally. It was a Wednesday night, Thanksgiving eve. It should have been a lot of fun, one of Mike's classmates had something smart to say about Mike's colleagues, Stevie, Tony, Floon and me. So Mike, being backed by some very devoted friends, was egged on to do battle. Mike clobbered the preppy punk and another jumped in to help. I gathered him up and not only did I punch him, I punched the guy standing next to him that neither he nor I knew. That got this guy active and he started hitting anyone near him. At first it would have looked like a part of the rally.

It continued to grow and I remember hearing a voice over a bull horn saying all good Poly boys should gather to their homerooms. So to our homerooms we ran. Ours was on the Biddle Street Bridge. The next day at the annual Poly-City football game held in Memorial Stadium (then known as Babe Ruth Stadium) some guy asked, "Did you guys attend last night's rally?"

"Attend it, we were part of it."

Mike, Everett and Stevie quit school and became members of the working community. They got jobs along with others at a drugstore supply house. If that supply house never had shrinkage in stocks, it would have them now. Stevie was ever so bold, he was taking orders around the neighborhood, orders to be filled by the trio. I don't know how much they were making in wages. I would give a guess it wasn't as much as this new enterprise. The enterprise ended when the firm took inventory and found a lot of merchandise never went out by way of customer orders. That was about the time Mike went to a more serious job that allowed him time to attend night school as a working father. Everett followed suit by getting his girl in the motherly way and he too had more serious things to take care of. Stevie, being a brilliant kid found refuge in the Army and of all things; the quarter master corps. As for me, I just figured, somehow, life goes on.

Since my last year in school, I have carried a guilt that with this writing is now released. It was October and Halloween time. We had a change in our homeroom class at school. Mr. Marine, one of my favorite teachers, had become ill and to this day I don't know whether or not he ever returned to school. We did, however, get a substitute teacher who was a real strange dude. He was a young guy in a dark suit with thick horn-rimmed glasses and his complexion was either red or constantly flushed. From his first day at school, it seemed as though he needed to hyperventilate. I only saw this teacher for about three days.

It was Halloween and I managed an evening off from the drugstore. A night of fun was upon us and I met some of my unholy few and it was off to the famous block to play. I had in mind all the naughty things that might happen down on Baltimore Street on Halloween. After all, Six Bits magazine had announced Baltimore's block was bawdier than Chicago's.

To get to the block from the Flying Saucer Restaurant on Charles Street, you had to pass through Queers Park, better known as the Mount Vernon Square. A monument to George Washington stands in the center of the square, the second one erected to the father of our country. The first monument was built in Boonesboro, Maryland and the one in Washington, D.C., was the third. A little-known fact to most Baltimoreans is the approach to Mount Vernon from the east. It clearly shows why Washington is the father of our country. (In the evening when the shining of foot lights on the monument clearly display a scene), we boys called a fags dream. The statue of Washington his arms merge in front of him gave the appearance of an enormous penis. I'm not positive if the monument lured the gay population to the square, but they would be there for sure. The year was 1954 and gays were very much in the closet.

On this particular occasion I was filled with anxiety about sex and making a score on the block. After all, I was sixteen and most knowledgeable, plus, I was carrying at least fifteen bucks. When we arrived in Queers Park, we were detained by two lovely ladies about eighteen years old. I don't know what I said that was so cool but, within minutes, one girl and I were embracing. She had stuck her tongue in my mouth and was not about to take it out! I was accompanied by Dave Startus, fresh from the reformatory and his brother, Larry. They were looking for some action, too. Dave's brother seemed upset at my wanting to break up our group by leaving with this most gamely candidate. I got her phone number and it was Splitsville.

Before I caught up with Dave and Larry, I could see they were talking to what looked like two men in the distance. It was dark and I wasn't sure who or what it was they were facing. If it was fags, I was going to be out of there. I wasn't interested in fags. Holy shit, one of the two men in the silhouette was my new substitute teacher. I called him by name, leaving the other man looking somewhat surprised, he asked, "You two know each other?" The teacher replied in the affirmative, adding that I was one of his students. With that the other guy belted out a "Let's go, we're already late." They hurriedly went on their way and I asked Dave what that was all about. He explained his brother was stopped by these two men seeking directions to the train station. That incident began to haunt me. Why would these guys want to know how to get to the train station when it was just up the street? I believe the teacher was a fag. What's more, I had asked what was he doing in Queers Park.

We finally reached the famous block where we managed to peek inside some of the bars featuring strip shows until the bouncers chased us away. We got some excitement when we saw a boy take a bicycle from a smaller kid. The boy was about sixteen years old and looked pretty bad. He just went up to this little kid who was about twelve and pulled him away from his bike. The kid started shouting for help, but no one paid any attention to him. He looked right at me and crying asked for my help. I was afraid to help and enlisted Dave to help me. Dave grabbed the thief by the hair and pulled him off the bike. The bike rolled to the opposite side of the street. While Larry ran across the street to retrieve the bike, I lent a hand in hitting the thief. The thief must have been wearing U.S. Keds for he was out of sight in no time. Larry now had the bicycle, and for some reason lifted it up to pass it around the tail end of a pickup truck loaded with junk. By accident, Larry dropped it onto the truck and the truck rolled off as the traffic light changed. Hollering to the truck was useless as the whole of downtown was alive with noise. The truck, with bike, was now disappearing from view.

The kid was now crying and screaming at us for trying to help him. I really felt for the kid so I offered him a five dollar bill to help out. He took the five and said I owed him ten more. "The bike cost fifteen dollars, you cheap cocksucker, so give me my money." This commotion began to attract attention and soon people began to gather. One man asked, "What's the matter, son?"

While pointing to me, the kid told him, "That son-of-a-bitch stole my fifteen dollars and won't give it to me."

Like a dummy I answered, "I gave him five."

The man, looking as if he was about to kill me, said, "Give him the rest of it."

Another guy, looking like this brute in miniature, came up and said, "What's the matter, Dad?"

"That son-of-a-bitch stole this kid's money and won't give it to him," he replied.

Quickly, I handed the rest of my money to the little bastard and we headed for the Greyhound Bus Terminal. I borrowed two bucks from my pals and we ended our evening in the bus terminal cafeteria with coffee and pie.

The next day, I went to school, but wasn't surprised to see we had another substitute teacher. The guilt I carried since my sixteenth October was that maybe the substitute teacher never returned to the all-boys school because of my seeing him in Queers Park.

My Buddy

My buddy, Tony Vespi, and I met when I was only nine years old and he was eight. I used to see him playing behind the florist shop on Chase Street. A chubby little blond-haired kid. It was impossible to imagine I would be friends with this spoiled brat. His parents, I thought, owned the florist shop and, like the Jews who owned the grocery store across from the shop, wouldn't allow their kid to play with me. You learned prejudice in this neighborhood at an early age. I imagine that is true of the blacks today who are not in constant contact with whites, Hispanics, Asians, etc. Boy, was I wrong about Tony. Until he was about ten years old, he was the only child in the Vespi family. Spoiled? Perhaps. Prejudiced? Never! A family with money? No. If anything, the family was from good Italian stock.

Tony's dad was a taxi driver and his mom was a good homemaker. The flower shop was Tony's uncle's business and Tony's dad helped in the shop when he wasn't on duty with his cab. Tony was a caring kid and if he liked you enough to call you friend, you had a friend for life. His grandparents were a very colorful lot. At one time they were one of the larger landowners in Anne Arundel County with several businesses, but an unfortunate circumstance occurred and all was lost. Grandma Vespi was a madam, dealing in imported Italian Ladies of the Night' and in the early days of the Twentieth Century a change of politicians made her give up her very lucrative business. Fines were imposed and protection from prosecution fees soon made short the families accumulated wealth.

This added to the heritage of the quality of the characters in our gang. You see, we were not your run-of-the-mill poor whites. When we did something, it was with style and grace, even if we stole it.

One day Tony was climbing up the Chase Street hill retreating quite rapidly from the railroad. Several freight cars had been broken into. What an Epicurean's delight, a fresh cherry carrier, a Tastykake carrier, and a frozen strawberry carrier. The Blatz beer car was the only thing that held no interest for us. Tony, accompanied by one of the Solon brothers, was wearing soldier's combat fatigue pants with large pockets bulging with cherries when he was stopped by a police patrol car. The police officer got out of the car. Tony's pants were dripping at the pockets with a red liquor from the crushed cherries. The cop spoke, "You boys see anyone with cherries that may have been stolen?" Tony and Vernon replied in unison, "No, sir!" Tony added to it by saying, "We didn't see nothing. Can we go now?" The police officer, about to explode with laughter, said, "Call me if you see anything." The railroad had their own police and many times the city police seemed uninterested in the petty crimes happening on railroad property. This cop was going through a drill. In reality, the cop didn't want to get involved, as it was a matter for the railroad dicks.

Most of the families in the Ward had three, four or more children. Tony was lucky, in a sense, having only two kids in the family. I mean, the money didn't run out as quickly. Having a car, Tony's dad was able to take him to events and enter him in some things I only dreamed about. He played baseball for a well-organized team hosted by the famous Aunt Mary. Tony also learned to play drums and bugle. By the time he was twelve, his family moved to Little Italy and, for a few years, he was away from the Ward. When he returned at age fifteen, he was quite different in appearance. He had lost his baby fat and was quite muscular. His blond hair was now a darker sandy color and he had a smile like that of Kirk Douglas, complete with a dimple in his chin. His good looks complemented anyone in his company. Tony became an acquaintance of mine and by the time he was sixteen, we were good friends. At sixteen Tony got his own car and we often traveled together.

I made mention of his being well-taken care of, but Tony lived a sheltered life. Once, when we were headed for an adventure, Tony had to go home and eat some prunes. His mother told him to and he obeyed. I still kid him about that some forty years later.

Tony always had money and it wasn't from his parents. He worked evenings at the Yellow Cab on Preston Street filling the cabs with gas when he was only thirteen. I guess his dad helped him get the job, because I went over there and they wouldn't even give me a chance and I was fourteen.

Another summer job Tony had was as an overpaid shoeshine boy. He would set up his shoe box on Greenmount Avenue and Preston Street and the same customers would appear each day. His first customer would arrive at noon. Tony referred to him as the "Daddy in the hat." He would give Tony a large white paper carton that looked like a pint-sized ice cream container. Then dozens of customers would give Tony his dime for the shine and a folded paper that may have contained a greenback or two. Tony said he never looked in to see what it was. Tony's shoe shine business was a front for illegal gambling. The daddy in the hat was a bookmaker. The last customer was again the "Daddy in the hat" and he would pick up the container. Tony never really shined anyone's shoes too well. However, he collected a dime from each customer for a quick brushing of the leather. The "Daddy in the hat" always paid twice. One day the "Daddy in the hat" didn't show up, so very few people wanted shines. Eventually the shoe shine business was going the way of the buggy whip and Tony gave me his shoe shine box.

Tony was a top-notch mechanic whether it was an automobile or a bearings laden transmission, they didn't come any better. He constantly looked for mechanical things to work on. He often stated, "You don't learn mechanical engineering from watching television."

I'll never forget the time it was Tony's sixteenth birthday and his dad gave him one hundred dollars. Tony told me it was to buy a motor scooter. We went to a shop on Mount Royal Avenue to look at an Italian scooter. It was on sale for only one hundred and fifty bucks. While en route, we got a lift with Herbert Litz, an idiot we knew from school. Herbert was driving a souped up '37 Chevy. It was really a cool car. He said it was a coincidence it was his father's birthday and he was selling this load to get his old man a new set of tools. Tony asked "What kind of tools?" I could tell his mind was racing to figure out a way to get the set of wheels. Herbert replied, "A full set of Craftsman wrenches and that kind of stuff."

Tony said, "Your worries are over. I have a full set and can let you have them in exchange for the car." We drove back to Tony's house on Mura Street to inspect tools. They were nice, but didn't satisfy Herbert's demands.

Herbert said, "I know what set my old man needs and I will show you." We drove up to Sears on North Avenue and in the big window was a full hardware display of tools and a big red roll-about cabinet to hold them. Herbert said he would need at least a ten-dollar deposit to consummate the deal. He would accept Tony's tools and fifty dollars or a set exactly like the one in the display.

The next day Tony called for the hardware manager and was informed he was on vacation but the assistant was on duty. So Tony asked the assistant if he had the display ready for pick up by the vocational school for the Maryland Hardware Fair. The assistant manager was available and said he didn't know anything about it. Then Tony explained, "The fair! The Hardware Fair at school. It starts at one o'clock. One of the student assistants will be over to pick it up. Will it be ready at your loading dock or what? It's Catalog Number Craft 01134542. Matter of fact, it's the same one as in the big window on North Avenue." The assistant manager said he was aware of the set but would have to get the display department to remove it from the window. Tony said it would be a good idea to include the signs with it. The assistant manager agreed. By eleven o'clock Hymie Glick was at the loading dock picking up the special school project, for which he was paid ten dollars. Then he drove back to pick up Tony and me, then off to make the exchange.

Herbert was waiting outside the garage on Gay Street where he suggested we meet and seemed very anxious. He said he was having a little trouble with the battery and not to shut the engine off until we got it back to Tony's house. Also, he would bring the title over tomorrow after he got his dad to sign it. Tony, being a trusting soul, didn't question Herbert's statement about the title. I only wish he had. As we headed down Preston Street en route to a garage Tony had rented from a friend, our conversation was on what we would be doing to this new and wonderful set of wheels.

A cop on a three-wheeled motorcycle pulled up along side of us when we stopped for a traffic light. Tony got nervous at the light and blew it. When the light turned from red to green he popped the clutch and we ran out into the center of traffic. Tony managed the gear and clutch before the car would naturally shut down from acceleration. The overweight cop dismounted and began to walk over to the car. He told us to pull over to the curb and shut the engine off. As he walked toward us, we stopped the car and Tony turned the key off, but the engine didn't stop running. The key was not a whole key. It was a piece of a key stuck into the key slot to look like a key. Tony quickly reached to feel the crossed wires under the dashboard and said, "Herbert sold us a hot car."

In an effort to keep the cop from looking inside we got out of the car. The cop immediately addressed Tony saying, "Give me your driver's license and registration card." Suddenly, from nowhere, Norman Solon, the car thief of the Solon bunch, was watching from a vantage point. He had been sitting under the traffic light on Greenmount Avenue and Preston Street. When we got out of the car, Tony put his hands over his head as if he was under arrest. Norman saw this and drove into the three-wheel police cycle, sending it rolling in a wayward direction and falling on one side. The cop turned to see what was going on and raced back to the cycle. Righting the cycle, he yelled for us to stay where we were until he got back. He was in pursuit of Norman who, by now, was racing into alleys and out of sight. We got back into the car, drove it to an alley about eight blocks to the west and nearer to Charles Street. The alley formed an H design behind the buildings and was not visible from the street. We disconnected the wires shutting down the engine and left the car there. We were a block away from the motor scooter shop. Next door was a clothing shop. We went in and Tony bought us both very loud shirts, which we changed into at the store. This was in case we were spotted by the motorcycle cop. He certainly would have remembered these shirts. Since we didn't have them on before, he would be sure we weren't his guys. Tony was really disappointed about the car deal and decided he didn't want a scooter either. We ventured into the Flying Saucer to have a meal on Tony. Tony waited a few weeks and with his dad's help bought a car from an honest car dealer, if there is such a person.

Months passed and we met up with our old pal Herbert Litz. Neither Tony nor I noticed Herbert coming out of the auto parts store, but Herbert made the mistake of calling to us as though we had seen him. We didn't. Herbert acted as if he was more than happy to see us. Reality must have reached this pot-smoking-son-of-a-bitch because Herbert began running. When we first noticed, he had a bulge in his coat. The bulge began to undo and a small box began to fall out. Looking back at the store, a clerk was in a full chase of Herbert. Herbert had just confiscated some small items.

Herbert entered a car that was waiting his arrival and the clerk gave up the chase. The car was determined by us as a get-a-way-car because the rear tag was covered by a brown paper bag. Tony said, "Let's chase 'em and when we catch 'em, we'll kick the shit out of 'em and take whatever they stole."

We got into Tony's newly acquired 49 Ford and raced like Hell down Eastern Avenue. Herbert must have told his accomplice to beat it out of there as he was running at fifty to sixty miles over the speed limit. His car hit a center strip in the road losing control flipped onto the side. Suddenly the regaining of Tony's loss was the last thing on our minds.

We approached the vehicle not knowing what we'd see. Peering in we see Herbert and his friend Billy Hershey, another nut from school. They were unbelievably all right. The first thing Herbert said to Tony was, "Where the heck have you been I've been looking all over for you."

"You guys alright?"

"Yeah Tony, I'm okay how about you Billy, you okay?"

Gasoline was leaking from the car. We helped the two out of the car. By now a crowd began to collect when a man yelled. "Get the hell away from that car. It is going to explode." We raced to get away as it did just that. Fire was streaming from the car as Herbert explains, "That's Billies mothers car. How about giving us a ride to his house. We can tell his mother the car was stolen. You guys can help verify that by offering to be witnesses. What do you say?"

"We say fuck you."

An after thought about Norman Solon. Norman ws a real scumbag of a person. Once he was involved in an accident and would have ran if it had not of been for witnesses. He exited his car after sideswiping a parked one. First thing he did was to ask if anyone knew who owned the car. Assured that the owner wasn't in the group, he wrote this note:

I just hit your car and promised the people here I would leave a note on the windshield. Here is the note like I promised.

Private Fazzio Will Protect Us

Not long before Stevie joined the Army, Tony Vespi and I went to see Stevie and his brother. They had moved to Holbrook Street, half a block away from the Preston Theater. Being hungry and talking about coddies, we walked down to the bookie joint—I mean green front store—to feast on coddies. As we walked to the corner, we saw some men unloading barrels of beer from a truck. The beer was for a private club in the back of the store. A wooden gate on a high board fence to the back yard of the store was the entrance to the club.

Stevie said, "My stepfather belongs to that club, let's help them unload the beer," with a grin that was saying "Let's steal one of the barrels." We hurriedly rolled a barrel into the private club's yard. Then back to the truck for another, and being real good fellas, we hurried this barrel toward the yard. By closing the gate, our chance came and we rolled this one past the yard and up the street to Stevie's house, through the house, out the back and into Tony Vespi's car. We took the barrel to Hymie's, who was extremely happy to tap it for us. Within an hour the whole gang was alive and well. And we planned a mother of an adventure. At eighteen you could drink in Washington, D.C., or D.C. as we called it. We would also refer to Baltimore as the Big B. Gerald Solon tells about the time he went to a cocktail lounge in D.C. and ordered a cocktail. He said, "I went in and sat up at the bar. I was so nervous that I would be asked to show an I.D. proving me to be eighteen, I started to ask questions as soon as I sat down at the bar. I hoped the barmaid would think I was eighteen or even older, I started right into a conversation and said, "I think I'll have a cocktail." The barmaid asked, "What kind?" I said "Shrimp."

Here we are, about twenty of us all smoked up from sucking on this keg of beer when Stevie told us his uncle owns the very club that is the talk of every kid from Dundalk to Alexandria, The Rebel Room of Fourteenth Street. The party started to dwindle down and Stevie began to tell us, "If we could go to D.C. before I leave for the Army, my uncle would treat us all to whatever we want." We parted in Tony's car, me, Stevie, Floon, Spanky and Ollie Owl. While cruising, Tony thought he had permission to take us all to D.C., and we don't realize we're heading down the expressway until we're on it. Big Jake a.k.a. Ollie Owl asks, "Where we headed?" To which Tony replies, "D.C.! I want to meet Stevie's uncle." To which Stevie is quick to explain, "He's not there and the guys who work for him are all new and they don't know me and . . . "pause" . . . and, hey, that's right, he sold the place. I almost forgot he don't own it anymore. That's right, ain't it Jackie?"

Stevie is going to be gone for a long time so my backing him up in a lie won't hurt anyone anyhow. "Sure that's right Stevie, I don't know how you could forget your uncle sold the joint." I don't think Stevie even knew where the place was or had ever been to Washington. We get into D.C. and Floon and Tommy Knoops a.k.a. Garbage Pants asked Tony to find some-place they could take a leak. Tony pulled over on New York Avenue near Capitol Street and Floon, Big Jake and Tommy began to urinate on the side of a building. Too bad for the three of them, it was not just a red brick building, but a red brick police station building. A cop no sooner stepped out of the side of the building, grabbed Big Jake by his belt and arrested the trio for disorderly conduct. Floon's brothers will probably come over for the three of them, but not until tomorrow. Tony was very cool-headed when this all took place and we just slowly drove away.

We circled the block a few times, but decided the best thing in our favor was we were not arrested too. On down the road we stopped at a red light and Stevie started into a conversation with a woman who was stand-ing on the corner. She seemed to be enjoying his conversation.

We parked the car and were invited into her apartment on New York Avenue, a second-floor front. We weren't in her living room five minutes, when the door to the apartment was being jiggled as if someone was trying to come in. The lady then said, "Oh no, it's my husband." Tony and I ran through a door and found it not to be a large clothes closet, but the bath-room, no windows either. Stevie jumped behind her sofa. Tony and I had our ears glued to the closed door, and found we were actually game for being shot. The nerve of this bitch inviting us into a who-knows-what trap.

Tony whispers very low, "I'm going to open the door, just do what I do and we're out of here. Okay." I shake my head in approval. I figure with Tony and Stevie, we can probably take this guy if he isn't armed.

Tony opened the door and in a soft voice to my amazement said, "Hey lady, I told you it was probably too much toilet paper. See, I didn't even need my tools to fix your toilet. I told the owner that's been the case with most of these apartments. Well call the owner if it happens again, Hey, this your husband? What a swell place and such really nice people. I hope I can have a place like this when Betty and I get married."

Shaking the man's hand Tony continued, "Come on out to my car and I'll give you something for the toilet." With a dumbfounded look, her hus-band took Tony up on his offer. He begins to accompany us outside. As we walked to the car a half-block down New York Avenue, Tony turned and noticed Stevie was just a few steps behind. He yelled, "Stevie you get that one on the next floor opened?".

"No. We should have brought the tools."

"For crying out loud, Lets go back to the shop and get my dad's tools."

"Hey mister, Look, I was going to give you a plunger but I just remembered, I didn't bring one. We'll be back in about an hour and I'll bring you one. Okay?"

"Huh okay, I really didn't know we had a problem or even think anything was wrong, but I guess you fixed it. Thanks a lot, thanks."

"Yes sir. We fixed it, I guess you could say, I fixed it."

The next week, Stevie decide to pull a caper and broke into an unmanned refreshment stand in the Mount Royal Train Station. He almost got away with twenty cartons of cigarettes and a mound of candy bars. But instead, his luck changed. The judge asked him what he intended to do with the loot and Stevie's reply got him off the hook.

"Your honor, I'm to go in the Army in a week and I needed some extra money. The cigarettes and candy could have been sold around my neighborhood and that's all. I ain't no real crook. I used to clean that place and know the people, I didn't mean them no harm. In fact I would have sent the money to the people at the station after boot camp. I really would have."

"If I sentence you. You will be wearing a uniform—and not one of the U. S. Army. Where do you live?"

"In the Tenth Ward, sir."

"My God, I see the chance to rehabilitate a Tenth Ward boy. You ever been in trouble before son?"

"No sir, your honor."

"Bailiff, where is the so-reported loot?"

"Down the hall in the police stores your honor." "Do you smoke Fazzio?"

"Yes your honor."

"Son, I find you guilty as charged and sentence you to a minimum of three years" . . . pause . . . "in" . . . pause . . . "the service of your country."

"Bailiff, get a carton of the butts for recruit Fazzio. Fazzio, Are you going to be a good soldier?"

"Yes, your honor, the best."

The Flying Saucer Restaurant

In the small towns across the U.S. the focal point for news is often found in the local barber shop. In fact the barber is somewhat a celebrity. The barber gets to know every customer by virtue of his closeness. If the barber calls you by name while cutting your hair, consider yourself a made man and if he tells you jokes then you're really in. In my describing the Tenth Ward you could compare it to a small town within a big city. There were several barber shops in the community, but three stand out in my mind.

Rockie's barber shop was on the upper end of Greenmount Avenue, Paul's was on the lower and Shell's barber shop was between the two. Depending on which had the shortest waiting line was where I made my choice for a haircut. You could get all the latest scoop on what's happening in and around town from any of these masters of tonsorial arts. I must have been an okay guy in the fellow's eyes since they liked me enough to tell me jokes. One barber told me a very funny story about a kid's mother coming to his shop. The story went something like this:

"My nephew was playing with a kid and the kid had money to get his hair cut. My nephew ask the kid to finance the both of them, my nephew and this kid, see, to the movies ya see? Well at first the kid says he has to use the money for a hair cut and my nephew says, Hey, I'll cut your hair, my uncles a barber and he showed my how'. . .Next thing I know, his mother . . . she is in my shop with this kid and a head full of chip chopped hair . . . and she says, Look what your nephew did to my Joey.' The only thing I could do was give him a shaved head and hope it grows back over the summer."

It is apparent that as we were coming of age we would need a more sophisticated place to frequent or have as our hangout. Like, I mean the corners of Brentwood Avenue and Biddle Street were okay when we were twelve and Aida Potatoe's place was not classy enough for our life style so we ventured to a more lively-open-all-night-joint, the Flying Saucer. I have made mention of the Flying Saucer Restaurant throughout these vignettes, now I will describe it and it's unique characters and style.

The Flying Saucer Restaurant was our hangout on Charles Street. I remember once while getting a hair cut, (we guys took such pride in our hair) Johnny Stallone a.k.a. The Slobbering Slop Top entered the barber shop and speaking to me exclaims, "What the hell are you doing in here at this time of day? I thought Charles Street guys were vampires." Turning to the barber, he asked, "These guys stay out all night. That restaurant stays open twenty-four hours."

"What restaurant, Johnny?" He asked.

Johnny, in his usual defensive voice, answered, "The Flying Saucer. You think we got a lot of high style punks over here at the bakery corner? You ought to go up to Charles Street. Shit, man, I thought I was poor or something. That place is for gangsters. Take Marlon Brando here, (referring to me) I saw him and Vernon Solon and his brother, Gerry, standing together. For one split second, I thought I was seeing a scene from on the Water Front', being rehearsed or something. It's those guys from down on Biddle Street, Warden Street and from over on Brentwood Avenue, I'm telling you, they dress and look like a scene from "Guys and Dolls'."

The Flying Saucer was a delicatessen that catered to the night club trade. I met a number of the entertainment people from Baltimore's nightlife there. You wouldn't believe the crap Lou the owner had to put up with from the clientele. I don't know if he was making money or not but if he did make money, he deserved it. I recall one rainy Wednesday afternoon a bunch of us were sitting around in the place when I got an idea. "Let's play a practical joke on Lou."

There were three pay phone booths in the place. I used one of those pay phones to call the restaurant. Not fully intending to place an order or to cause any grief, I asked in a sissy voice, "Do you have carry-out orders?" Lou replied in the affirmative. Then I asked if they sold hamburgers and again Lou responded that they did.

"I want forty-nine hamburgers and forty-nine glasses of orange juice. I want the orange juice extra cold in paper cups. I'll be over soon, maybe an hour or so, to pick them up. The orange juice must be cooled to thirty-seven degrees and the hamburgers piping hot. So, how soon will they be ready?"

"Where are you calling from?" Lou asked.

"From the hotel across the street. Are you that cute little fat man I see in the window?"

Lou paused and continued, "When you come over I'll get the order started." Lou hung up the telephone.

I knew Lou was bursting to tell the gang about this faggy character who called and asked for the impossible. Lou headed back to where we were and was wearing that particular grin for which he was famous. As he started to speak, the front door opened and Lou went back to the front where the grill was located. The grill was actually in the window where it would be visible to passers-by. The waitress was looking at us and wondered what we were up to. Lou was talking to a skinny-looking fellow in a Hawaiian shirt and from his facial expressions, Lou was telling him something in a hostile manner. When the fellow in the Hawaiian shirt exited, Lou again approached us.

"You see that son-of-a-bitch who just left here?"

"Yes." I was about to talk over Lou's head so we could all have a laugh at the practical joke when Lou told me to shut up and listen.

"That son-of-a-bitch just called me up. He came in and asked for a hamburger and a cup of orange juice. I asked him what the hell happened to the forty-nine hamburgers and cup of orange juice he ordered. He asked me if I had been playing with myself and I told him to go to the drugstore on the corner and get himself a hamburger suppository. The nerve of that fag son-of-a-bitch."

We all became very cool about any more practical jokes. Matter of fact, it ended there for me.

Lou had recently married and his wife was at least twenty years younger than he. She was very pretty and sexy. If Lou got any pleasure from the business, I suppose it was working with his young and beautiful wife. Lou was a hard worker and kept his place clean. Spotless, actually. Lou never closed. He told me that on the one night he did close for a cleanup job, it was about three-thirty in the morning and he was scrubbing the floor. He had a couple of his people helping so he would only be closed for as long as it would take to clean. Some guy in a suit came up to the door and tapped on the glass. Lou told him he was closed, but the guy showed a badge and said he wanted some information. Lou opened the door.

"Are you Lou Cost?"

"Yes."

"Do you know Bob Sipe?"

"Yes."

"When did you last see him?"

"He came in yesterday and asked for a meal and a fifty-dollar loan. I told him I don't make loans. He said he was down on his luck and had to leave town for a while. He was broke and hungry so I gave him a meal."

"Did you buy his television set?"

"Yes."

"Sipes is in jail. Where's the television set?"

"In the storeroom."

"Let's see it."

Lou took the detective to the storeroom where he looked the television over and informed Lou he was under arrest for receiving stolen goods. The stolen goods being the television he bought for fifty-dollars. He was booked and released. It was apparent the authorities figured Lou to be a victim of a foul play by Sipes.

One day I was in the game room. Lou had a game room in back with pinball machines, which paid off to the regulars. Those not known were out of luck when it came to cashing in. I was there at six o'clock Sunday morning. I went there because I had the feeling the jackpot was about to be won. There was a one ball machine that had been warming up for the past week. If all the lights were lit across the trademark, the machine would pay

300 games if one ball landed in hole number fifteen. When I was there the evening before, one light remained to be lit. I entered the game room and all the lights were lit but one. Why someone would leave the machine open like that made me wonder. The last player must have gone broke.

I got a dollar's worth of nickels and proceeded to try my luck. Understand the minimum wage was seventy-five cents an hour, so nickels were like dollars to me. I got lucky on my fifth nickel. The games racked up to 300. Jackpot!

The cashier just looked at me when I tried to collect. I gave him the high sign but he only stared at me. I realized this guy didn't know me, so my chances of getting my winnings were poor. Going back to the machine, I began to play slowly to while away the time until Lou arrived. Then I would get my winnings. I was really on a winning streak. When I lost twenty games, I decided it would be better to stop playing and since I was the only customer, nobody would bother the machine.

Going to get change for a dollar, I noticed a new coin changer on the wall. It gave five nickels for a quarter. Obtaining my change from the cashier, I inserted a quarter and was about to slide the handle down to release my nickels when I sensed someone behind me. I let go of the slide lever and turned to see Jimmy Grogan. Jimmy was a very handsome young man. His broad shoulders and blond hair complemented his fair skin. He was every bit six feet tall and gave the appearance of an athlete. Jimmy Grogan was the kind of guy you could really learn to like, but as soon as you did he was ready to screw you. Jimmy was the ideal confidence man, although he was always without funds. I told him not to touch the one-ball machine. Jimmy went over to admire my fortune and I slid the release lever again. Looking in my hand I saw seven nickels. I repeated the action. Not wanting to arouse any suspicion, I walked over to the one-baller, looked in my hand and saw another seven nickels. I handed five of them to Jimmy. "Here, take these nickels and play that five-ball machine. We're partners. If you hit, we split."

Going back to the quarter changer I slid the release lever fully after inserting a quarter. Five nickels appeared. Then I inserted a quarter and slowly slid the lever down halfway. When I released it, two nickels fell out. Continuing to pull the lever all the way down, I received an additional five nickels. I repeated this again and again. Each time, I got a total of seven nickels. I know it was early in the morning, but this was not a dream. I stopped so as not to arouse curiosity. Jimmy had just hit the five-ball machine for 200 games when he turned and exclaimed, "Oh, shit! Lou is pulling up out front."

"Great. Now I can get my winnings. Hey, where the hell are you going?" Jimmy hurriedly made a dash out the back door yelling, "You don't know? Lou caught me balling his new wife!"

When Lou came in, he asked me if that was Jimmy who just left.

"Yeah, why?"

"He's one no-good son-of-a-bitch."

I told Lou he owed me twenty-five bucks and he went to the game room and clicked off the games. He told me to go to the counter and wait and order something and he'd give me my money in the change. I started feeling sorry for Lou, but after I got my winnings, I couldn't resist getting a couple extra quarters and making some more change. Only then did I call Lou back to the game room. I showed him the extra nickels I received for the quarter. He was amazed.

"You can probably empty the machine for a quarter. Each time you pull the lever half way down, out pops two coins."

"So, why didn't you empty it out?"

"How much would I have gotten? How much do you keep in there?"

"Fifteen dollars. That fucking Jimmy, he probably fucked my changer, too!"

Mervy Gets His Own Car

Mervy Domore was a real cool cat and everyone respected him. He also hung out at the Flying Saucer. He was sixteen and experiencing family changes. His mother was dating a man she decided to marry. Mervy, by arrangement, was to stay in their rented house and his dad would move in with him. His dad, wanting to become friends with his boy, immediately tried to seal their friendship by buying Mervy a car. His dad was quite the salesman, however he was a few bricks short of a full load.

There was a story about his going to a wholesale baking company that sold to stores and retail outlets. I remember this one also sold pies, cakes, and bread, etc. door to door.

Without the consent of anyone, Mr. Domore entered Chesapeake Bakery armed with what appeared to be a roll of blueprints, a ruler, tape measure, pencils, and paper. He walked around the place as if he owned it measuring the ovens, the floor, the drive-in bays and even enlisted some of the help to aid him in his efforts. He summoned the plant foreman and had him give him specifications on the ovens and then take him to the president's office. He said, "Tell the boss Domore is ready to see him." The plant foreman did just what Mervy's dad suggested. The president was in awe. He didn't know whether Mervy's dad was with the city engineers office or the F.B.I. Domore had his complete attention.

Domore explained, "Now see here, I have a plan to increase your total gross business by 75 percent." The president of this small bakery was at Domore's complete regard. "I intend to achieve this goal by using my truck and allowing you to put my name, Domore's Great Cakes, on your label."

I don't know all the particulars of that incident, but I heard the president threw him out of the building.

When I had the pleasure of meeting him, he had just moved in with Mervy and he had another kook with him whom he introduced as his partner. Together, they were going to be the mayonnaise kings of the Eastern Seaboard. They were moving large mixing bowls and giant electric blenders into Mervy's rented house. They impressed me. They had labels with DOMORE'S MAYONNAISE in bold colorful letters on the label. I never knew anyone with their name on a label. Who knows what great achievements were put to the wayside when Mr. Domore's partner suddenly and permanently quit. His partner had his right arm pulled from it's socket in an accident with one of the large floor-model mixer machines.

I realized Mr. Domore was some kind of nut when he gave me a jar of his Domore's corn product. The product supposedly contained a miracle ingredient known to cure the common cold. Mr. Domore had a stack of letters addressed to him and some addressed, but never sent to the then-governor attesting to the miracles achieved by eating Domore's corn product. Mervy told me his dad was buying this stuff at a wholesale grocers' exchange. It was really Niblets and his dad merely reprocessed it in the kitchen.

Hey, Mervy was not unique. A lot of guys had dads who, for the most part, were totally stupid. Mervy's dad was nuts, not stupid.

Back to Mervy's dad buying him a car. What a car. It was a 1950 Lincoln Cosmopolitan. It was late summer and the evening was a rainy one when I played hooky from the drugstore to go over to Mervy's to see his car. We went out and sat in it. The car was a real dream. It was almost too much car. It was a rich person's car fully loaded and had everything you could imagine on it.

We sat in the front seat and talked about all the things that would be available to us now that Mervy had wheels. Mervy produced the key and inserted it into the ignition and started the car. The sound of the engine produced a temptation too great to resist so we ventured out on the road. Within minutes we were racing through Druid Hill Park when we discovered a new thrill. The car had a passing gear.

"Hey, Mervy, how and when did you get your license?" I asked.

"October," he stated.

"October?"

"Yeah, October. I'll be sixteen in October then I'll get my license."

We cruised around awhile and Mervy said his dad would be home soon so he'd better park the car as close as he could to where it had been.

About a week later, I got a call from Tony Meatball asking if I had heard about Mervy's car.

"Hey, not only do I know about it. I rode in it!"

"You ain't heard nuffin'. We takes da car out fer a ride. We gets to Wyman's Park. BAM! We hits a tree." Tony tells me how they covered up the accident, "Gino gets out some tin-a'foil from a pack a butts. Breaks a wire under da dash and wraps the tin-a'foil around the wires. Made it look like da car was a stole car."

I told Meatball to shut up the talk and to keep it to himself, then I called Mervy. I asked him, "What about Meatball telling me your car was stolen?" He confirmed it was stolen and was being repaired.

In the coming months we took a few rides around town on Saturdays while Mervy's dad was at work. Once, while going the wrong way on a street in South Baltimore, we were stopped by a cop. He stepped out on the street and instructed us saying, "Pull in that alley. You're on a one-way street. You got a license to drive?"

"Can I get to Pratt Street through this alley?" Mervy asked.

"Yes, two blocks over," replied the cop.

"Boy, I thought he had us," gasped Mervy as he cautiously drove through the alley. Within a few months Mervy got his license and it was on the road for the chosen few.

Mervy was now in charge and was sought out by a host of butter-upping friends. We soon drag raced everything imaginable. We were getting bored with the riding around thing. My riding was limited since I worked a confining job.

Sometimes, I would stay out late during the week. On one occasion, to fight the boredom, we came up with a caper that was really the limit. In our Charles Street gang we had a guy who was the epitome of Joe College. J.C. is what we called him. He looked out of place with our mobster-looking bunch. What we saw in him or what he saw in us was the sixty-four thousand dollar question. Anyway, he was to be our subject for a fake kidnaping. We set up a plan for the caper and J.C. was not only very cooperative, he should have been given an award for his performance.

The Belvedere Hotel was a very fashionable hotel on the corner of Charles and Chase Streets. We told J.C. to walk to the entrance of the hotel and stand around until he was noticed. He was to ask if the lobby had a tobacco stand. (We knew it did.) The entrance had a marquee and a uniformed doorman. J.C. was to walk inside, purchase a pack of cigarettes, exit slowly from the hotel and walk on the floor mat to the curb. Hopefully, the doorman would ask if J.C. wanted a taxicab. Two guys would be waiting off to the side of the entrance wearing double-breasted topcoats. The Lincoln would be parked down the street. When J.C. reached the end of the mat, the Lincoln would speed up to the entrance. The door on the curb side would open and the two guys waiting next to the entrance would rush up and push J.C. into the car. No one was to make a sound except for J.C.. The car would then speed off, tires squealing. If the light at the corner was red, we would race through it. That would certainly add to the dramatics. The scene was set.

Everything went off with commando precision. Only thing wrong was, the doorman was not outside and no one seemed to give a damn. We got some excitement from the act, though.

I was about to become disinterested in riding around with Mervy especially since my time was limited to when I wasn't working. I really believe it was because Mervy was a dangerous guy. I still can't believe we drag raced another car on Key Highway and wound up missing a freight train by inches at a speed of nearly eighty miles an hour. I didn't see much of Mervy after that. I did, however, take him a carton of cigarettes when I heard he was being held as a guest at the Fallsway Apartments.

Mervy in jail, that was some sight. He was locked up for burglarizing the sandwich shop where he worked. To some that may seem a just reward. Mervy didn't think of it on his own. One of his so-called friends talked him into the burglary. There sat Mervy in a blue denim suit, looking so forlorn it was sickening. He opened his mouth to speak and had to spit. Blood came from his mouth as he explained he had been beat up that morning in an act of self defense. We talked very little. Mervy told me he was going to be held for a few years as he had no defense.

I really felt broken-hearted as I watched my friend slip into depression. I guess that was my first real jolt of what life is about as I told Mervy he probably had the wrong idea of his fate, he would be out soon. "When you get out, you can stay at my house." I added. I said good-bye, encouraging him to be cool, not to take any crap off anyone in there. I turned to walk away when I heard my name being called from a distance. I turned to look back at a large line of youths walking in a procession. Not once but many times my name was being called. I must have known at least a dozen of the inmates in that march to wherever. I pointed as I returned their calls and suggested to Mervy, "Look those guys up. They are friends of mine I haven't seen in a long time."

Ridin' 'n Fightin'

At the time it seemed the very existence of being a teenage boy in the inner city required either having taken part in or having an interesting gang fight story to tell. This held true about a breed of boys whether from the Tenth Ward, Towson, Catonsville or across town. "Impress your peers with fear" was probably the name of the game. If you doubt it, ask your son. Fear was a living, breathing thing that followed me around. It seemed like others who heard about you would make up stories about them and you.

In the summer of '55 while working in the mail room at a credit reporting agency downtown, a guy told me he had a friend who knew me. In fact, the guy claimed to have beaten me up and stuffed me in a hamper at the old Hecht Company on Pine Street. I worked there during Christmas of '54. A few weeks after hearing this story, I was riding on the Charles Street bus in the company of Floon and Blackjack when the guy in question came up to me and identified himself as a friend of mine from the Hecht Company. He also told me we had a mutual friend at the credit agency. With that, I grabbed him by the buttons on his shirt and at the same time belted him on the chin with the same fist.

"Care to tell me about the hamper stuffing thing at Hechts?" I asked.

"I don't know what you're talking about," he informed me and quickly added his friend is a terrible liar.

Monday, when I returned to work at the credit agency, his friend greeted me, "I heard you got beat up and thrown off the bus."

I imagine my experiences in fighting promoted a short fused temper in me. That was because I never wanted the worry of someone being after me with a vengeance. I wanted arguments finalized, then and there. Most of my colleagues knew this and only a few times took advantage of this weakness. Tony Meatball was probably one of the most trusted friends I had. I was a full head taller than Tony and outweighed him by at least twenty pounds. The girls knew him as a cute guy. The gang knew him as a jerk. I knew him as insecure and in need of friends. The trust I had for Tony was limited to faithful, like being honest to me and not a liar or thief.

Tony was not a fighter but he could talk about a good fight. Stevie, Floon and Little Louie must have been really bored when they pitted Tony and me in what seemed to be mortal combat. They pushed Tony into me and my reaction was to push him back. After three or four times of this I slugged Tony with a hard right and a direct hit to his nose. Blood streamed out and I immediately rolled up half a matchbook cover and told Meatball to put it under his lip to stop the bleeding. He did. These three so-called pals were all laughing about the mean thing that had just taken place. I walked Tony home and stayed with him until he was okay. His grand-mother, who was also his legal guardian, couldn't thank me enough for all my help. Tony told his grandmother, "Five niggies jumped me and pulled me in da alley on Brentwood Avenue. Jackie happened along and we battled them." Tony's grandmother then gave him this advice. "You should have kicked them in the shins." I believe I had heard that somewhere before. "You can't hurt niggies hitting them in the head!"

Then came the a day I learned just how far my trust for Tony could go. A limit was now to be established. When I say "trusted" I don't mean backing me in a fight. It would have been better if I could have kept an eye on him, too! If the odds were against us Tony would run away. We used to go up to Carlins' Roller Rink on Sunday afternoons. The roller rink was in an amusement park known as Carlins' Park. This was a swell place to meet girls and have a lot of good clean fun. I remember the first time I went to Carlins'. I remember a girl named Eva and I skated together. I was only thirteen years old but by the time I got home, I was lovesick. Eva said she lived on West North Avenue. I had her address, but not her phone number, which was common at this time because not everyone had a tele-phone. Tuesday night I wrote and mailed Eva a letter. Today, I still recall some of the lovesick words that the letter contained. Not fully understand-ing the meaning of what I was writing I began:

When I saw you in your skating skirt with your lovely auburn hair flow-ing, my heart began to throb. Truly, you remind me of a blossom in the dust.

I went on to tell her to call me on the telephone and apologized for asking her to since girls didn't call boys. Furthermore, I told her we could meet in a theater on West North Avenue. It was later brought to my atten-tion that the theater I mentioned was patronized only by coloreds. I imag-ine her parents were wondering who the hell was writing their daughter. Eva wasn't at the roller rink the next Sunday and I never saw her again.

On a cool Friday night in November about three years down the road, Mervy picked me up at the drugstore when I got off work. It was urgent! Tony Meatball was going to be beaten up at Carlins' by a bunch of punks from Walbrook. Walbrook was a section of West Baltimore at the end of North Avenue. We rounded up what guys we could and headed for Carlins' Park and the roller rink. By the time we got there, we had laid out our battle plan. Mervy would park the car some distance from the entrance and Blackjack would stay with me until Mervy joined us. Little Louie would stand by the door so as not to be associated with us. Louie had a zip gun Mervy kept in his car and he now had it under his shirt tucked neatly in his pants top.

Gino went inside. Gino had never been to Carlins' before so no one would recognize him. Gino summoned Tony Meatball to come out, which he did along with four other guys. When Tony saw me and Black Jack, he began introducing these four guys to us. The same one's alleged to wanting to jump him. Gino and Little Louie were still not joined with us and kept themselves back as we had planned.

"Who was going to jump you?" I asked.

"Hey, that's all been settled. When these guys heard I was from the Ward, they said everything was cool."

"What was it all about?" I questioned. "This one fella broke bad with me because I had on my Pig Town jacket," said Meatball. "I don't understand. You were going to do Tony in and then, when he made a phone call, you punks got hip to being in bad trouble," I said.

"Yeah, well, we changed our minds. We didn't know he was from the Tenth Ward. Then he told us and we changed our minds.

"You changed your mind after the phone call?"

"Well, yeah. He should have told us he wasn't from Pig Town. We don't want their trash out here."

"So like, what are you telling me, youse guys own this place."

"Yeah, this is our territory."

"No way punk, not your territory, not now, never was. How about it Tony, you want to rumble with these punks?"

"No, we settled it already."

I interrupt with, "Nothings settled. You punks want to go a couple of rounds?"

Trying to impress me the assumed leader of these punks began to speak in a manner associated with toughs, a type of jive talk, "No need to do battle Daddy-O. We is cool with Tony and you guys are cool too. Besides there are only two of you. We like Tony and, anyway, he is hep to our jive. You dig? Now if you still want to want to rumble we can all go over to across the way and we'll settle it once and for all!"

That sounded like the best idea I'd heard since we got there. "Only thing different is you and Meatball are going to rumble," I stated.

By now Mervy a.k.a. Stonewall had parked the car and was coming up the hill toward us.

"Hey, Stonewall, which one of these punks you want to chew up?"

"What's the beef? We rumbling or what?" Stonewall asked.

Quickly, Tony turned and ran inside the rink. The punk I was talking to sucker-punched me KABOOM! My lights went out. I was on my ass. By now, two guys were holding me down and one bastard was kicking me. He kicked me in the nuts and I almost went out cold. They ran back to the rink, I thought.

When I tried to stand, I fell back down. Thank God there was a bench at the curb where I could sit until I regained my senses. Looking down the road, I could see a figure walking with a stagger. As the figure neared, I could see it was Mervy. "You all right?" he asked.

"No! Where'd everybody go?"

"I'm not sure. I got jumped by at least four of them, they knew we were coming. That fucking Tony ran right past me. He's a low-down rat!"

Gino and Louie were coming out of the rink when Louie said, "You see them punks take off when I pulled this gun out? They were about to jump me when I pulled it out. Hey, Jackie, you okay? Where's Blackjack?"

Just then a car came speeding down to the entrance from the back of the rink. It stopped for a few seconds then Blackjack emerged holding his face, blood streaming from his nose. The car took off and we all looked at each other assessing the damage. It was obvious some of us got the shit knocked out of us. What we didn't know did hurt us and it happened fast. There were two cars sitting up the street from the parking lot. The cars contained a bunch of guys, at least ten of them. They were there to back up these Walbrook punks and they did.

Hey, I couldn't believe my eyes when another car came racing down the drive and five guys jumped out swinging chains and ropes with what looked to be fishing weights affixed to the ends. Louie took a hell of a chance and pulled out the zip gun. If these guys had guns, we were dead.

"I'm shooting the first who wants it, in the face.!" Louie exclaimed and quickly ordered them to drop the chains. I didn't know it, but the gun was loaded. Knowing Louie he would have shot the first one who tempted him. Two of them retreated to the car and seeing no one got shot, the others followed. They started the car and then it stalled.

While running to the car, they had dropped their chains. We quickly scooped them up and advanced to the car. The driver rolled down the window pleading with us not to hurt the car as it belonged to his dad. One guy started to get out and received a chain across his face for the effort. After that, they just stayed in the car looking on while we dented the doors, broke out the lights and busted the windows. The cops were coming and it was time to go, but not without busting a bottle of booze the punks had. We poured it in their car so the cops would have something to investigate.

Running in high gear we made it to our car. All of us stayed low while Mervy, driving like an old lady, took the long way across town to our neighborhood not without stopping in Waverly first. Waverly was a community near the stadium and sported one of the first shopping centers in Maryland. We arrived in Waverly to get a sandwich with our friends on Thirty-Second Street and found "Brother Rat" Tony Meatball waiting for a bus to go home. We really should have hated him but we didn't.

"Why did you run? You could of yelled we were getting into a trap or something," Mervy asked Tony.

"I didn't think it would do any good. I figured you guys hated me by now. Besides, if I'm gonna get beat up it ought to be from you guys, my real friends."

In the car I asked Tony, "Did you learn anything tonight?"

"Yeah, I learned I'm a coward. I'm sorry I asked you guys to help me and then ran out on everybody. I ain't never going out by myself so fuck roller skating."

On the Job Training Equals
a Crash Education

Over the next few weeks I became very ill with a virus infection and was home for about two weeks from school and the drugstore job. While recuperating and working with my drawing tools, I remembered a few of the things that concerned me most. One was money. I didn't have any. The other was I felt the school I was attending was not as progressive as it should be. The courses were dull and uninteresting and the drafting teacher wasn't a real draftsman, only a mechanical drawing teacher. In an attempt to make up for my lost time from school I obtained some lessons and was about to start on them. Before I did so, my brother Jim read them and told me he found they contained a few mistakes and I must correct them before returning them to school. I was ashamed to tell Jim that I hadn't worked on them as they were my teacher's handiwork. I had obtained them for a drill. You see, Jim was opposed to me going to this school in the first place. I was a very confused sixteen year old. School wasn't any fun and I had no steady girl and if I had a girlfriend I wouldn't be a pleasure. Who would want to date a guy who's always broke? I realized I wouldn't become a celebrity and for the most part I was feeling very sorry for myself and never returned to school. I was ready to accept every East Baltimore boy's fate—working in one of the steel mills, breweries or tin factories.

When I applied to an advertisement, I was told I had to be eighteen years of age. Should I lie? No! This was now real life. A lie wouldn't be strong enough to build my future on.

My first job upon leaving school was as stock boy in a department store, which lasted about four months. I had a good record with this company and could probably have had a career there but it was not very exciting. I still maintained a part-time position at the drug store, which was soon terminated, as I couldn't keep up the pace. I wanted something more challenging. I took a day off and went to the Industrial Building a block from my house and was hired immediately as a folding machine operator in a printing plant. That job, too, went by the wayside within three months. In that job I was surrounded by a bunch of uneducated people who were always hollering at each other. I was tasting life as it would be on an assembly line. Although this operation may have been important to the firm, it made me feel as if I didn't exist. I quit and looked for another job.

Mail clerk in a credit reporting agency lasted four months. The job was great. It didn't pay much, but there was an unending supply of girls. I quit this job after much dating and playing around. I wasn't able to save money and the job seemed unproductive to me. The drugstore lost their evening help so I talked to the druggists and they agreed to let me work for them again, evenings. This way I could take a day job Mervy told me about. Bicycle delivery boy lasted two weeks. I took this job since no one really wanted a delivery boy's job on a bicycle. Mervy was working in a sandwich shop and clearing some forty bucks as a delivery boy. He said it was a great job and I could have one for the asking. It was true. I asked and got the job. I cleared over forty bucks which was almost double what I took home as a mail clerk. The Doc at the drugstore really helped me get the delivery boy job by intervening on my behalf. He wasn't sorry when I quit it some weeks later and retained the drugstore job. The only thing, I was quitting the drugstore, too.

One of the deliveries I made was to a payroll service. The secretary there was trying to operate an Addressograph machine and had a plate stuck in it. I always had a knack for things mechanical so I volunteered to help. I also showed her how to load the machine. She went in and summoned her boss, who was the owner of the firm. He asked me if I was also the young man who worked in the local pharmacy in the evenings and I said I was. He thanked me and that evening he came to the pharmacy and offered me a job. I immediately quit the sandwich shop and gave notice at the drugstore to become a clerk in a payroll service. I found a home at this place.

Since I quit day school, I had been reading from a tutorial on English and eventually entered an English course in the evenings at Baltimore City College. I had become accustomed to rigorous hours and was enjoying regular with this new job. The firm was on Calvert Street just four blocks from my home. I went to school at night and took an additional course in business machines. Somehow, I still longed for adventure. I knew there had to be something better in life than just being a clerk. I joined the U.S. Army National Guard hoping that would fill the gap. It didn't. Then I thought about becoming an entertainer.

With all the show people I had met on the strip of Charles Street, I certainly wouldn't have any trouble. I started writing jokes, some of which were very good. I read the works of Joe Miller and a few others and I had some cards printed suggesting I was a Master of Ceremonies. Then, it happened. I got my first gig. I would be the M.C. for a midnight spook show held at the Pennington Theater in Curtis Bay. The famous Magician Danteeni was to perform. Actually, it was his show.

My adopted uncle, one Al Caminitte a.k.a. Al Knight, was my manager. Al was a swell guy. He wasn't any relation to me, but you have to understand the neighborhood and the Italian philosophy. If a Capo takes a liking to you and makes you a member of his family, you are now blood and nobody—and I mean nobody better lay a hand on you. Al was about fifteen years older than I and since I had brothers close to his age, I had no problem communicating with Al. He was a Baltimore nightlife celebrity. Through Al, I met a lot of entertainers.

I did my first show and Al said I was great. A month or so went by and I did my second gig. Another spook show in a larger theater, The Westway, on Edmondson Avenue Extended. Once again, I was a natural. At least, that's what Al told me.

I was contacted by Danteeni and some really weird-looking guy who actually scared me. They wanted me for a movie they were shooting in New York. I told my mother about it and she advised me to check it out first. Later she told me a motion picture actor was passing through Baltimore and tried to make contact with me from the Pennsylvania Railroad Station. My mother was deaf in one ear and partially so in the other and said she couldn't make out the full conversation, so that ended that.

I was contacted by a number of good people wanting me to do benefits. I wish I had done them all because I loved that life. I did one at the War Memorial Plaza in which a jazz band performed, an opera singer sang, and a religious group lectured. Over the next weeks I received several calls from the jazz band asking me to accompany them on some jobs. The opera singer invited me to Washington to meet the people who owned the restaurant where he was singing and the gospel group wanted to enlist me in becoming an evangelist.

I answered all these callings in this manner. I needed a union card to perform with the band and couldn't afford the dues to join. I didn't have any transportation or funds to support a trip to D.C. and I was afraid the "religion" might get the best of me. In other words, I didn't realize my full potential.

On my eighteenth birthday I asked permission from Mr. Dover, the owner of the payroll service, to take off a few hours to register at the Selective Service Local Board Number Nine. While out for the day, I applied for a job at Bethlehem Steel in Sparrows Point. I quit the Dover Payroll Service and was now ready to earn my living as a man. As a steel worker and member of the union, I was up in the morning at four and rode two buses and a streetcar to the giant steel plant at Sparrows Point. On the job by seven, (I was late every day) off by three, and with another hour and a half streetcar and bus ride (if I was lucky), I only lasted two weeks!

Next I became a shipping clerk for a scent company. The scents manufactured here were perfume-soaked cardboard cutouts that hung in automobiles. I worked there about two months. What a bunch of crooks those people were. They had at least three names and addresses and operated under all three. They were their own competitors and offered deals to the field representatives. In turn, they offered better deals to the same representatives under a different package. They received mail at a dentist's office on Preston Street, at a doctor's office on Saint Paul Street, and of course, at the factory address with an additional mail stop at the post office.

I didn't realize just what was going on there but I caught hell from them when I packed a shipment for one of their field representatives under a competing company's label. I think they were telling the distributor that they were setting him up as an exclusive dealer. They also duplicated their offer under another label. Thus, they played on the representative's greed to corner the market on car scent materials.

I quit this firm one morning. I got up to go to work and walked out to the Biddle Street Bridge and I just kept on walking until I got to Charles Street. There I purchased a morning paper, read the want ads and saw a job for an assistant manager at an art-type theater. It was less than two months until the Reserve's summer encampment. So, if I got the job and it was as I believed a dud, nothing would be lost. I got the job. The hours were from ten in the morning until midnight while in training. I stayed about five weeks. I learned almost every line of the motion picture "The Lady Killers." This art-type theater served complimentary coffee and the clientele were, for the most part, the city's upper crust. During my tenure, I met two very naughty but nice usherettes who were quick to help me understand the facts of life. It was a good thing the summer encampment was just around the corner because their husbands were just as close, too! While at the theater, I read where the whole crew of crooks from the scent factory were arrested in a scheme. They were selling stocks in rocket fuel alleged to be endorsed by Werner Von Braun.

When I returned from summer camp, I got a job with a typewriter company. This time I was sure to build my future with a firm that offered fair wages, training, insurance and camaraderie with a great group of people. I liked this place enough to recommend it to Tony Meatball, a guy who, as yet, had never worked a day in his life. Tony came on board in the supply department and lasted only a few months. He had stopped going to Reserves drill earlier in the year and it caught up with him. The M.P.s picked him up and he was activated to regular Army duty.

I now had my future laid out for me. I made a lot of friends at the summer encampment and I believe it helped to fill the need for companionship. Somehow, I must have grown up while at boot-camp, because I came back about ten pounds heavier and with some knowledge I didn't have when I left. Knowledge such as team work in combat situations, the workings of the M-1 Garand and becoming an excellent rifleman. Wiring and communication skills were also my specialty. I learned to drink about a six-pack of beer before getting a buzz.

I worked my job with the typewriter company and again entertained the idea of looking for the right girl. I dated a little Italian girl from East Point and found the competing for her was heavy and not having a car was a burden in dating.

My Bodyguard

Mervy came home for a visit from the male reformatory in Hagerstown. He had an old friend, Norman French, drive him down to Biddle Street to see me. Norman was a poor man's Allen Ladd, a short but handsome guy who was so stuck on himself that it was a wonder he didn't marry himself. Mervy looked good and was managing to survive the jail sentence. He would be out within a year and he had his girlfriend with him. We drove him up to Bel Air where he was staying with his mother and her new husband until he had to report back to the facility in Hagerstown.

Norman became familiar to me and he would come down to my house on Sundays where we would have jam sessions. My mother usually went to Annapolis where my brothers were building a new house for the Lundon family, so our house on Biddle Street was ideal for small gatherings. Al Knight would bring his guitar or bass and Norman would attempt to play our old player piano while I beat my snare drum. I had a tape recorder and taped our sessions for the evening.

After a dance at the famous ballroom, I almost blew it by telling someone we had these sessions and were planning another one that night. When I got to my house there were at least forty people there with cases of beer invading all the bedrooms. My mother, upon arriving home within minutes of the bash, ordered the party over.

I had a very busy schedule during this time. I was traveling with Russel Filbera a.k.a. Gino, Silent Sam and Tony Meatball and we were almost inseparable. The only thing I wasn't aware of was Silent Sam and Gino were not allowed to be in each other's company. I went to Silent Sam's home to meet him and his mother asked me where we were going and with whom. She asked if Ralph was going too. I said I didn't know any Ralph. Silent Sam entered the room and his mother asked him if Ralph was going with us. Turning to me she asked, "Do you know Ralph? Ralph is such a nice young man." I answered with a negative reply and as we left the house. Sam replied back to his mother, "Jackie hasn't met Ralph and yes we're meeting Ralph later." I asked Sam, "Who the hell is Ralph?" To which he answered, "Ralph, is Gino, I'm not allowed to associate with him since we were locked up together at the reform school. Gino called me once, slipping he told my mother who he was on the telephone and all hell broke loose. I told my mother, Russell was merely looking me up. To keep us from getting together she had our telephone number changed to non-listed." Silent Sam had told his mother, Russell was Ralph. His name was Ralph Gino. As we were leaving, his mother stated, "Make sure we stayed away from that God Damn Russell Filbera!" He said he promised his mother he wouldn't ever associate with Russell Filbera. I agreed that makes a lot of sense.

Silent Sam got his name because he seldom spoke. That was true if he didn't know you, but I couldn't get him to shut up. He had a problem with pronouncing words and I found out later it was because he was partially deaf and couldn't hear the sounds. In most cases, people made fun of his way of speaking but not so with our crowd. Hell, knew we weren't perfect.

Sam had a job in a dental laboratory making false teeth, etc. He also was a cleanliness nut. He wasn't an ugly guy. His being quiet and his hook nose made him a not so acceptable type. Sam liked to wear dark clothes: black shirts, white ties, dark blue pinstripes suits and the like. These things helped him maintain the gangster image he so desired. I knew him to be a real caring and warm person. He was the perfect example of "Don't judge a book by its cover."

Gino, who in reality was Russell Filbera, lived in West Baltimore and was a fun guy. He was a mechanic for a cigarette lighter firm. He actually repaired cigarette lighters. He was also a trumpet player and enjoyed modern jazz, plus he had a girlfriend who was very fat and muscular. She picked him up at the Y.W.C.A. and it was love at first sight. Matter of fact, she used to manhandle Gino. She actually carried him once when he was loaded. As I said, Gino was very funny in a strange way. He was a dead ringer for James Dean, so I don't know why he even bothered with her. One of my chums asked me why I hung around with Gino. I remember him telling me he was at the Maryland Reform School with Gino where everyone called Gino "Goofy Fill."

Goofy or not, there was a period when my life depended on Gino. I had received a barrage of telephone calls from a guy who threatened to kill me. At first I thought it was a cruel prank. But the prank got ugly and the calls kept up. I wouldn't leave my home unless in the company of Gino, Silent Sam and Tony Meatball.

I told my uncle Al who seemed very disturbed by this. In fact, he was really pissed. He gave me a gun, a small .25 revolver to carry. I was afraid of what may become of me carrying a gun and left it in my drawer at home.

By accident I happened onto the alleged assailant by myself. He was standing in the doorway of the Flying Saucer Restaurant. He called me by the name he used on the telephone, so I knew him immediately. Every one of the calls started with, "Hey lover." And the word lover was constantly used.

On first encounter he said, "Hey lover, we gotta talk." His chant of lover caused me to immediately reflect to an incident of a few weeks before: One evening I met this girl in the Flying Saucer. She was at least twenty and I struck up a conversation with her. Max, one of the bouncers from a club down the street, suggested I take the chick out to a movie. I asked with what and he dropped a ten-dollar bill on the counter and said with that. I smiled and palming the bill thanked him. I asked the girl if she would enjoy walking down to Baltimore Street with me and she responded positively. As we were strolling, she told me she had just been discharged from the Women's Army Corps and she had been dating a Pat McHenry. I couldn't believe what I was hearing, this guy was a first-class bum. I asked her what she saw in him. She then told me a story about the guy. Pat told her he was a steel worker and was in love with her. However, he was heavy in debt and she told me she was supporting him on dates. By the time we arrived at Baltimore Street, she had told me one of his friends said Pat is so in love with her he was actually thinking of getting a job.

We continued our conversation about Pat and went into a bar I frequented. The bar was in an alley near the Lord Baltimore hotel and was known as the Monkey's Butt. I went there because they wouldn't ask me for an I.D. We shared a few beers and I walked her to her apartment. My original intention was to put the make on her, but I felt too sorry for her. She had gotten tangled up with a bum and that was enough. She was really in love with him and suffering with a broken heart. As for me, I was just a new friend she found on the rebound. I elected to be a gentleman and saw her to her apartment. Having her own apartment and a few bucks of her own was probably why McHenry found her so attractive. She had made the discovery of what she was getting into with Pat and fortunately called it off. I walked her home and I said good night. I never saw her again.

Here I was face to face with a creep who threatened to kill me. I knew he may have imagined me as being the architect of his demise with his girl friend. Little did he know the truth. That wasn't going to change anything now. He was here and so was I. When you come from this environment, you're not as likely to be afraid of the elements as a stranger might, but man, I was now afraid for my life. He was a Charles Street bum who loafed in a pool hall, a place where you could get anything for a price. For all I knew, he was a bad character.

How did I get into such a predicament, as I stared into his face I felt vengeance. I could think only of my mom being terrified by his telephone calls. My heart started to pound and part of me wanted to hit him and part of me wanted to run. Pat went on talking to me. Frightened, all I could hear was blabbing coming from someone who had driven me to the point of hate. I turned and walked fast from his presence. Almost to a slow jog, I could hear the sound of someone walking quickly and close behind me. It was Pat, still blabbing away about the need to talk. Then he shouted, "Hey, I'm sorry!" But from the tone of his voice he was pissed. I thought this was perhaps a trick to get me by myself and maybe kill me. Here in front of the restaurant I was safe. He claimed he was getting pissed off at me for not accepting his apology. Apology, I wanted no apology for his threats. I wanted his blood. I was just afraid to take it. I was now at the steps of Mount Royal

Park. In my rage I lead him to my battlefield, a place where I had achieved many victories. Had I gone there out of fright. Certainly I was too much the coward to actually be there out of desire. I stopped and turned. Pat was now really pissed at my actions and pulled out a knife and I was now engaged in what could become mortal combat. Quickly, I pulled my jacket off and using it as if it were a whip, I slung it at Pat, jerking it back by the sleeve. The jacket made a cracking sound and the zipper made a large gash down Pat's face. Bleeding, he now shouted, "I'm going to kill you."

Once when I was a child, my brother Jim told me, "If anyone ever bothers you and they are bigger than you, pick up a board and hit them with it." Bigger than me was not so much the case, as was Pat's reputation for being a tougher older guy. Plus he hung with what was possibly the local mob. I saw what looked like a board and picked it up. Pat backed off. I said, "Come and get it you lousy bastard." Stopping in his tracks Pat explained, "Look I told you I was sorry. You wanted this, I didn't."

Out of control I really wanted to hurt him both mental and bodily. I began to yell things while I got into a position close enough to swing the board. I made him really take notice, he began to scream his anger while I shouted, "You're mad because I had beer with your broad. I not only had a beer with her, but I fucked her. I fucked her in the alley behind her apartment. I fucked her in a car. I fucked her in her doorway and I fucked her in the men's room at the flying saucer and my troops also fucked her. Swinging the board I knocked the knife several feet out and away from Pat's hand and the connection with his arm made a cracking sound. I was in a position to let him have it again when Pat shouted, "I've had enough I think my arm's broke." Pat, grabbing his arm again he shouted, "Fucker, I think you broke my arm."

"That's right and I'm going to break your face!"

"No more. You mother fucker, can't you know I'm sorry?" Pat was still holding his arm and repeating he was sorry.

"So why did you follow me? Why didn't you just leave me alone?"

In agony he managed to get out, "Max, Max told me to leave you alone, and to apologize to you. That's why I followed you. Now Max is going to be pissed because we fought."

"Okay, I accept your apology. Okay?"

"Yeah, sure. Fine and I'm sorry too! Look what you did to my arm."

"No shit, Max told you?"

"Yeah, Max! I was telling Max about calling you on the phone, asking him what I should do when I met up with you. Max said, "That's my boy and you better not hurt him! Hey, I didn't know you were in with the crowd!"

"Something else you didn't know, my Uncle Al gave me a gun to blow your fucking head off with but now I won't have to."

"Your uncle Al? Who the fuck is your Uncle Al?"

"You'll find out. In fact, when he finds out it was you scaring the shit

out of me, he'll probably have you fitted for a new pair of cement shoes."
Maybe I'll tell him to call it off and maybe I won't.

"Hey did you really screw her?"

"Nah. The broad was in love with you. I just said that stuff because you deserved to hear it. Where's she now?"

"She left town."

I left Pat standing holding his arm and went home and got in bed for a well-deserved rest. I hadn't slept too well in a couple of weeks. When the dawn rose and I lay gaping at the ceiling it also dawned on me. Max gave me the dough to take Pat's girl out. Max was the architect of that whole mess.

About a week passed and while I was headed for Charles Street a man approached me to tell me Pat McHenry got the living hell beat out of him late last night. He said, "McHenry was in the bus terminal's coffee shop on Howard Street bragging to some of his cronies about scaring someone half out of their wits by telephone over a period of weeks. When he left two guys who were in the place drinking coffee followed him out, dragged him into an alley and went to work on him."

"Was it a robbery? Did they rob him?"

"No, they said they didn't like his story. They didn't think it was very funny."

"So, why you tellin' me this story?"

Laughingly, he said, "Oh, I knew McHenry was a friend of yours and thought you might like to know."

"Okay, thanks for telling me." I changed my destination and decided it would be a good idea to go home and call Gino and tell him about McHenry. Funny thing, Gino already knew all about it.

Going Steady Sucks

Recently, looking over a picture of my wife's junior high school class, my thoughts went back to some of the kids in the picture. One in particular was my first serious girlfriend, Lois Starcher. Years later my children referred to her as Bug Eyes, a name they obviously got from my wife. Lois was introduced to me by Georgie Emerson. Georgie had a girlfriend named Sally and Lois was Sally's sorority sister.

Georgie told me I had a secret admirer who wanted to meet me. Please don't get me wrong, but I had a lot of girls that admired my dancing. I was very popular due to the dances and the television shows I attended. Georgie was with me when we saw a girl on the Fallsway at Preston Street. She was waiting for a bus and happened to recognize me from the television show. I talked to her for a few minutes and introduced her to Georgie. Georgie was at this time passing himself off as Chuck. I don't know whether "Chuck" was already embroidered on the front of his jacket or if Georgie had it placed there. Anyway, Chuck, a nickname usually used for boys named Charles, did eventually become Georgie's nickname. As for his jacket, it was a beautiful purple high school jacket formerly owned by a Mount Saint Joseph Student until Georgie heisted it. So much for that tidbit, back to the girl. Her name was Sally and she later became Georgie's wife.

Georgie and Sally planned to get Lois and me together. After meeting Lois, I was very infatuated with her. She was attending Eastern High School and was in her junior year. I dated her a couple of times and she asked me if I liked her enough not to see any other girls. I should have known she was not for me. She was overwhelmed by my boldness and popularity but her parents were scared stiff when they met me. I had a duck's ass hairdo with sideburns and was wearing a black corduroy jacket with TENTH WARD in large lettering on the back. The lettering was not bad, but the reputation of that part of town was.

For all practical purposes, I was a walking billboard for the hoodlum population. Hey, what the hell. Tony Meatball's jacket had PIG TOWN written on the back because that was the part of town he originally came from. His family eventually moved into the Tenth Ward, a step up, obviously.

The rest of my attire was a pair of black slacks pegged at thirteen inches at the bottom and a pair of blue suede shoes. In addition, I smoked cigarettes. I guess Lois' parents were ready to take gas when they met me.

One evening they came to pick Lois up at my house on Biddle Street. It was the first time Lois had come to my house for dinner. They arrived unexpectedly saying they "Just happened to be in the neighborhood." Bullshit! When they came in the door, you wondered if they worked for Sherlock Holmes or something. Their eyeballs looked up, down and all around. I really didn't think they would let Lois go out with me again, especially now that they had seen my neighborhood and environment.

With exception of the little money I gave my mother, I spent every penny I earned on Lois trying to entertain her. I just left school and was working as a stockboy at The Hecht Company warehouse when Lois came into my life. We went steady from November 1954 through May 1955. Lois' mother and father were beginning to treat me as though they were accepting the fact I might be there to stay.

Just when everything was going okay, a couple of pals of mine got their names in the paper for shooting windows out of a passing passenger train near Preston Street. Lois' parents asked her about these two guys since the newspaper gave the location. She said they were friends of Jack's.

My salable stock, for whatever it was worth, was at a new low. Christmas was coming and Lois asked me for a hint of what I wanted most. I told her I wanted a black onyx ring with my initial in the center. I also told her my mother might get it for me. Lois told me to tell my mother not to because she'd been to a jewelry store in Waverly and I would be very surprised at Christmas.

Boys in the 1950's paid for the night on the town. It was an unwritten law that girls didn't shell out for expenses of movies or dinner. I managed to show Lois a good time and tried also to save a few dollars each week to get Lois exactly what she asked for, a Brownie Hawkeye camera with flash attachment. Christmas came and Lois gave me a small box from the jewelry store in Waverly. It contained a pair of Swank brand cuff links. I don't know what happened to the ring. I was so very disappointed, although I acted like it was the nicest thing anyone ever gave me. Please understand, these rings cost close to twenty dollars. Lois had a part-time job at the dime store that was next door to the jewelry store. She didn't pay board to her parents so why didn't she give me the ring she hinted she was purchasing? She bought herself one.

When we'd get together, Lois would begin to quiz me on things such as how you pronounce a certain word or some other subject like biology. She stayed far away from history. As a matter of fact, she walked around history. Good thing, too, because I would have made her feel stupid! I guess she was finding that I was too illiterate for her.

On my way to night school one evening I stopped at her house where I was informed she was meeting me at the malt shop up the street. When I got to the malt shop, I was informed she was on her high school campus with another guy. I became enraged and I ran to the campus. By the time I got there, I had collected my thoughts and realized she had used me. The guy she was with had just been released from jail. I told him I wanted to talk to her alone and asked her to return my ring. Not wearing it she said she would. She also said I was jumping to the wrong conclusion and asked me to call her tomorrow. I went on to school. I remember I was very upset and hurt when I thought about my time spent on this girl, but I was not unique. Although, as Little Louie told me, "Jackie, you can have any girl in the Famous Ballroom," I really only had one thought in mind and that was Lois Starcher. I went home and listened to Sinatra records and cried myself to sleep. Funny thing, when Lois' parents started to treat me like they might be accepting me, Lois turned me OFF!

The next morning I took a good look at myself in the mirror. I had let this girl change me from what I really was. I was no longer the major Daddy-O of Charles Street but a Joe College square. My hair was cut short and my clothes all matched. I would have to stop this change before it was too late. I really started to develop a new attitude, one of a rebel. I bought myself some new Lee jeans and sweat shirts. I got back with my crowd and met a few new girls but it wasn't any fun because I still had Lois on my mind.

It was late spring when I started to give more thought to Lois and what she might be doing, so I called her up and made arrangements to see her. Georgie said Lois had been inquiring about me. She was working a summer job for a finance company on Saint Paul Street. It was convenient for me so I decided I'd go to see her. While en route, I met up with Mervy and told him about this girl. He said he wanted to see the girl that put me down. While repeating and reliving the affair to Mervy, I totally blew it.

We finally arrived and when Lois came to the counter smiling and saying how nice it was to see me, I looked at her and said, "Yeah, so what? Gimme my ring." She looked again and still smiling suggested we talk. I held myself back from touching her hand and telling her I missed her. Instead, I turned my head once in Mervy's direction and again back to her and with a jackass' chuckle I exclaimed, "Just gimme the ring so I can get the hell away from you." She reached down to her hand and removed the ring from her finger. Deep down inside, I was starting to fall apart. I grabbed the ring, turned and walked away. I looked at Mervy and said, "Let's get out of this fucking place."

The fall of the year came and Georgie told me Lois was again asking about me. That "asking about me" part kept wearing at me for days. I guess I was mostly ashamed of myself for showing off in front of Mervy. I finally called her. I don't think I had any idea what nerve was. I never had to get up nerve to act on anything, I just acted. I talked to her for a long time and we both lied to each other about all the romances we were having. Only I wasn't lying. I had five girls I was seeing regularly. Sometimes I would be romancing one and call her by another's name.

On Friday evening I arranged for a date with Lois to go to the Boulevard Theater and I tried to look as plain as possible. When I arrived at the

Starchers' house, the reception was somewhat cold. Lois' mother seemed to be asking Lois what I was doing there. I could hear her asking questions of Lois regarding some other boy. When Lois re-entered the room, I asked her what her mother was referring to. Lois said his name and that he was the son of a prominent doctor. We exchanged a few kind greetings and then with tears coming from her eyes she mentioned, "Maybe we shouldn't be doing this."

"Does that mean you would rather not see me?" I asked while searching her face.

"Yes, I believe it would be a mistake for us to go out."

"Hey, okay, don' worry about it."

I put on my topcoat and headed for the door when she asked, "Aren't you going to tell my parents you're leaving?"

"Nah, you tell em." A few weeks passed and Mervy's girlfriend was at the Famous Ballroom. I was standing, watching a few dancers and trying to make up my mind which girl I wanted to ask to dance. Turning to walk away, I almost walked into this gorgeous chick with a smile that could talk an Eskimo into buying an icebox. It was Mervy's former girlfriend, Diane. I hadn't seen her in a year. She was beautiful.

"What are you doing here?" I asked.

"Looking for you."

"You're kidding. How did you know I would be here?"

"I got a letter from Mervy. He's in jail up at Hagerstown but he always knew I had a soft spot for you. In his last letter he mentioned I could probably find you here."

I went completely head over heels. Mervy used to take me along to see Diane at her home in Wilson Point and they always had a girl there for me. Being the gentleman I was, I never tried to push myself on Diane. I wanted her in the worst way but she was Mervy's girl and that was good enough for me. But now, she was giving herself to me. Believing myself to be the luckiest guy in East Baltimore, I was unofficially Diane's guy.

I was working a very decent job and making a fair wage at the payroll service. I could afford to take Diane on dates and since she had a car, it made life a little less complicated. Diane informed me we were not going steady but we were not seeing anyone else either. Whatever the arrangement, it was okay with me. I had put Lois out of my mind.

Diane wanted a picture of me so I had her drive up to Gorsuch Avenue to Lois' house. My adorable Diane presented herself to Lois and asked for, and received the large photograph of me. Mean old me, having Diane drive up in her brand new 1956 Ford Victoria Crown top to pick up my picture. Mean or not, there was some poetic justice in the act.

The time came when I would have to stop going to the Ballroom on Sundays. There was a wolf pack at the dance after my Diane. I danced a few dances with my adoring Diane and when I returned from a break to the men's room, I went into a rage. This guy kept coming over and asking

Diane to dance and I'd have to tell him to get lost. But now I had only been gone a minute or two and he was back at it. She had just given him an empathic "No" when he grabbed her by the hand. I came up to him.

"Hey, get your hands off her."

"Fuck you."

Two more punks came from nowhere and were all around me. These guys must either be nuts or knew something I didn't because as far as I was concerned, this was Rome and I was a centurion. Like a precision drill team Gino had a knife in each of his hands and placed himself alongside me. Silent Sam was behind yelling, "Jackie, get dat sum bitch!" I grabbed the guy by the front of his clothing, tie, shirt and suit coat and up and away he went. The clown must have gone three or four feet in the air. I couldn't believe what I had just done. He was at least ten pounds heavier than I, although the same height.

The Ballroom detectives were all over us by now. They knew me and asked me to behave myself. Then they asked the three punks what was going down and they said they just wanted to leave and leave they did. Gino and Silent Sam went to the restroom to share a half-pint of booze and Diane and I left in her brand new Ford.

I don't know if Diane was a screwball or I was a dumbbell, but one evening while riding down Route 40, she asked me to marry her.

"Don't you think we should wait and just be engaged for a while?"

I was truly infatuated with Diane but somehow she demonstrated some kooky ideas that didn't set right with me. I felt I was wasting her time and called it all off between us. I understand she got married two months later.

I'm Goin' Home. Back Where I Belong

I returned to the friendships of my old neighborhood which by now was 80 percent black. I hadn't really left I was just using it as a bedroom. Upon taking a good look at the neighborhood I saw it was a changed neighborhood but I had changed, too. I guess, by now, I knew I was poor but it didn't make a damn bit of difference. I had already tasted life as it would be among competitive friends. It was not the warmth of friends who love you because you're you and not what you have or can do for them. Even our new neighbors shared this camaraderie and except for the color of our skin, it was our neighborhood.

Tony Vespi happened over to show off his new set of wheels. Tony was into hot rods. I wasn't, but I remember an incident that was quite a lot of fun. The Shriners were having their convention in Baltimore. Tony and I were driving by the Lord Baltimore Hotel when a group of Shriners standing near the hotel, asked me through the opened car window if we had room to take them to the Fifth Regiment Armory. Tony looked at me. Why not? We let them ride with us. There must have been at least five of them and they gave us a tip for the ride. We immediately went back to the hotel and picked up another group. This time I acted as a guide pointing out the sights and told some jokes along the way. One of the Shriners gave me his card and told me to come to Virginia Beach as he had a job in his night club for me as an entertainer/bus boy. Tony and I talked about going and said we would next spring.

The Last of Our Crowd

When I joined the Reserves, I didn't join alone. Vernon Solon, Tony Meatball, Silent Sam, Mervy and Jerry Salvo from the Charles Street mob joined with me. The adventure became a bonding of our friendships and for the rest of our teens we watched out for each other. I got a call from Silent Sam asking me to go to a dance at the YWCA on Friday night. In fact, we called Gino and the whole gang joined us. We had a great time and the people at the Y were great. They were sponsoring a dance on Saturdays, too. The Friday night dance was a record hop but the Saturday dance had a band. This was the perfect place for downtown kids to gather. In fact, they had just formed a club, The Saturday Sunday Club. It was for youths in their late teens and early twenties.

On Sundays they would meet for fellowship and discuss the coming weekend dance and plan the same. We were almost asked to leave at the very first meeting. Tony Meatball had been drunk all day and he was sitting behind some kid and started throwing up all over her. I gathered him up over my shoulder and carried him from the Y to his house, about two and a half miles away. He had passed out completely. The next week we apologized to the group and our apology was accepted.

We were told by the members that a group of Gypsies was beginning to frequent the dance and was strong-arming the dance members. There was also a story that they had raped one girl and she was afraid to tell anyone for fear of her life. Most were prejudiced toward Gypsies. So the Gypsies passed themselves off as Italians. When we got to the dance, it was noticeable that there was a group of dark-skinned high style dressers who appeared like they were trying to look like Cubans not Italians. There would be a mutual benefit to the Saturday Sunday Club if we joined up. After we established ourselves, we laid out a plan to instigate a fight, or better still, a battle with the Gypsies. We would do this on our own and not let the club know our intentions. In fact, if they had any idea of our plan to rid the place of Gypsies they wouldn't have allowed us to join. Since we were new and didn't know the strength of the Gypsy bunch, we would wait. The weeks passed and the opportunity was now ours for the asking. Silent Sam was shaken down by three of the Gypsy band in the back street behind the Y while on his way to the dance.

So that Friday evening would be D-day. Silent Sam was standing with Tony Meatball near the stage selecting records for the disc jockey when three dark-skinned so-called Italians confronted them and told them, "Make for the men's room." I was just coming out as two guys were entering. The men's room was empty except for those two guys. One was a very big guy, possibly twenty years old and weighing about 180 pounds. As a matter of fact, he bumped me on the way through the door. Silent Sam looked at me like he was about to get sick. He nodded to me. I didn't realize he was being forced into the men's room at knifepoint. Tony was now considering whether to break loose or break bad. At least he didn't run. As they entered the men's room, one of the Gypsies told Tony to give him his watch. He was going to give him two dollars for it. The men's room door closed.

Quickly our gang herded down the hall being quiet so as not to arouse anyone to what we were about to do. There were eleven of the Gypsies in all. We had kept track of them during the preceding two weeks. Jerry Salvo made conversation with them and didn't let on he was our confidant. Jerry entered the men's room to discover Tony and Sam had just been robbed. When we entered, the two were really pissed. Tony said the one Gypsy threatened him with a knife and made him sell his watch for protection against harm. Sam said the other one made him give him his wallet containing his whole two weeks pay of seventy-four dollars. But where were the five Gypsy punks? Sam said they went out through the fire escape.

"Not all of them," whispered Tony pointing to the toilet stall. One of them had been sitting on the crapper. When we opened the door, he was surprised when Gino told him to remove his watch. He did and it was retrieved by Tony. Tony exclaimed, "Hey, this fucking thing's a Bulova." Tony was still very upset and he started to beat the living hell out of the Gypsy. We went outside to look for the others when Gerry Solon and a few of the Solon gang were pulling up in the back alley. They had just confronted four Gypsies coming out of the alley and after beating them up made them disrobe. They had just driven their clothes up to the Orleans Street Viaduct where they sent them airborne.

The Gypsies, like bad pennies, kept turning up. The next Friday night at the Y there were about twenty of them standing on the corner. There were two new Buick automobiles that the Gypsies were congregating around. I imagined they were anticipating our arrival and we were anticipating something like this happening. As we watched from half a block away, Silent Sam went into a drugstore on the next corner and bought some camera film. He was laughing when he said, "I been want'n' to do dis for a long time." Stripping the film, he rolled it in some napkins retrieved from the drugstore. Sam then walked up to where the Gypsies were, but stayed out of sight on the opposite side of the street. Gino went to the telephone booth on the corner. He called the police and explained he was being followed and slapped a discarded auto tag on the ledge of the booth's inside while Norman French simultaneously dropped a milk bottle. Then Gino dropped the phone. We thought these sounds would mimic a gunshot and glass breaking.

Tony Meatball was in the drugstore calling the fire department about a car on fire across the street. When Tony reappeared from the drugstore, Silent Sam, running like a bat out of hell with a newly-acquired handful of flaming napkins dropped them into one of the Buick's open windows. Smoke began to billow from the Buick. Within minutes the whole street was a rush of cops and fire trucks. The cops were questioning the occupants of the other Buick and were making arrests since the car was hot. The smoking car was hosed down and was towed away. The large group of Gypsies that was milling around on the corner of the Y turned out to be Polish refugees. Man, did we make a mistake. While walking home with Tony Meatball, I told him I was glad he got his watch back.

"Hey, Jack. This is a Bulova!"

"Yes, like I said, I'm glad you got it back."

"Jack, this ain't my watch. It's a Bulova. Mine was a BINGO. I got it from a claw machine."

Something had really changed us. We were actually enjoying a dance and didn't even think about rumbling. Good Lord! We were becoming lovers.

It was not long after attending The Saturday Sunday Club that I met Mary Donovan. I fell in love with her the first time I saw her. I had seen her years before but at a time when I was too busy looking at myself. This was at the Saturday night dance and as Mary entered, I said to Gino, "Gino, there's the girl I'm going to make my girl!" I asked her to dance and told her I knew where she lived and that I would be at her house tomorrow, Sunday, to take her to the movies. When I introduced myself to Mary, she wasn't interested in meeting me or hearing what I had to say. She said, **"I DON'T WANT TO GO OUT WITH YOU. DON'T BOTHER COMING TO MY HOUSE TO MEET ME. I HEARD YOU ARE A BAD BOY!"** Needless to say, I went to her house the next day. Her brother answered the door, looked at me and said "Hi" as he closed the door in my face. I heard him say, "I know him. He's okay. He's a nice guy." He re-opened the door and allowed me entry.

During the evenings I would hang out with my old buddy, Tony Vespi, once more we plied the streets of Baltimore in his '55 Chevy looking for a drag race or a girl to embrace. We were the last of our breed. Tony liked cars and I liked to dance. The thought of Mary Donovan began to overwhelm me so Tony and I parted as friends once again.

I entertained myself by going to the dances at the YWCA on weekends. That is where my Mary Donovan would be. I was falling in love. In spite of her saying I was a bad boy, she is the girl I adore to this day.

One night about midnight I was awakened by the ringing of our front doorbell, and going to the window I could hear the rumbling sound of a glass pack muffler coming from an eight-cylinder engine. I looked out the window of the third-floor apartment my mother provided me in her house. The sound was coming from a street rod. It was my buddy, Tony Vespi!

Opening the window I called down to him, "Hey, Tony, what ya want?"

"Hey, man, come on out and we'll go riding!"

"I can't."

"Why not, man?"

"Because I'm married."

"Aw, man, what'd you do that for?"

End of Part One

The Gangs of the Tenth Ward

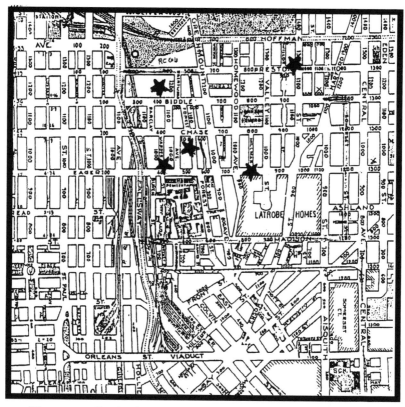

There were five basic gangs that made up the Tenth Ward as starred on preceding map. Each gang may have had several places where they frequently hung out.

The Biddle Street Gang

Our gang was the Biddle Street Gang and, for the most part, could be found in one of four places:
- — hanging out on the corners of Biddle Street and Brentwood Avenue, or
- — the park at Biddle Street and The Fallsway or
- — the Brentwood Lunch Room, a popular place on weekends or
- — the 1300 block of Charles Street.

Our gang was made up of some twenty-five boys, which included the Fictional Infamous Four Dot Gang, which was alleged to have terrorized Greenmount Avenue and Preston Street.

The Bakery Boys

The Bakery Boys was a gang that actually hung out in front of a bakery. It was the largest of all the Ward gangs inasmuch as the city housing projects were included in its make up. I believe this gang sometimes numbered as many as two hundred. They were also the most colorful. It had some of the nicest as well as some of the worst, some of the meanest and some of the dumbest guys of all. It was a real collection of characters that looked like they escaped from a Bowery Boys Movie. To identify the gangs of the Tenth Ward as one union, most were proud to wear the words "Tenth Ward" emblazoned in a prominent place on a garment. At that time the most popular garment was a Black Corduroy warm up jacket, like those worn by baseball teams. Once, when we had gathered to ready for a fight, we all met in Johnson's Square, a park in the center of the Tenth Ward. One of the Solon Brothers suggested we tie handkerchiefs to our wrists to identify each other. It didn't work. If some couldn't afford decent clothes to wear, then where were they going to get handkerchiefs?

The Solon or Warden Street Gang

The Solon or Warden Street Gang included, as its force, a family of six brothers who had their own following. Located across the street from the penitentiary, at times this gang numbered more than twenty-five. The Solon Gang, as they came to be known, were the Biddle Street Gang's closest ally. All the time I lived in the Tenth Ward there was a Solon brother in jail. The irony of this was Mr. Solon, the father, was a guard at the jail.

The Hollywood Gang

The Hollywood Gang was a very close-knit bunch made up of some ten or twelve guys from over on Forest Street near Eager Street. They were very secretive in what they did. These guys were always dressed up. During this period in time, Baltimore had a lot of clothing manufacturers. Rumor was, these guys were in the "hot clothes" business.

The Preston Street Gang

The Preston Street Gang, about equal in number to our own Biddle Street bunch, was one that hung out on Preston and Ensor Streets. They were very sports-minded and somewhat remote from the rest of the neighborhood. We were more diversified: sports, dancing, loving and fighting. What more could a kid want?

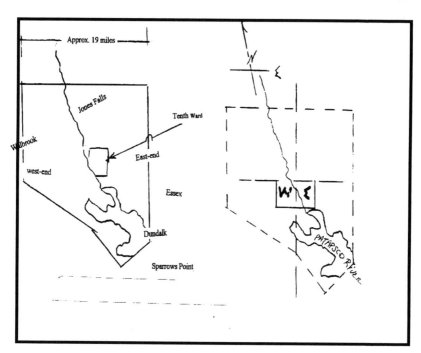

Baltimore City Outline for Illustration Only

Baltimore City is divided into sections as illustrated. The port of Baltimore is on the Patapsco River and the Tenth Ward was in East Baltimore and located about one mile North of the port's inner harbor. Six miles Southeast of the city by way of water is the Chesapeake Bay.

Follow up. . .

The characters, where are they now? Jack Lundon is a successful businessman and business consultant. Mike Campo became an Industrial engineer with a few patents that earn him a healthy income. Stevie Fazzio stayed in the Army and retired in Japan. Moe Thompson is a well rounded and obese bartender. Georgie Emerson owns a clothing store in Canada and is an absolute bore. Little Louie sleeps with the fishes. Warren Grimm is on the witness protection program. Larry Barely is a beautician and owns a gym. Gene Bork died of A.I.D.S. Big Jake works with an elephant act in Argentina. The Solon Brothers, Kipper and Norman in separate incidents died of unnatural causes. The three remaining own a pawn shop in New Orleans. Mervy Domore, sells slot machines and makes loans in Chicago. Everette Frayman claims to see snakes and demons when he isn't drinking alcohol. Hymie Glick is alleged to operate a floating card game. Hugo Footley sells used cars. Big Bob works on a banana boat in Costa Rica. Tony Meatball travels the U.S. as an escort for three strip tease dancers. Tony Vespi designs racing machines of all types. And me, the Author, I enjoyed writing this book.

The names of the characters in the stories are fictitious and similarity to persons living or dead is completely coincidental.

**Thanks to my best friends,
Charlie Longo
and
Tony Genco,
for making this book happen.**